TABLE OF CONTENTS

THE STORY SO FAR...

Once a year in Barrow, Alaska the sun fails to rise for a month.

In November of 2001, the promise of that darkness was too much to resist and a band of vampires descended upon the town, decimating the population. Stella Olemaun survived, but when her husband, Sheriff Eben Olemaun was infected, he chose suicide over life as a blood-sucking monster.

Stella wrote a book about the tragedy in Barrow, but the world (and her publishers) refused to believe her story. At her big release in Los Angeles, Stella learned that *30 Days of Night* was to be marketed as fiction. She persisted, determined to bring the existence of blood fiends into the light, but when the vampire queen offered her Eben's remains—and the means to revive him—in exchange for the evidence of their existence, Stella relented. She set aside her better judgment and shed her own blood to bring her beloved back to world of the living. Never one to stray too far from reason, however, she made sure to kill the queen first.

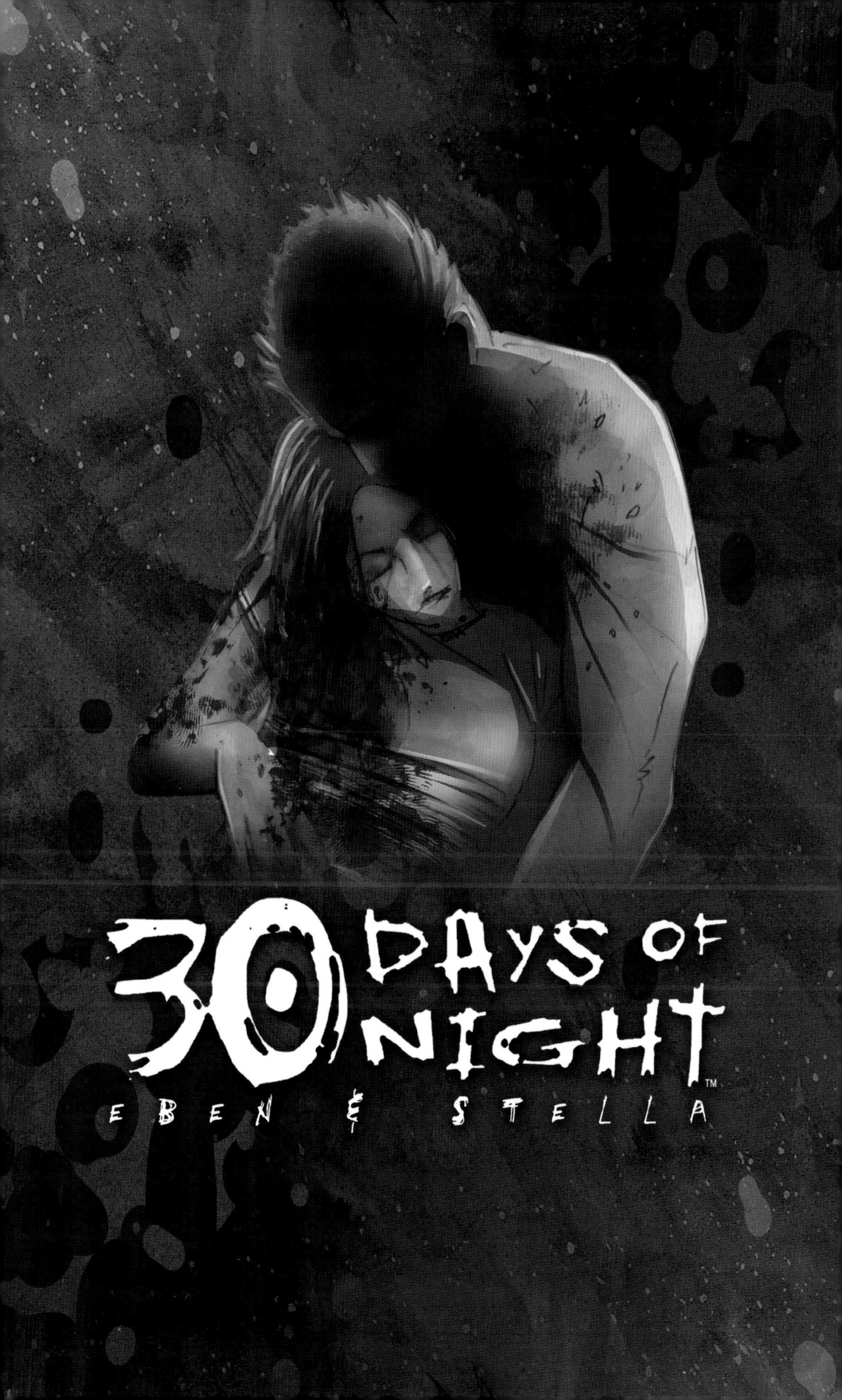
30 DAYS OF NIGHT™
EBEN & STELLA

30 DAYS OF NIGHT: EBEN & STELLA

WRITTEN BY STEVE NILES, KELLY SUE DECONNICK

ART BY JUSTIN RANDALL

LETTERS BY CHRIS MOWRY, ROBBIE ROBBINS, NEIL UYETAKE

EDITS BY CHRIS RYALL

COLLECTION DESIGN BY CHRIS MOWRY

COLLECTION EDITS BY JUSTIN EISINGER

30 DAYS OF NIGHT CREATED BY
STEVE NILES AND BEN TEMPLESMITH

IDW Publishing is:
Ted Adams, President
Robbie Robbins, EVP/Sr. Graphic Artist
Clifford Meth, EVP of Strategies/Editorial
Chris Ryall, Publisher/Editor-in-Chief
Alan Payne, VP of Sales
Neil Uyetake, Art Director
Justin Eisinger, Editor
Tom Waltz, Editor
Andrew Steven Harris, Editor
Chris Mowry, Graphic Artist
Amauri Osorio, Graphic Artist
Matthew Ruzicka, CPA, Controller
Alonzo Simon, Shipping Manager
Kris Oprisko, Editor/Foreign Lic. Rep

30 DAYS OF NIGHT: EBEN & STELLA
ISBN: 978-1-60010-107-6
10 09 08 07 1 2 3 4 5

www.idwpublishing.com

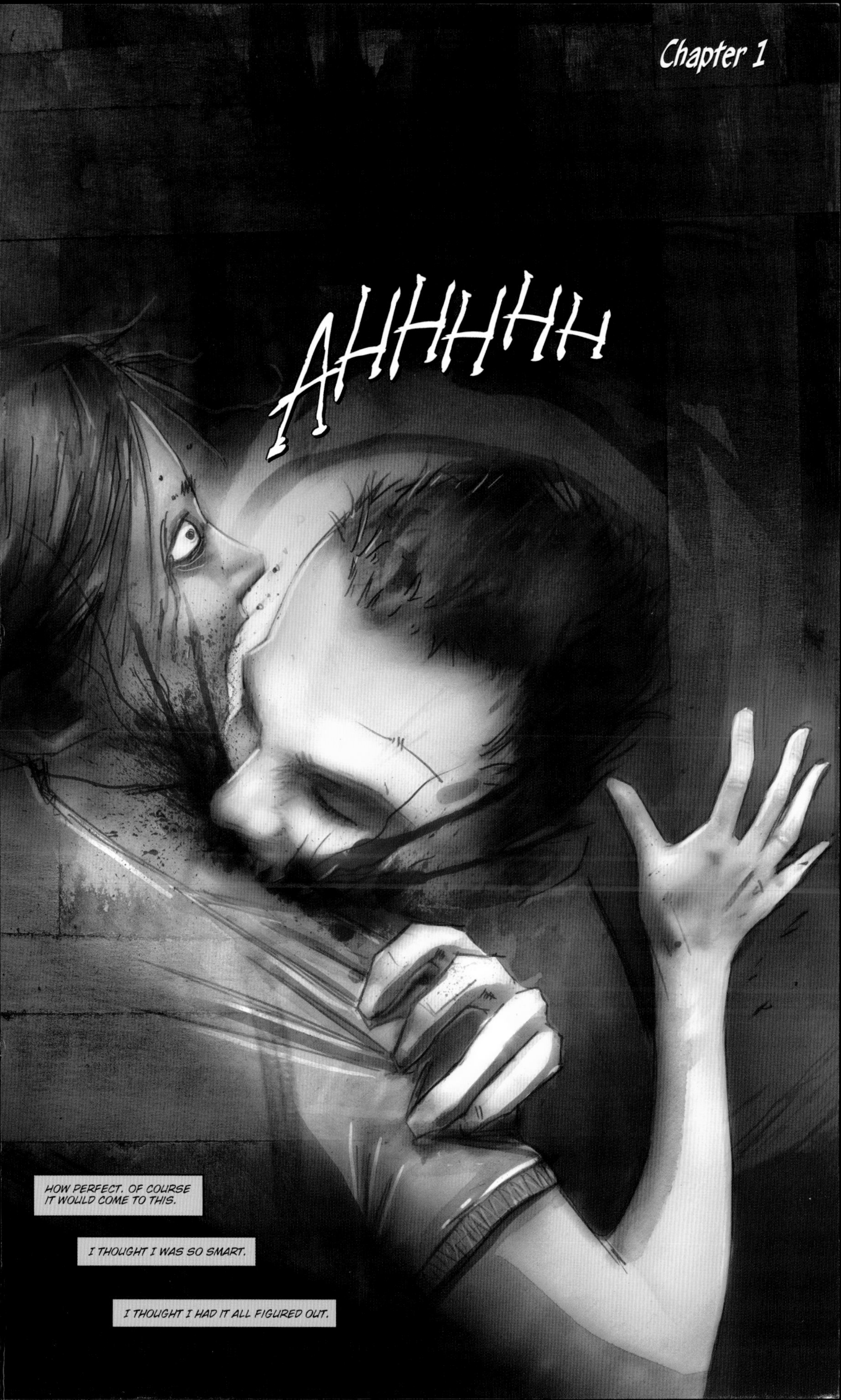
Chapter 1
AHHHHH
HOW PERFECT. OF COURSE IT WOULD COME TO THIS.
I THOUGHT I WAS SO SMART.
I THOUGHT I HAD IT ALL FIGURED OUT.

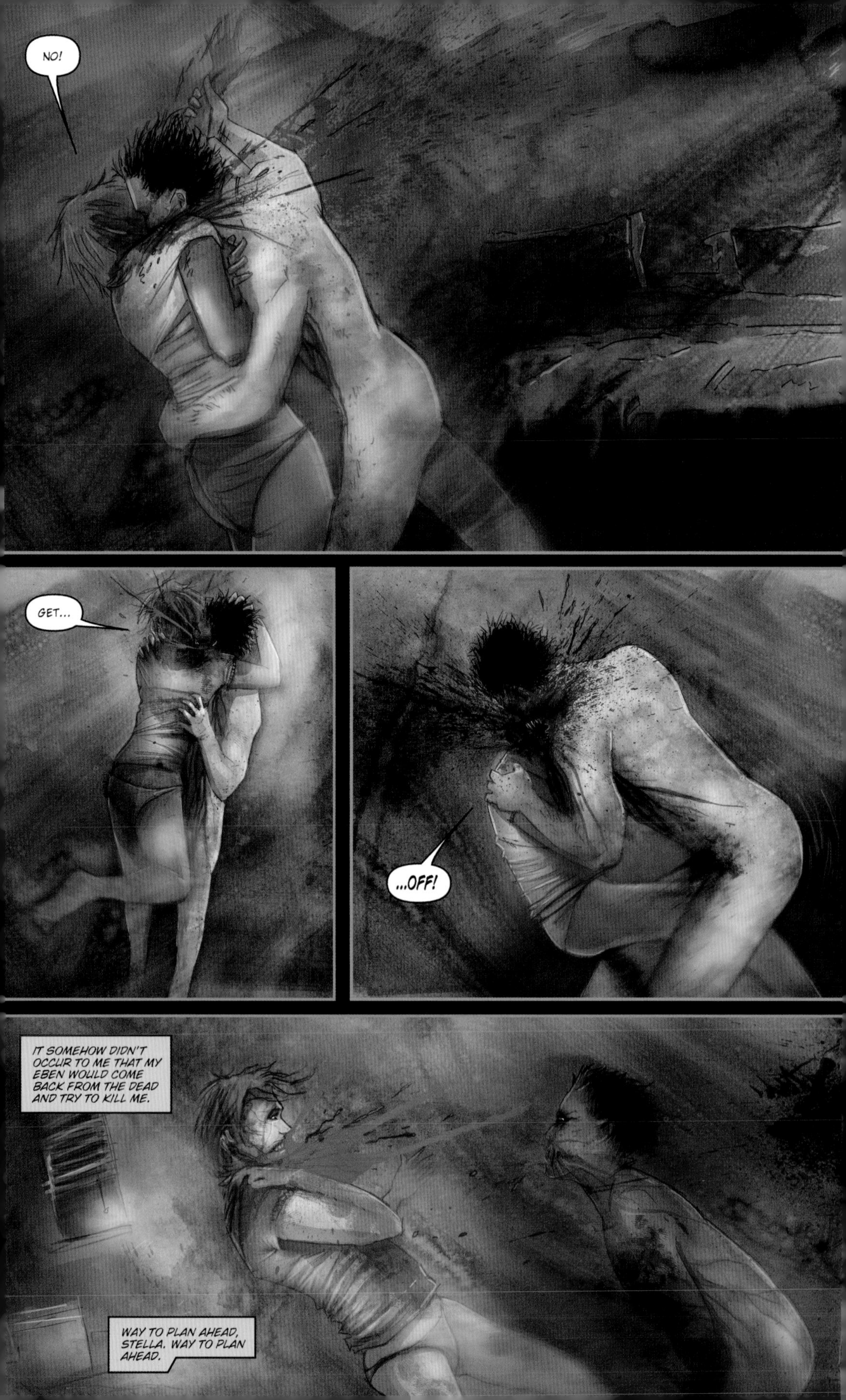
NO!
GET...
...OFF!
IT SOMEHOW DIDN'T OCCUR TO ME THAT MY EBEN WOULD COME BACK FROM THE DEAD AND TRY TO KILL ME.
WAY TO PLAN AHEAD, STELLA. WAY TO PLAN AHEAD.

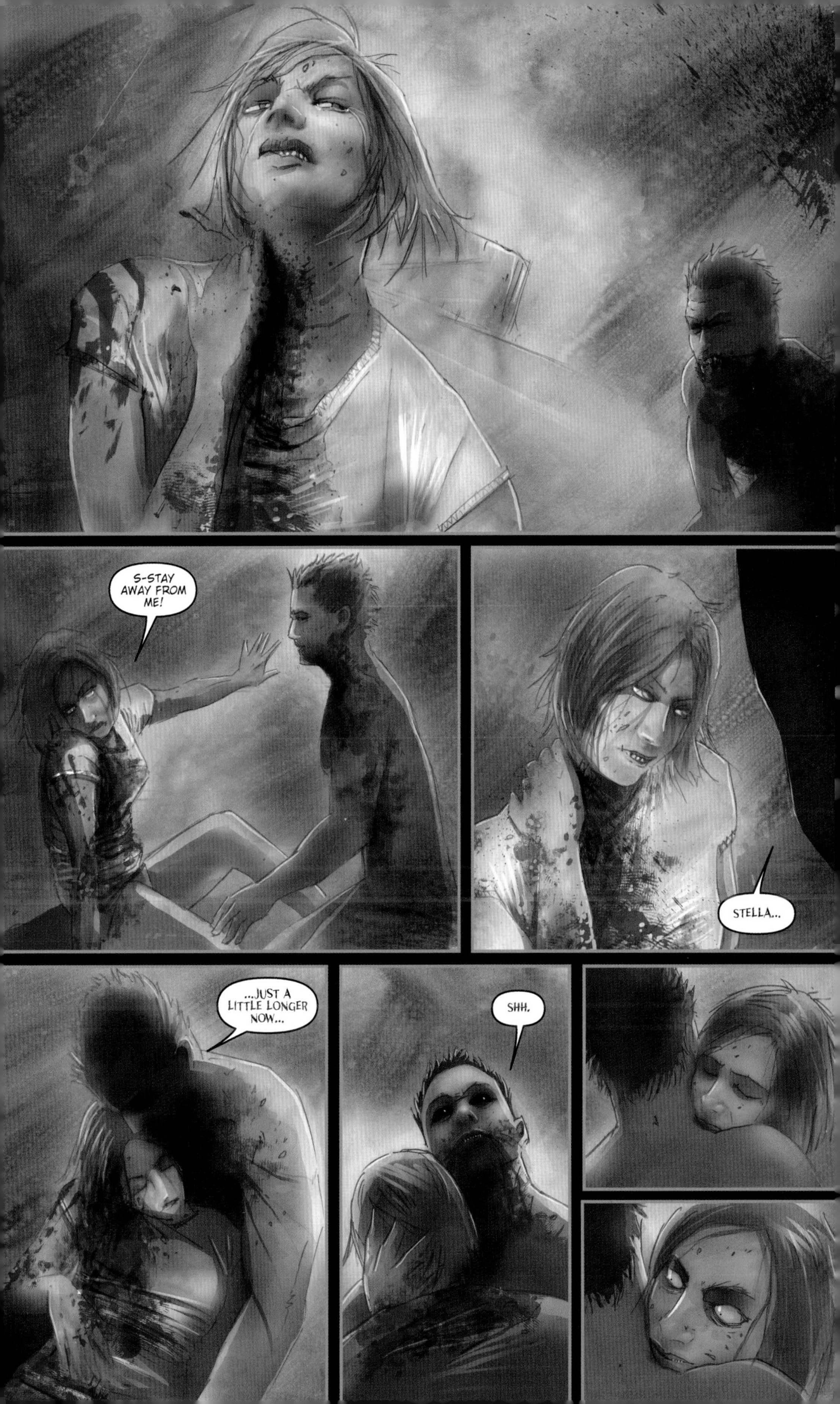
S-STAY AWAY FROM ME!
STELLA...
...JUST A LITTLE LONGER NOW...
SHH.

LOOKING BACK ON IT NOW, IT'S ALMOST FUNNY...

KAK

YOU...

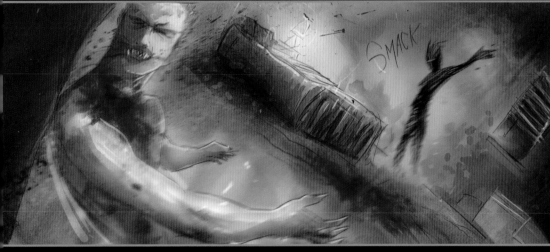

SMACK

...SONOVABITCH.

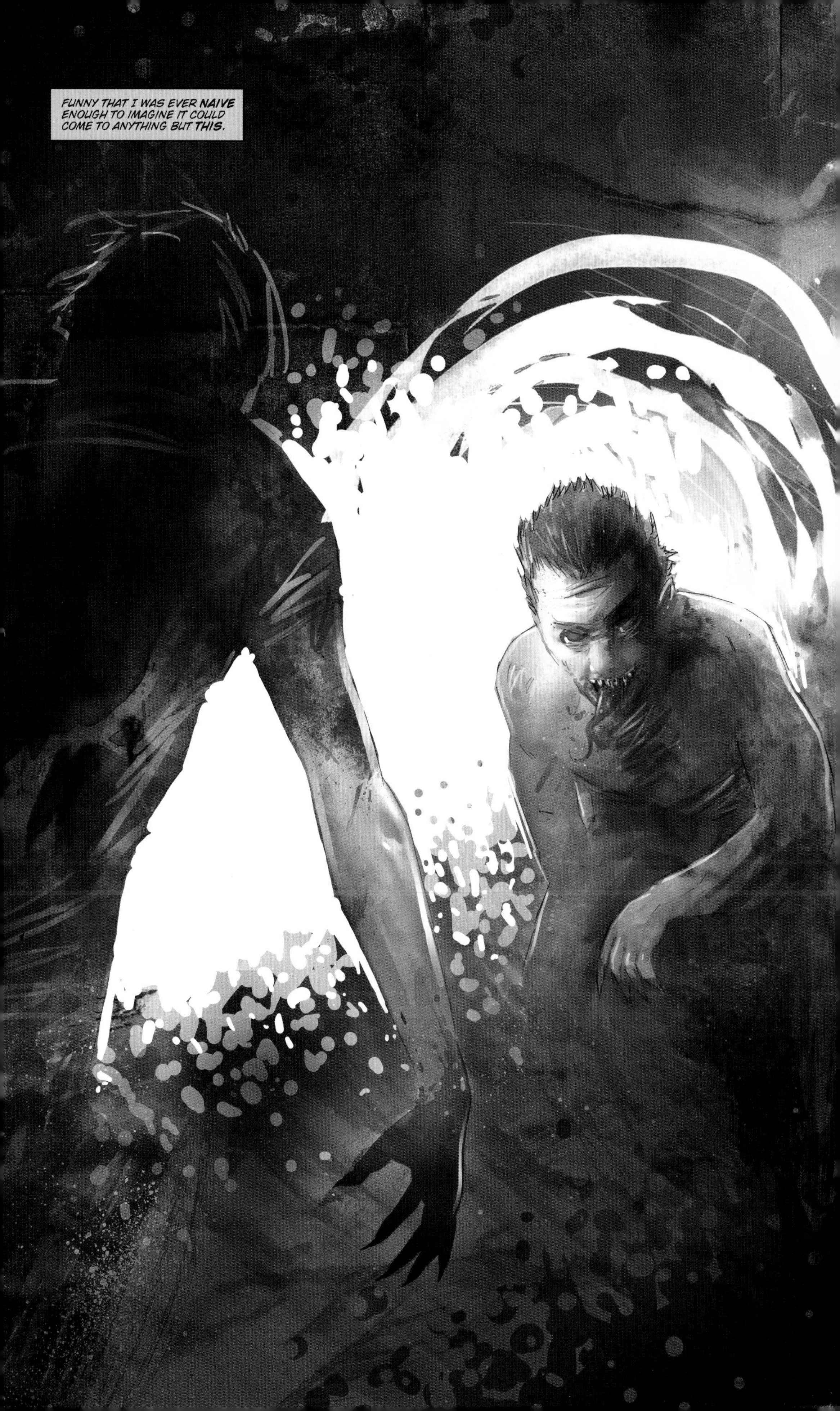
FUNNY THAT I WAS EVER NAIVE ENOUGH TO IMAGINE IT COULD COME TO ANYTHING BUT THIS.

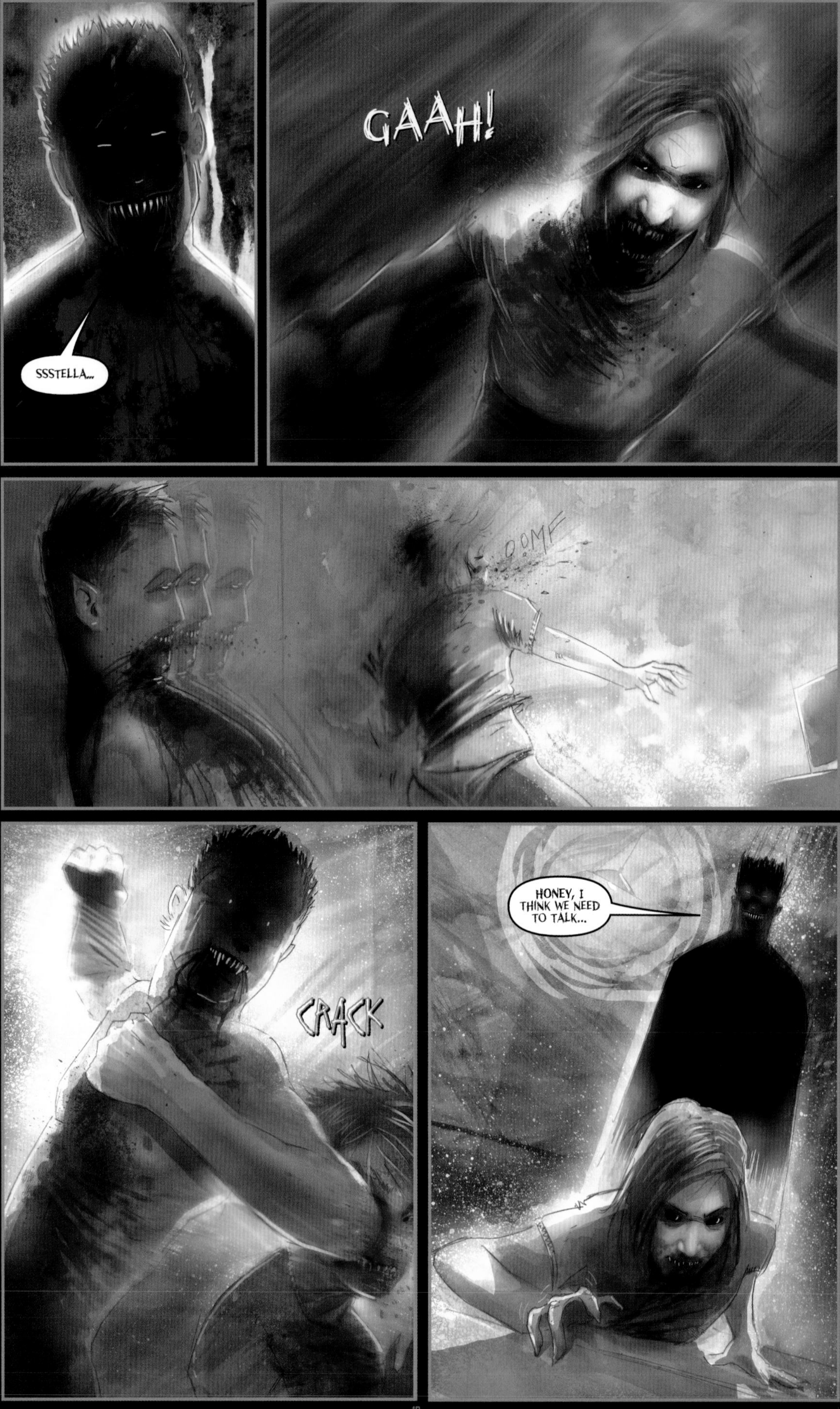
SSSTELLA...
GAAH!
OOMF
CRACK
HONEY, I THINK WE NEED TO TALK...

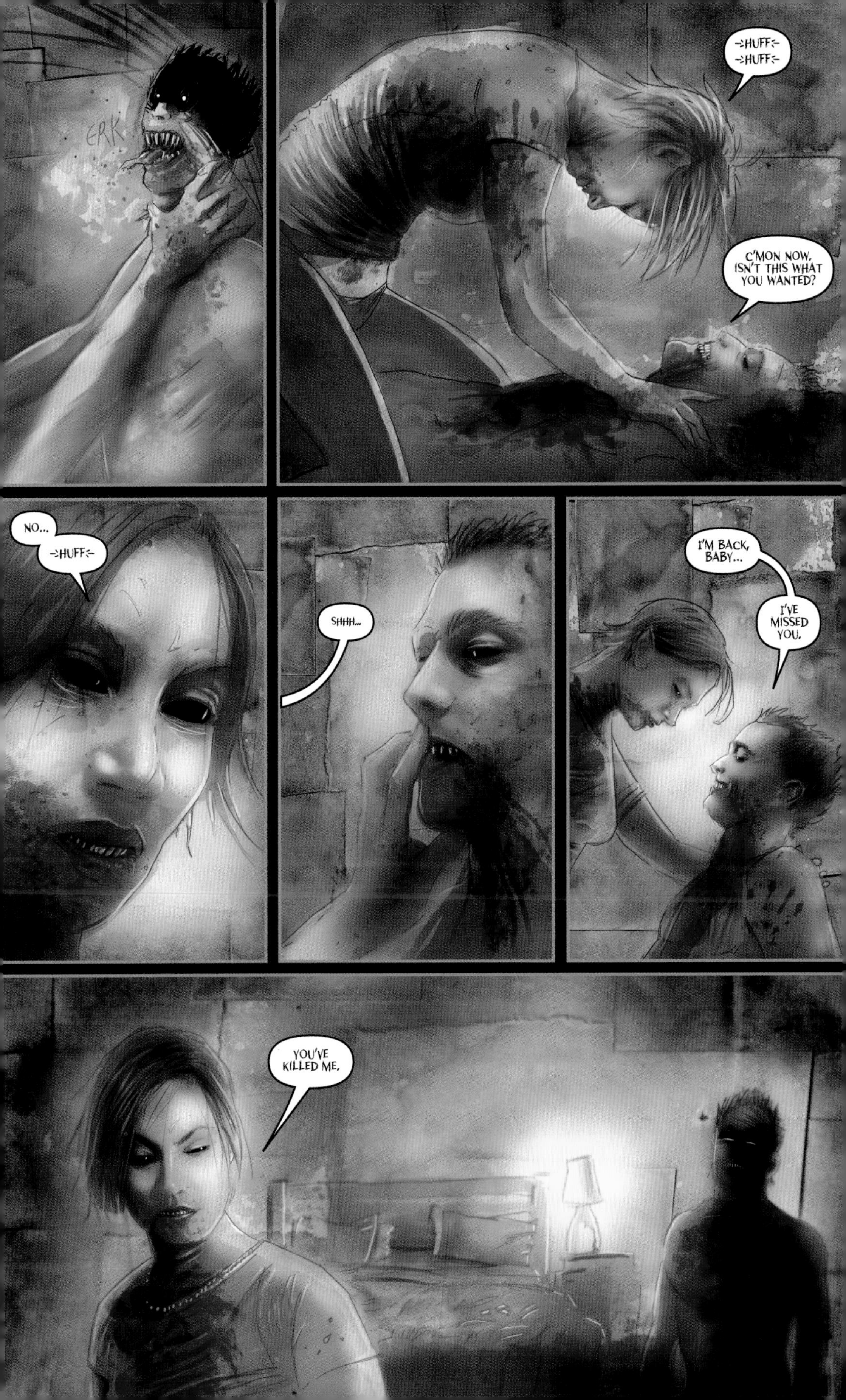
ERK
-HUFF-
-HUFF-
C'MON NOW. ISN'T THIS WHAT YOU WANTED?
NO...
-HUFF-
SHHH...
I'M BACK, BABY...
I'VE MISSED YOU.
YOU'VE KILLED ME.

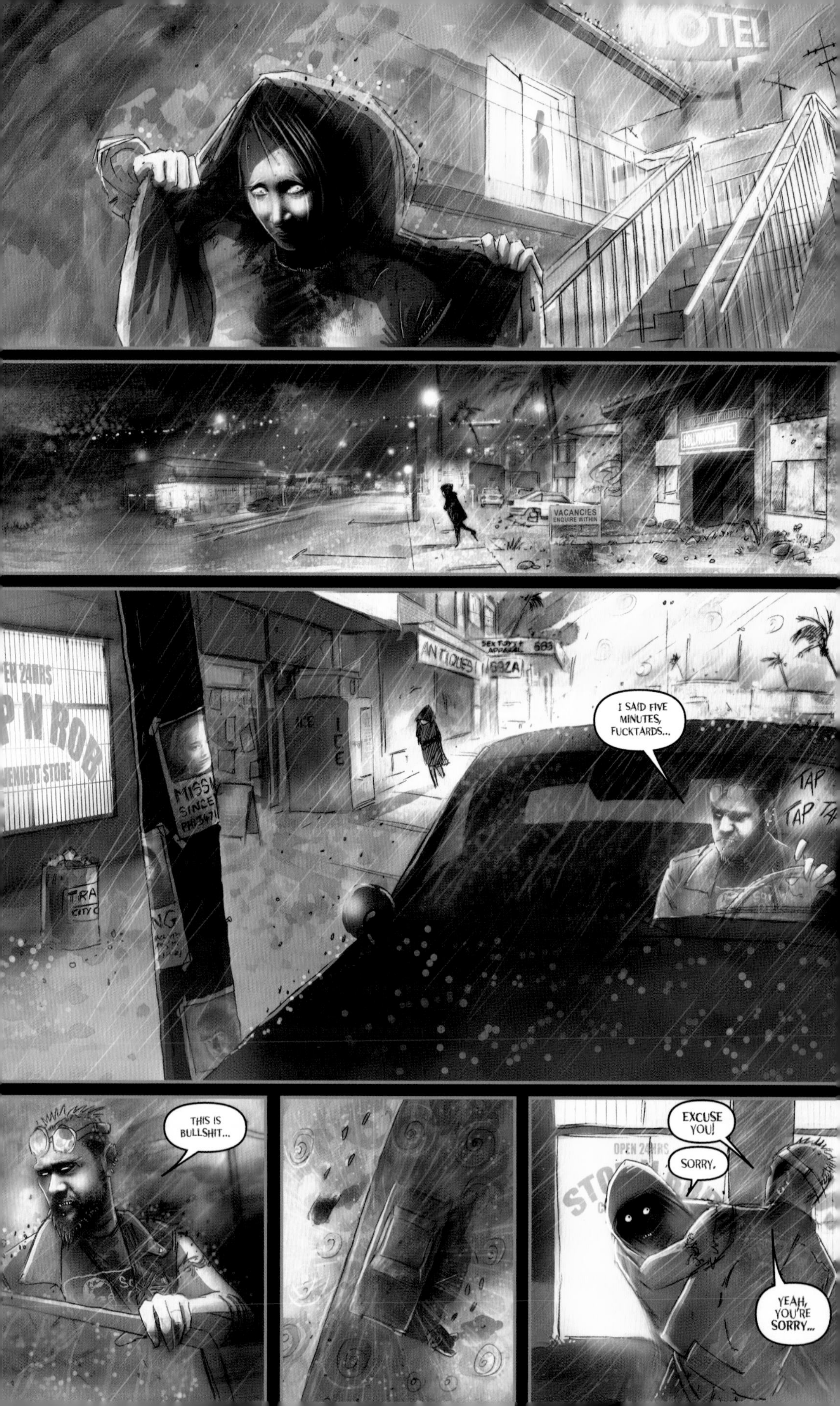
MOTEL
HOLLYWOOD MOTEL
VACANCIES ENQUIRE WITHIN
OPEN 24HRS
CONVENIENT STORE
ANTIQUES
692A
ICE
I SAID FIVE MINUTES, FUCKTARDS...
TAP TAP
THIS IS BULLSHIT...
EXCUSE YOU!
SORRY.
YEAH, YOU'RE SORRY...

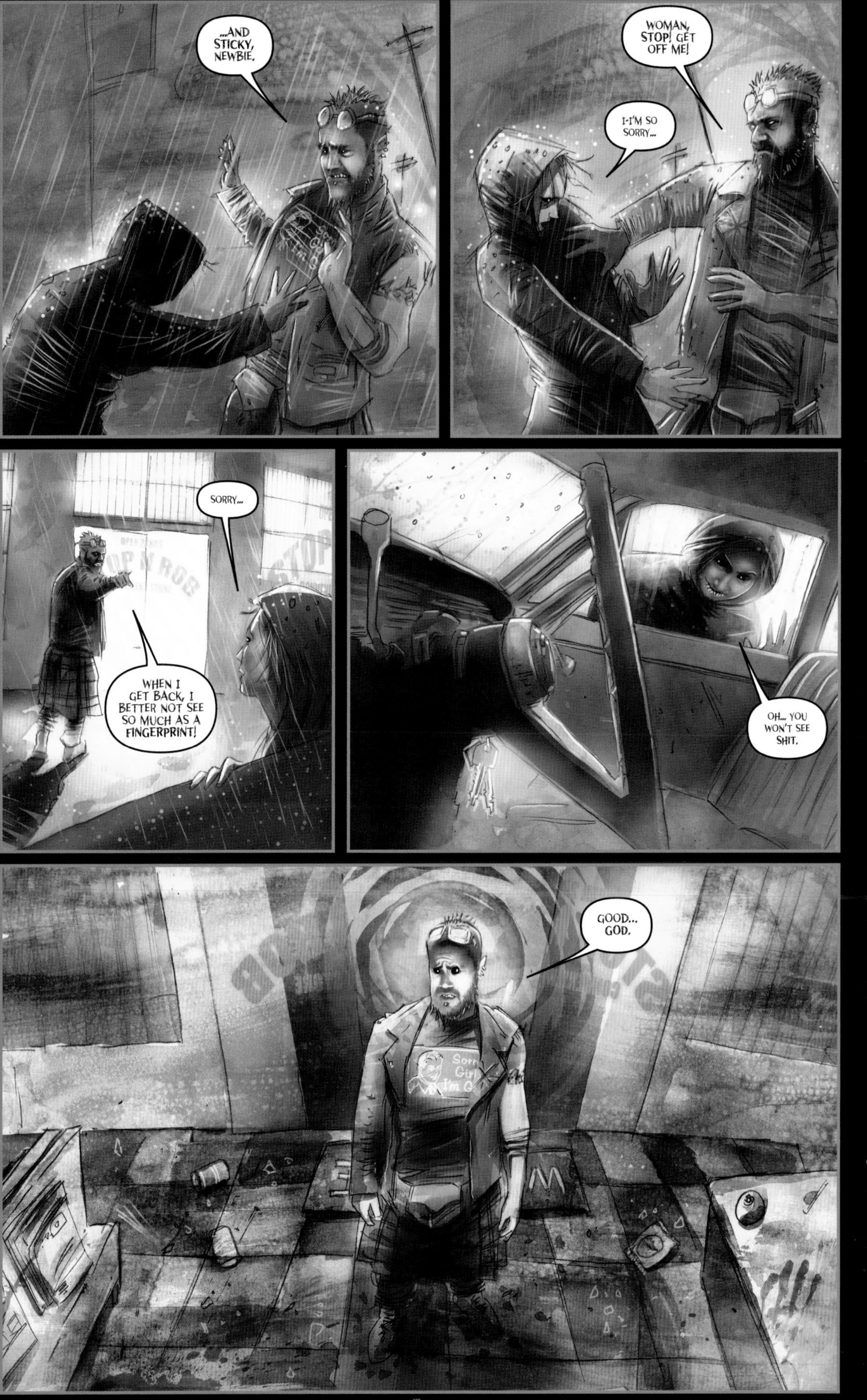
...AND STICKY, NEWBIE.
WOMAN, STOP! GET OFF ME!
I-I'M SO SORRY...
SORRY...
WHEN I GET BACK, I BETTER NOT SEE SO MUCH AS A FINGERPRINT!
OH... YOU WON'T SEE SHIT.
GOOD... GOD.

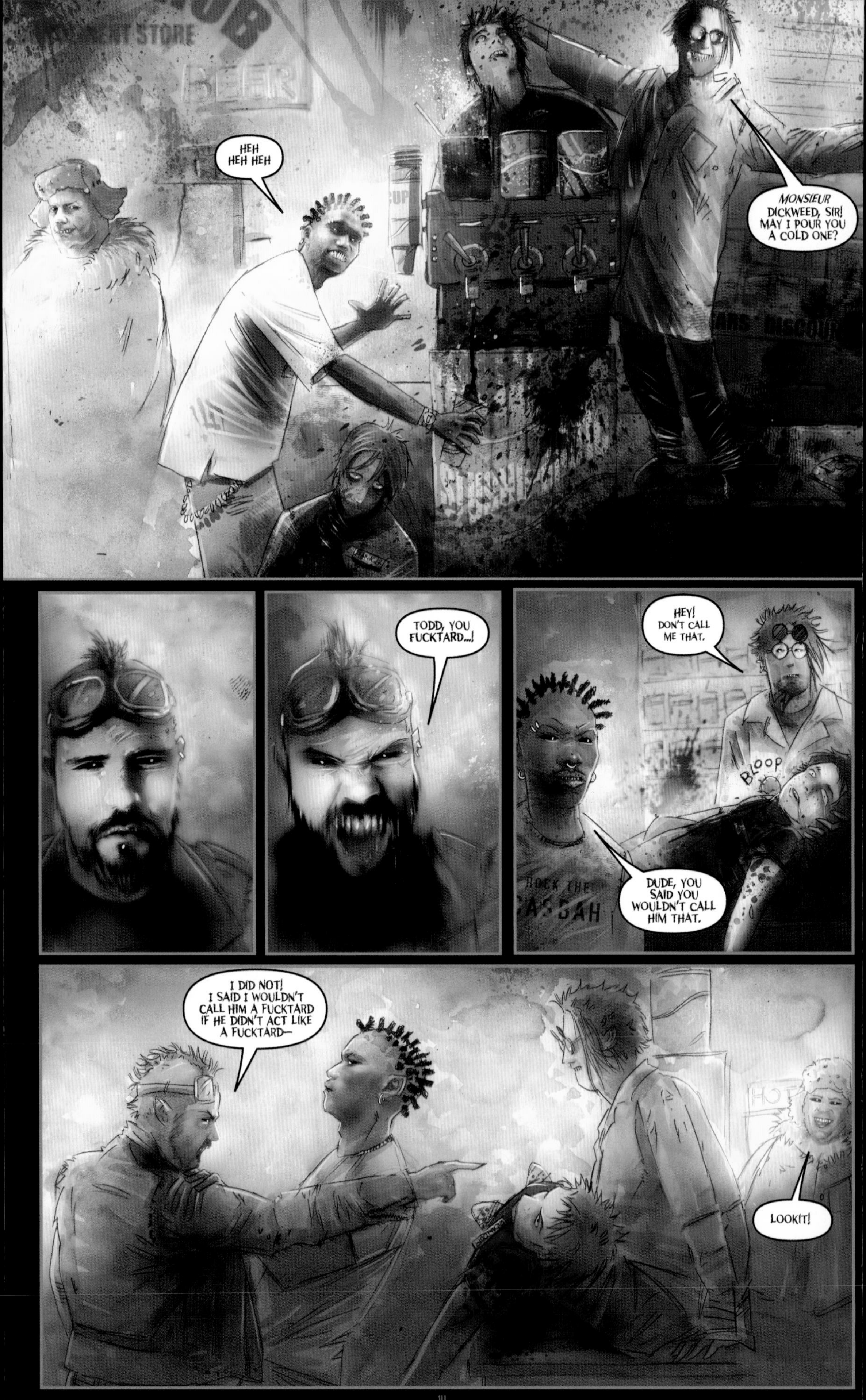
HEH HEH HEH
MONSIEUR DICKWEED, SIR! MAY I POUR YOU A COLD ONE?
TODD, YOU FUCKTARD...!
HEY! DON'T CALL ME THAT.
BLOOP
DUDE, YOU SAID YOU WOULDN'T CALL HIM THAT.
I DID NOT! I SAID I WOULDN'T CALL HIM A FUCKTARD IF HE DIDN'T ACT LIKE A FUCKTARD—
LOOKIT!

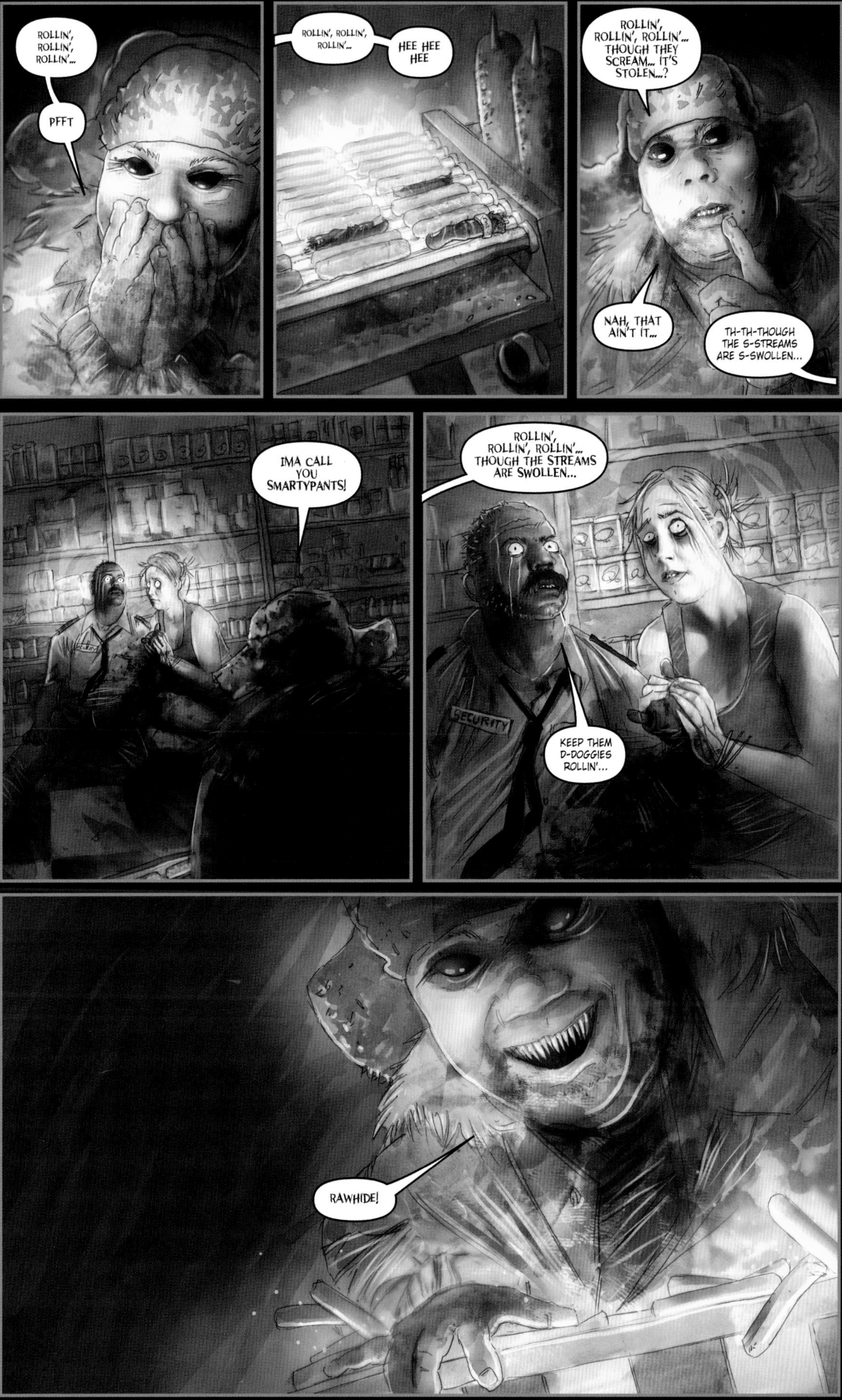

ROLLIN', ROLLIN', ROLLIN'...
PFFT
ROLLIN', ROLLIN', ROLLIN'...
HEE HEE HEE
ROLLIN', ROLLIN', ROLLIN'... THOUGH THEY SCREAM... IT'S STOLEN...?
NAH, THAT AIN'T IT...
TH-TH-THOUGH THE S-STREAMS ARE S-SWOLLEN...
IMA CALL YOU SMARTYPANTS!
ROLLIN', ROLLIN', ROLLIN'... THOUGH THE STREAMS ARE SWOLLEN...
SECURITY
KEEP THEM D-DOGGIES ROLLIN'...
RAWHIDE!

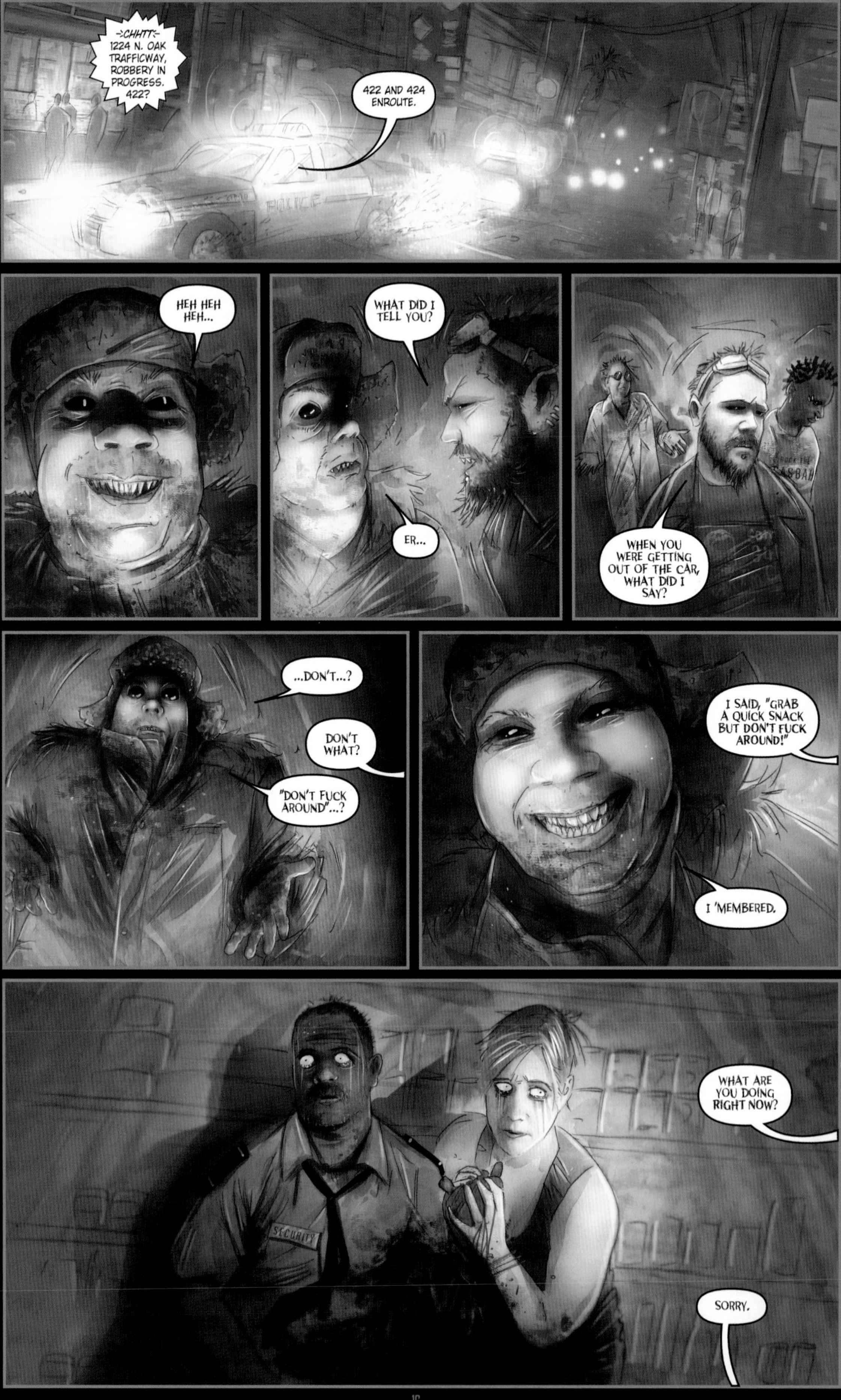
-CHHTT-
1224 N. OAK TRAFFICWAY, ROBBERY IN PROGRESS. 422?
422 AND 424 ENROUTE.
HEH HEH HEH...
WHAT DID I TELL YOU?
ER...
WHEN YOU WERE GETTING OUT OF THE CAR, WHAT DID I SAY?
...DON'T...?
DON'T WHAT?
"DON'T FUCK AROUND"...?
I SAID, "GRAB A QUICK SNACK BUT DON'T FUCK AROUND!"
I 'MEMBERED.
SECURITY
WHAT ARE YOU DOING RIGHT NOW?
SORRY.

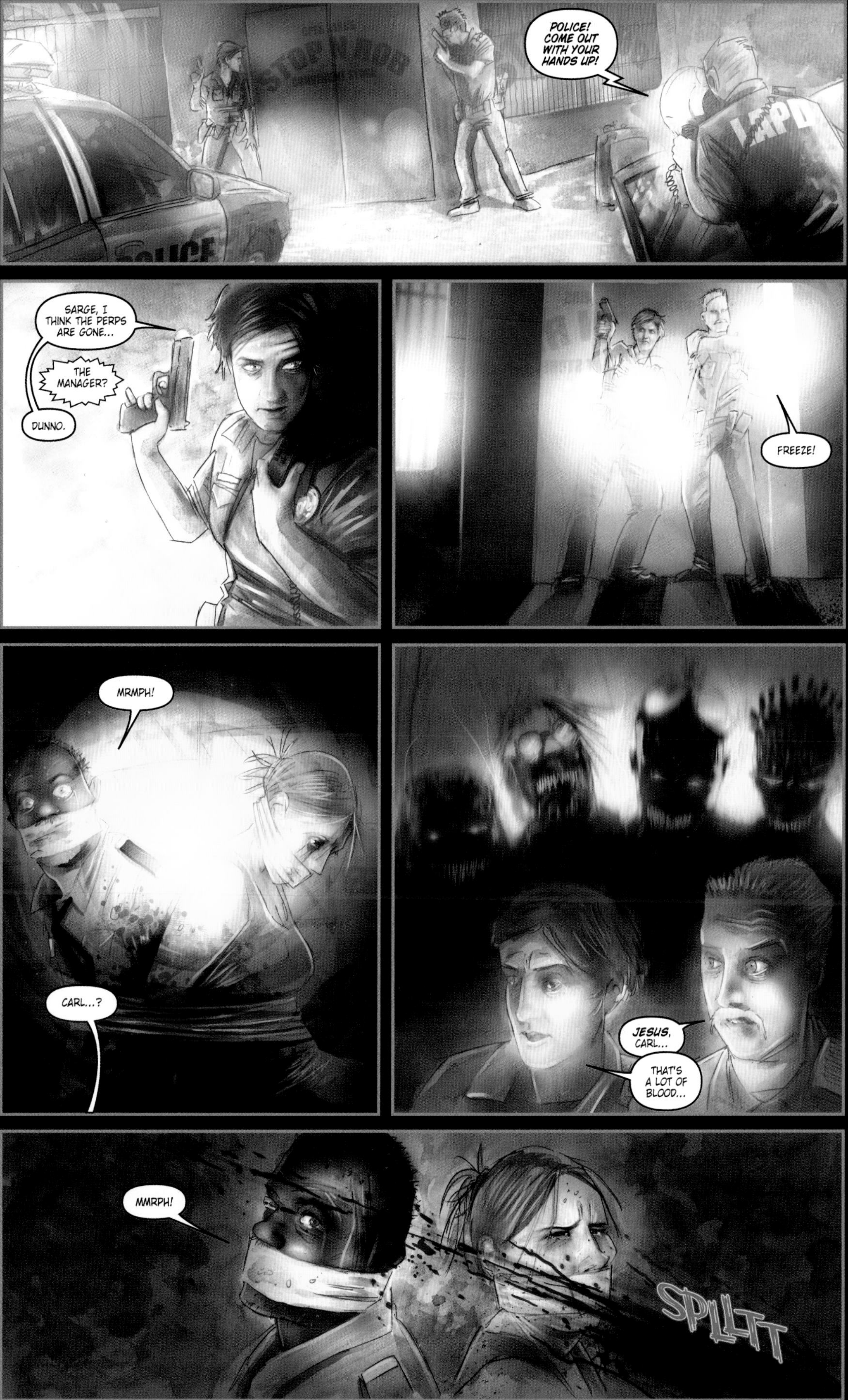
POLICE! COME OUT WITH YOUR HANDS UP!
LAPD
SARGE, I THINK THE PERPS ARE GONE...
THE MANAGER?
DUNNO.
FREEZE!
MRMPH!
CARL...?
JESUS, CARL...
THAT'S A LOT OF BLOOD...
MMRPH!
SPLLTT

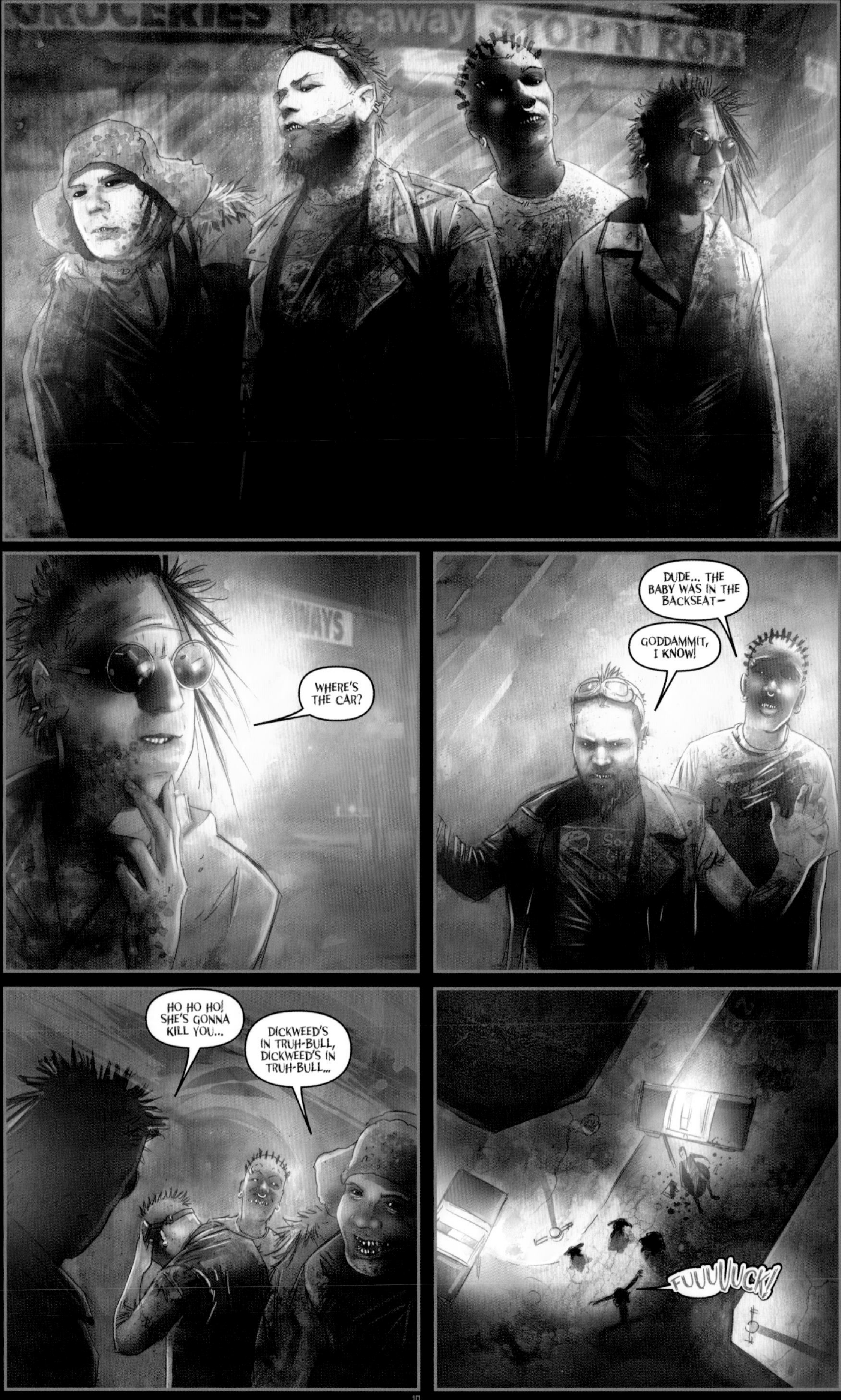
GROCERIES
Take-away
STOP 'N ROB
WAYS
WHERE'S THE CAR?
DUDE... THE BABY WAS IN THE BACKSEAT—
GODDAMMIT, I KNOW!
HO HO HO! SHE'S GONNA KILL YOU...
DICKWEED'S IN TRUH-BULL, DICKWEED'S IN TRUH-BULL...
FUUUUUCK!

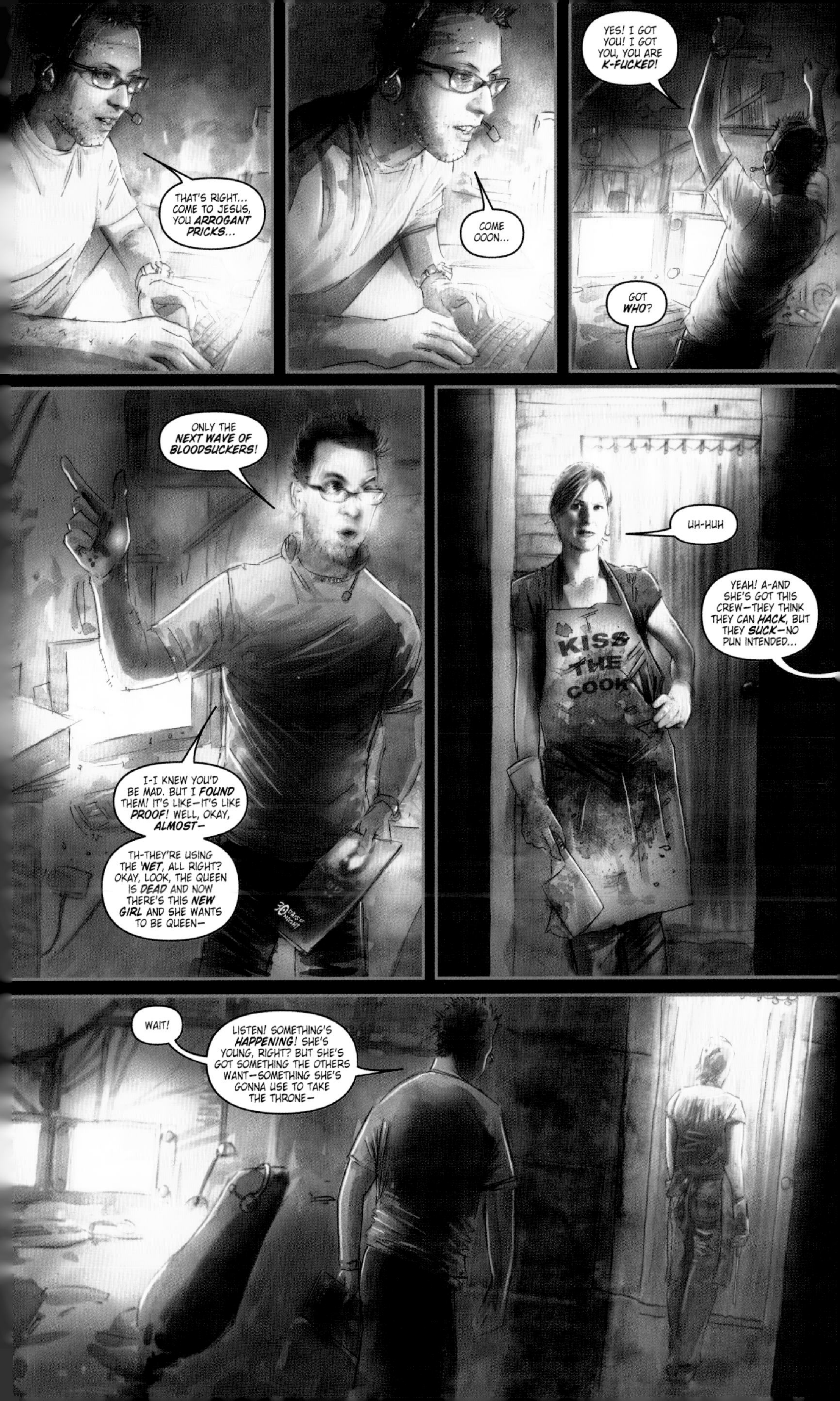

THAT'S RIGHT... COME TO JESUS, YOU ARROGANT PRICKS...
COME OOON...
YES! I GOT YOU! I GOT YOU, YOU ARE K-FUCKED!
GOT WHO?
ONLY THE NEXT WAVE OF BLOODSUCKERS!
I-I KNEW YOU'D BE MAD. BUT I FOUND THEM! IT'S LIKE—IT'S LIKE PROOF! WELL, OKAY, ALMOST—
TH-THEY'RE USING THE 'NET, ALL RIGHT? OKAY, LOOK, THE QUEEN IS DEAD AND NOW THERE'S THIS NEW GIRL AND SHE WANTS TO BE QUEEN—
UH-HUH
YEAH! A-AND SHE'S GOT THIS CREW—THEY THINK THEY CAN HACK, BUT THEY SUCK—NO PUN INTENDED...
KISS THE COOK
WAIT!
LISTEN! SOMETHING'S HAPPENING! SHE'S YOUNG, RIGHT? BUT SHE'S GOT SOMETHING THE OTHERS WANT—SOMETHING SHE'S GONNA USE TO TAKE THE THRONE—

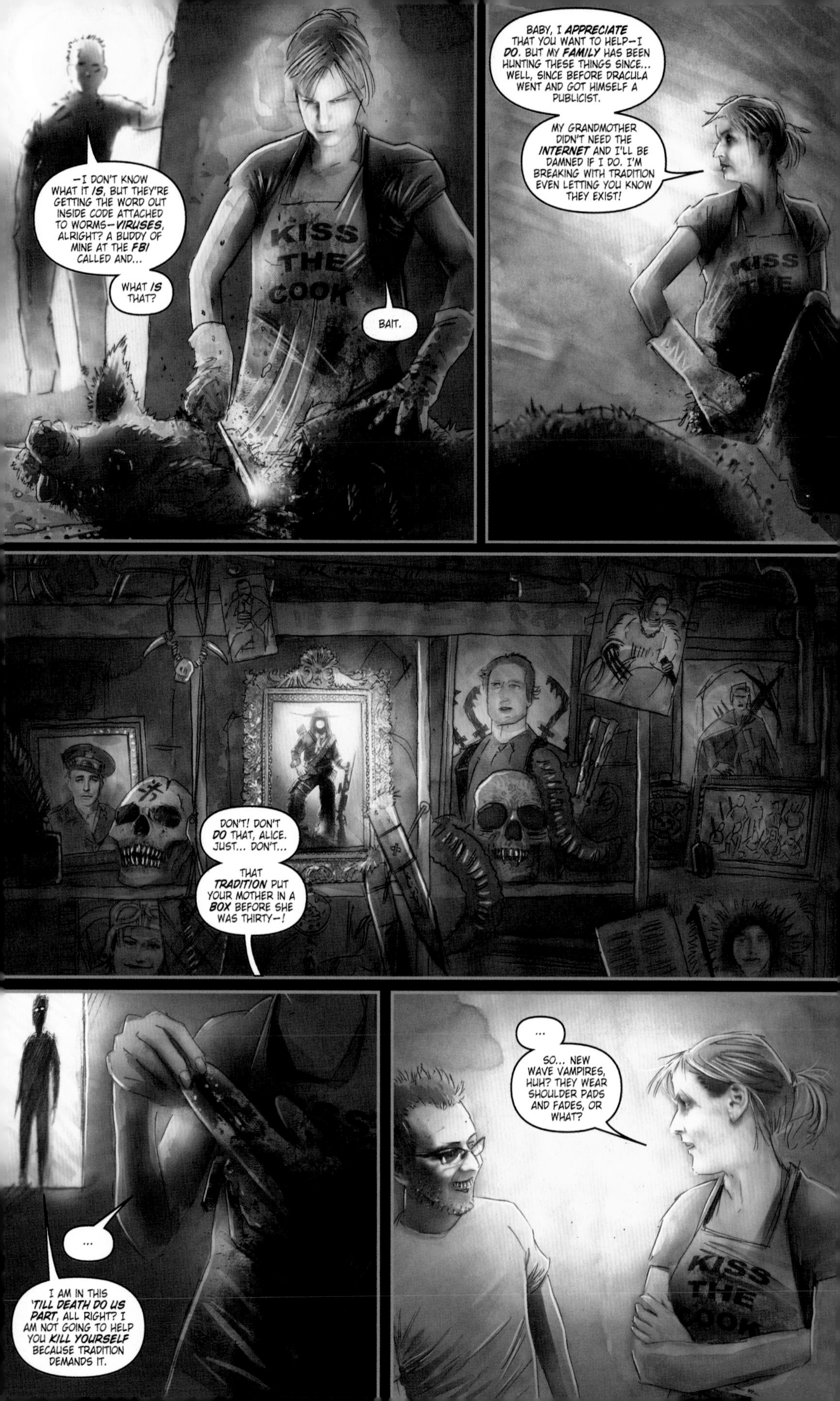
—I DON'T KNOW WHAT IT *IS*, BUT THEY'RE GETTING THE WORD OUT INSIDE CODE ATTACHED TO WORMS—*VIRUSES*, ALRIGHT? A BUDDY OF MINE AT THE *FBI* CALLED AND...
WHAT *IS* THAT?
KISS THE COOK
BAIT.
BABY, I *APPRECIATE* THAT YOU WANT TO HELP—I *DO*. BUT MY *FAMILY* HAS BEEN HUNTING THESE THINGS SINCE... WELL, SINCE BEFORE DRACULA WENT AND GOT HIMSELF A PUBLICIST.
MY GRANDMOTHER DIDN'T NEED THE *INTERNET* AND I'LL BE DAMNED IF I DO. I'M BREAKING WITH TRADITION EVEN LETTING YOU KNOW THEY EXIST!
DON'T! DON'T *DO* THAT, ALICE. JUST... DON'T...
THAT *TRADITION* PUT YOUR MOTHER IN A *BOX* BEFORE SHE WAS THIRTY—!
...
I AM IN THIS *'TILL DEATH DO US PART*, ALL RIGHT? I AM NOT GOING TO HELP YOU *KILL YOURSELF* BECAUSE TRADITION DEMANDS IT.
...
SO... NEW WAVE VAMPIRES, HUH? THEY WEAR SHOULDER PADS AND FADES, OR WHAT?

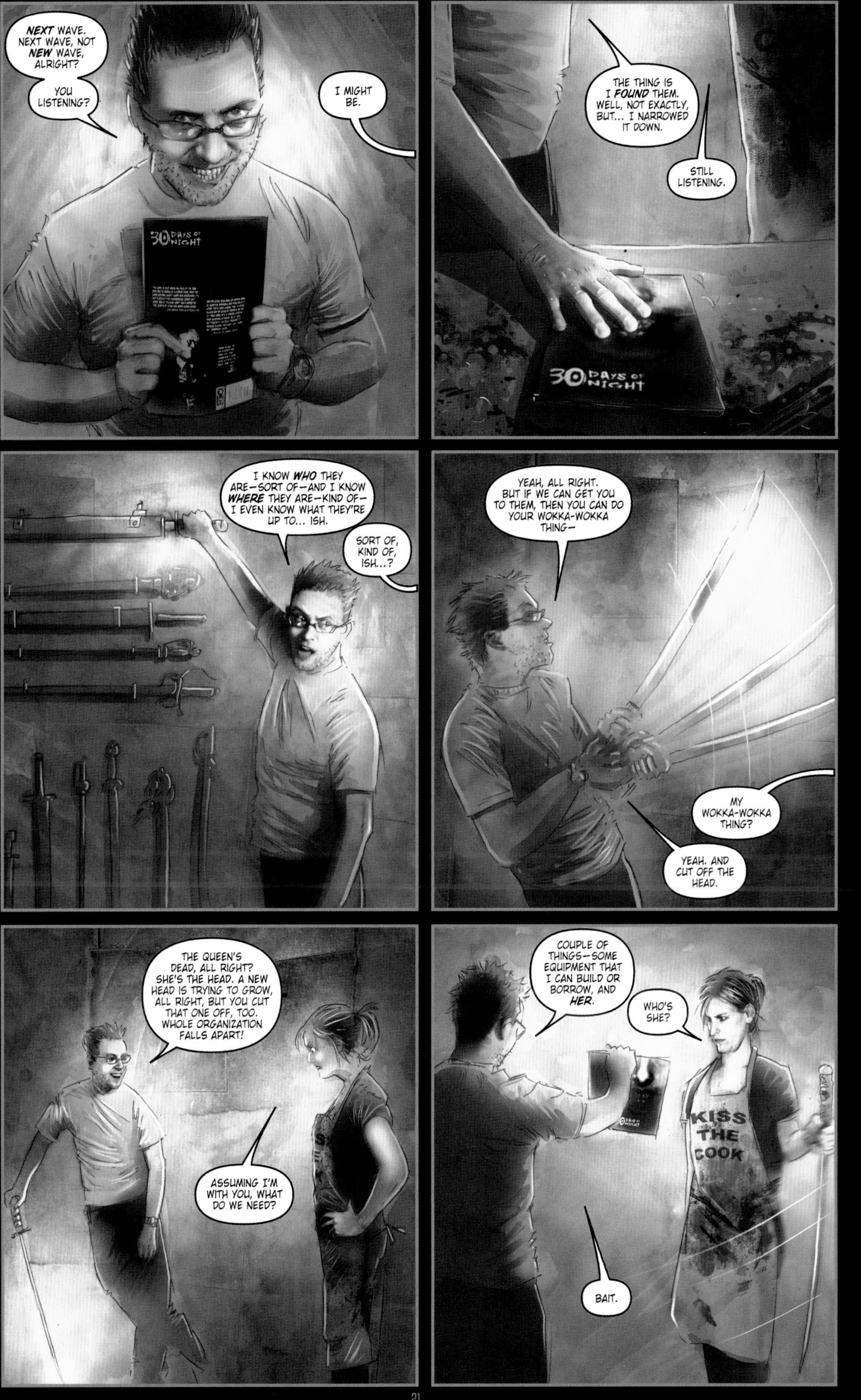
NEXT WAVE. NEXT WAVE, NOT NEW WAVE, ALRIGHT?
YOU LISTENING?
I MIGHT BE.
30 DAYS OF NIGHT
THE THING IS I FOUND THEM. WELL, NOT EXACTLY, BUT... I NARROWED IT DOWN.
STILL LISTENING.
30 DAYS OF NIGHT
I KNOW WHO THEY ARE—SORT OF—AND I KNOW WHERE THEY ARE—KIND OF—I EVEN KNOW WHAT THEY'RE UP TO... ISH.
SORT OF, KIND OF, ISH...?
YEAH, ALL RIGHT. BUT IF WE CAN GET YOU TO THEM, THEN YOU CAN DO YOUR WOKKA-WOKKA THING—
MY WOKKA-WOKKA THING?
YEAH. AND CUT OFF THE HEAD.
THE QUEEN'S DEAD, ALL RIGHT? SHE'S THE HEAD. A NEW HEAD IS TRYING TO GROW, ALL RIGHT, BUT YOU CUT THAT ONE OFF, TOO. WHOLE ORGANIZATION FALLS APART!
ASSUMING I'M WITH YOU, WHAT DO WE NEED?
COUPLE OF THINGS—SOME EQUIPMENT THAT I CAN BUILD OR BORROW, AND HER.
WHO'S SHE?
KISS THE COOK
BAIT.

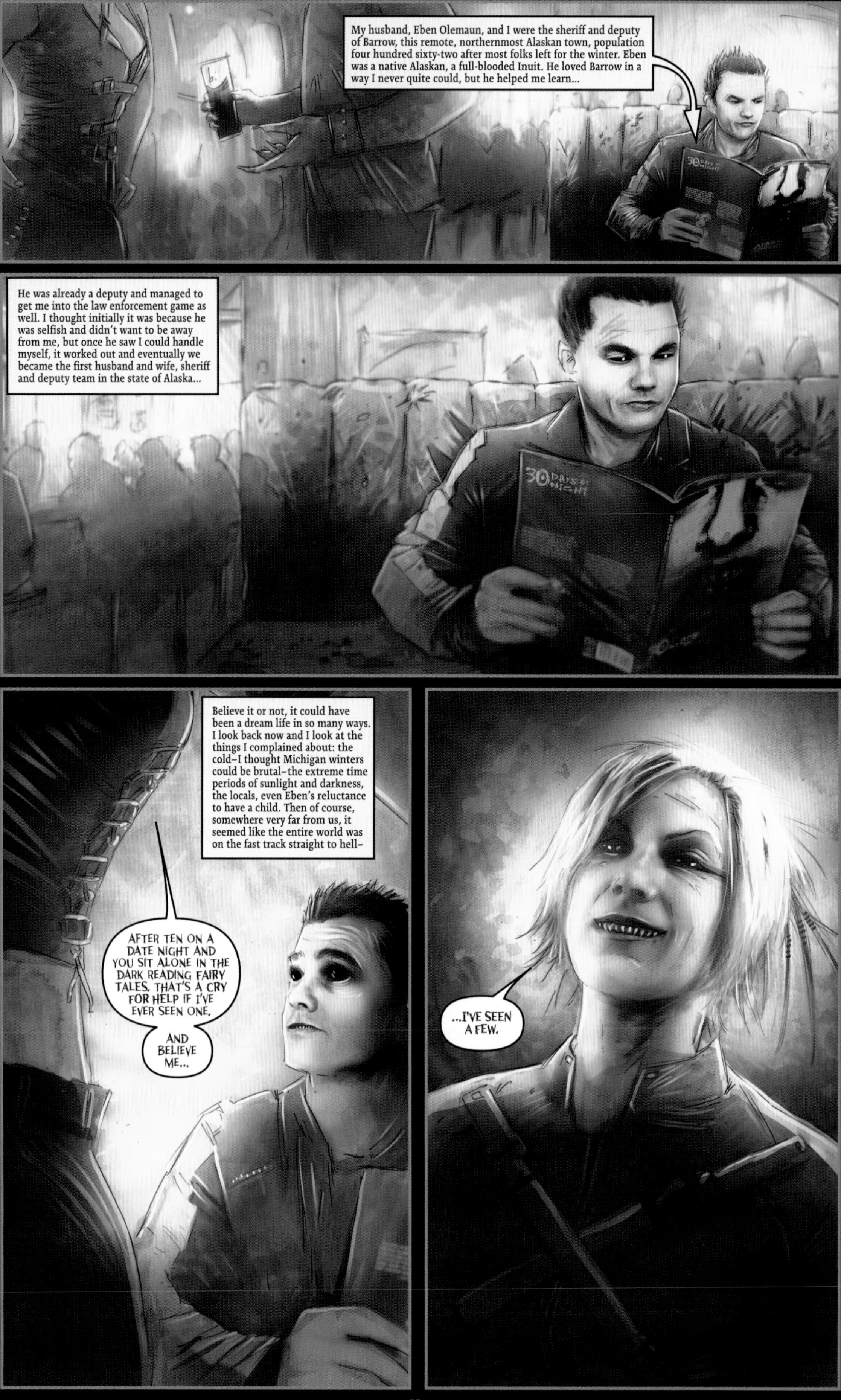
My husband, Eben Olemaun, and I were the sheriff and deputy of Barrow, this remote, northernmost Alaskan town, population four hundred sixty-two after most folks left for the winter. Eben was a native Alaskan, a full-blooded Inuit. He loved Barrow in a way I never quite could, but he helped me learn...
He was already a deputy and managed to get me into the law enforcement game as well. I thought initially it was because he was selfish and didn't want to be away from me, but once he saw I could handle myself, it worked out and eventually we became the first husband and wife, sheriff and deputy team in the state of Alaska...
30 DAYS OF NIGHT
Believe it or not, it could have been a dream life in so many ways. I look back now and I look at the things I complained about: the cold–I thought Michigan winters could be brutal–the extreme time periods of sunlight and darkness, the locals, even Eben's reluctance to have a child. Then of course, somewhere very far from us, it seemed like the entire world was on the fast track straight to hell–
AFTER TEN ON A DATE NIGHT AND YOU SIT ALONE IN THE DARK READING FAIRY TALES. THAT'S A CRY FOR HELP IF I'VE EVER SEEN ONE.
AND BELIEVE ME...
...I'VE SEEN A FEW.

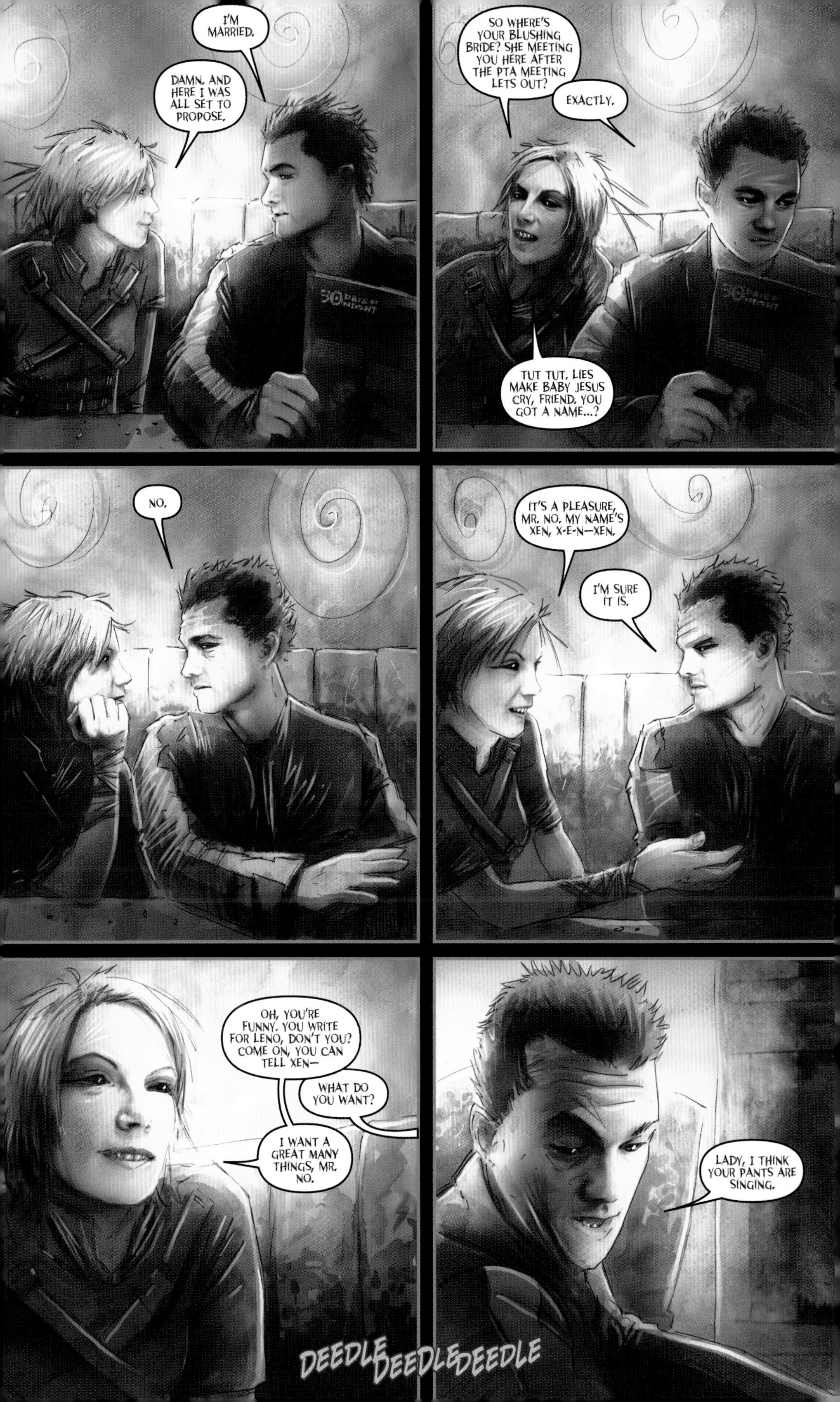
I'M MARRIED.
DAMN. AND HERE I WAS ALL SET TO PROPOSE.
30 DAYS OF NIGHT
SO WHERE'S YOUR BLUSHING BRIDE? SHE MEETING YOU HERE AFTER THE PTA MEETING LETS OUT?
EXACTLY.
TUT TUT. LIES MAKE BABY JESUS CRY, FRIEND. YOU GOT A NAME...?
NO.
IT'S A PLEASURE, MR. NO. MY NAME'S XEN, X-E-N—XEN.
I'M SURE IT IS.
OH, YOU'RE FUNNY. YOU WRITE FOR LENO, DON'T YOU? COME ON, YOU CAN TELL XEN—
WHAT DO YOU WANT?
I WANT A GREAT MANY THINGS, MR. NO.
LADY, I THINK YOUR PANTS ARE SINGING.
DEEDLE DEEDLE DEEDLE

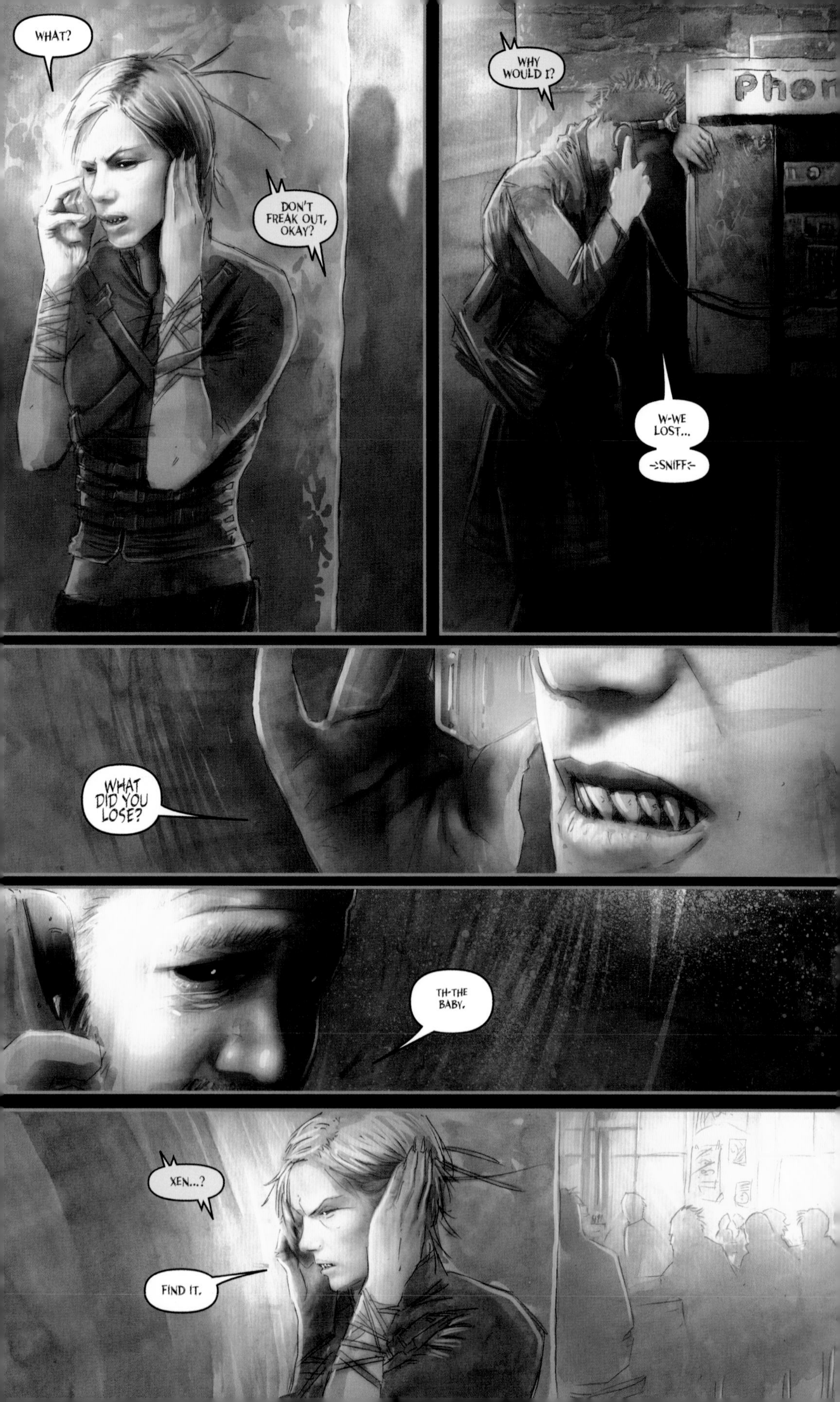
WHAT?
DON'T FREAK OUT, OKAY?
WHY WOULD I?
Phon
W-WE LOST...
-SNIFF-
WHAT DID YOU LOSE?
TH-THE BABY.
XEN...?
FIND IT.

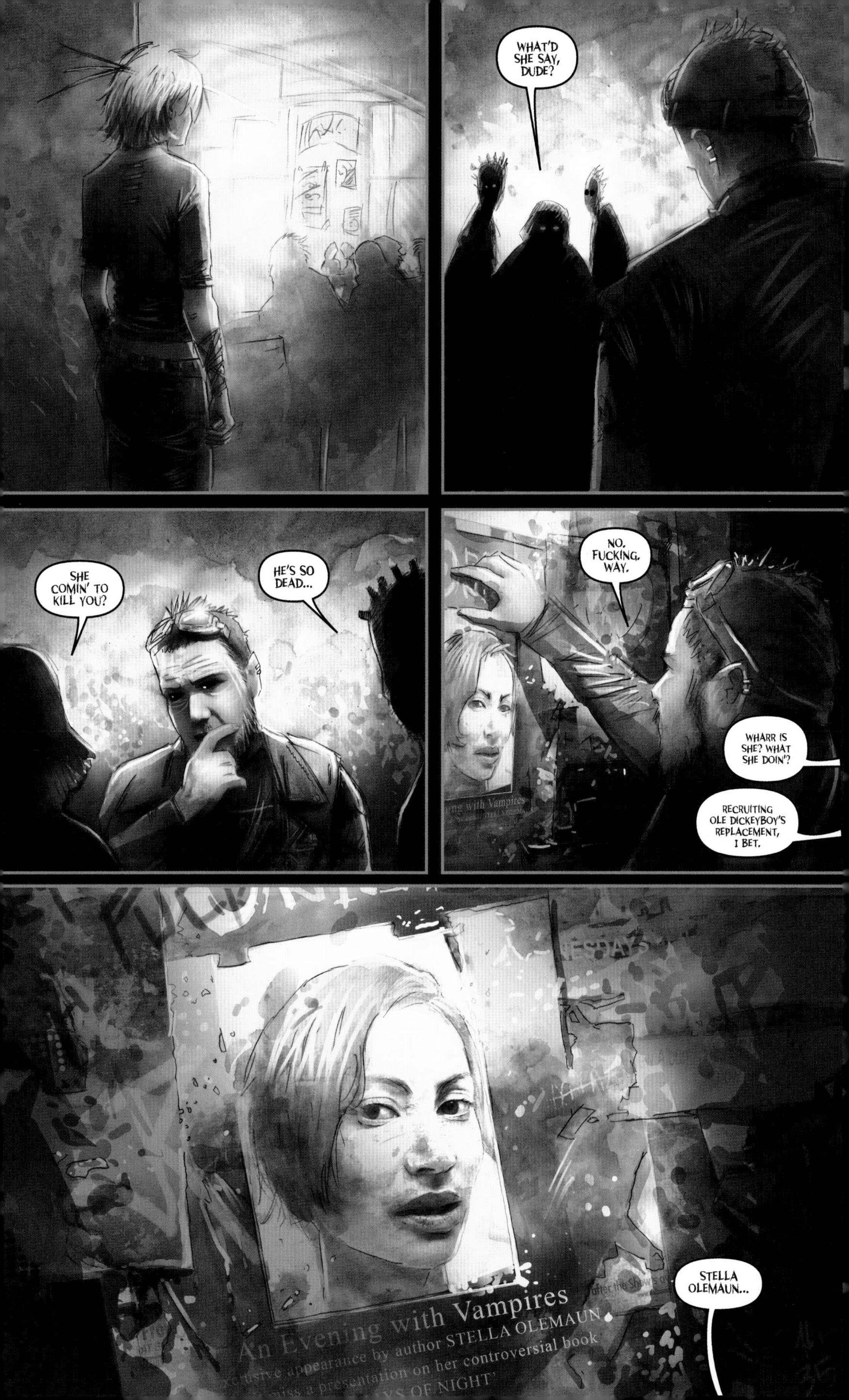
WHAT'D SHE SAY, DUDE?
SHE COMIN' TO KILL YOU?
HE'S SO DEAD...
NO. FUCKING. WAY.
WHARR IS SHE? WHAT SHE DOIN'?
RECRUITING OLE DICKEYBOY'S REPLACEMENT, I BET.
An Evening with Vampires
appearance by author STELLA OLEMAUN
a presentation on her controversial book
STELLA OLEMAUN...

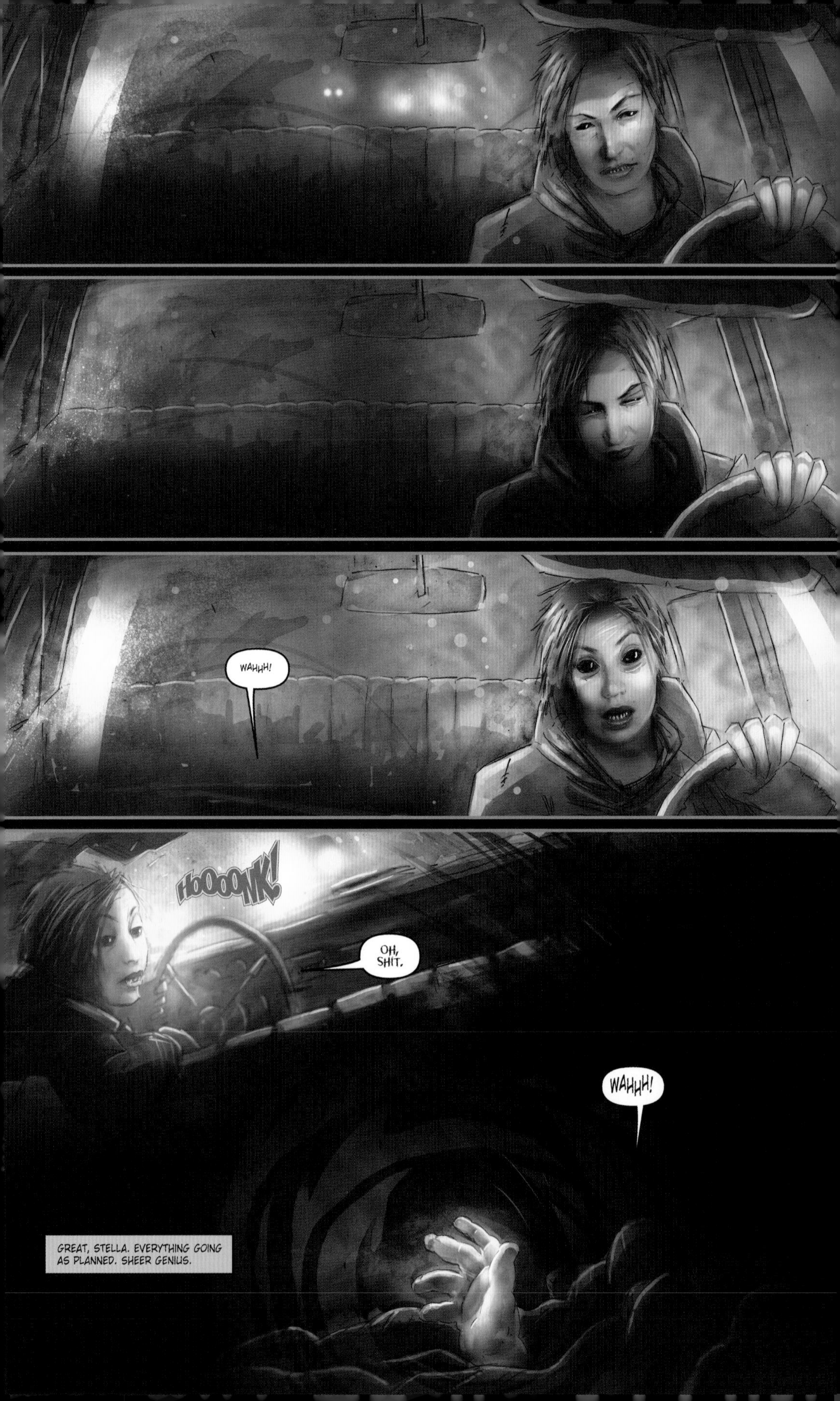
WAHHH!
HOOOONK!
OH, SHIT.
WAHHH!
GREAT, STELLA. EVERYTHING GOING AS PLANNED. SHEER GENIUS.

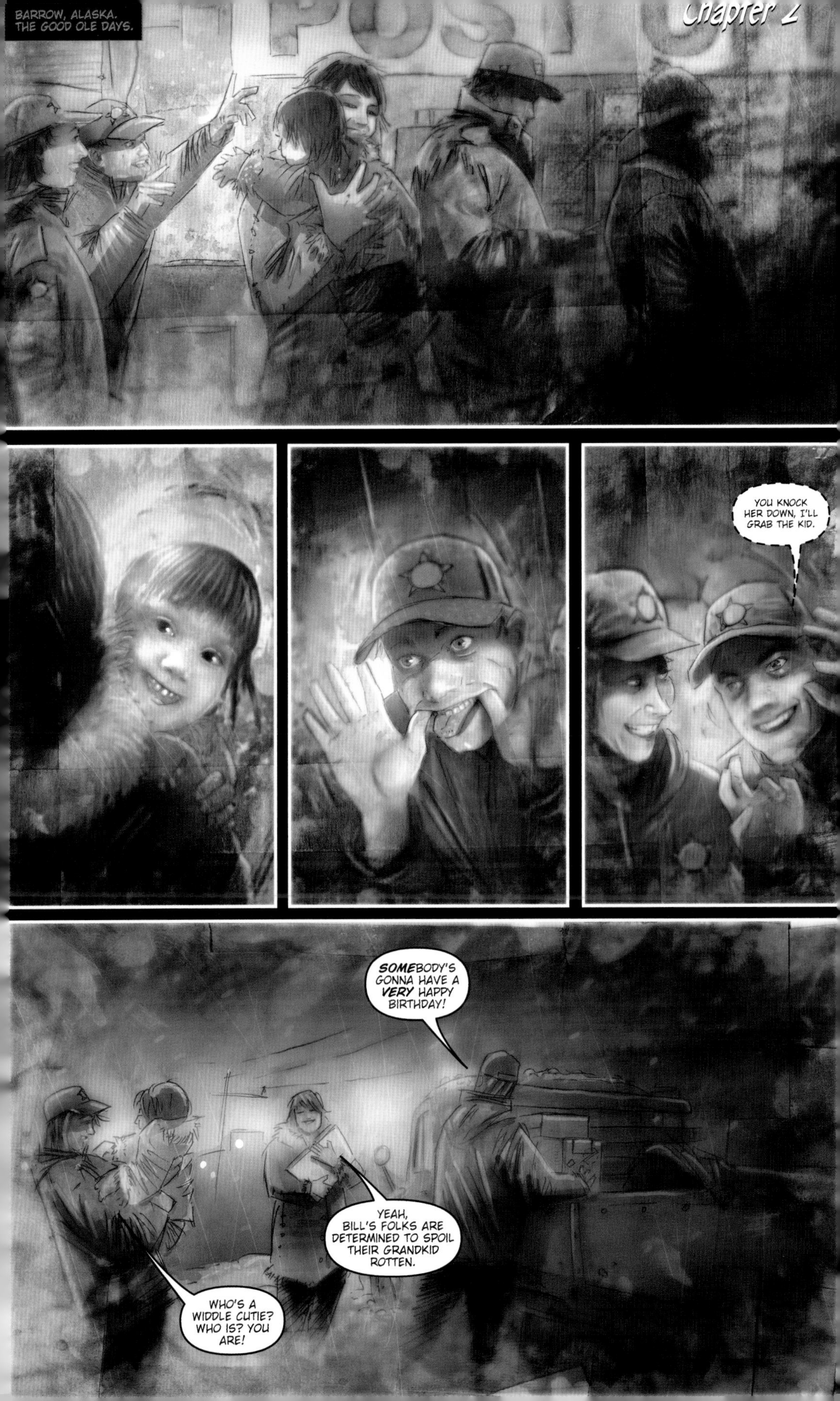
Chapter 2
BARROW, ALASKA. THE GOOD OLE DAYS.
YOU KNOCK HER DOWN, I'LL GRAB THE KID.
SOMEBODY'S GONNA HAVE A VERY HAPPY BIRTHDAY!
YEAH, BILL'S FOLKS ARE DETERMINED TO SPOIL THEIR GRANDKID ROTTEN.
WHO'S A WIDDLE CUTIE? WHO IS? YOU ARE!

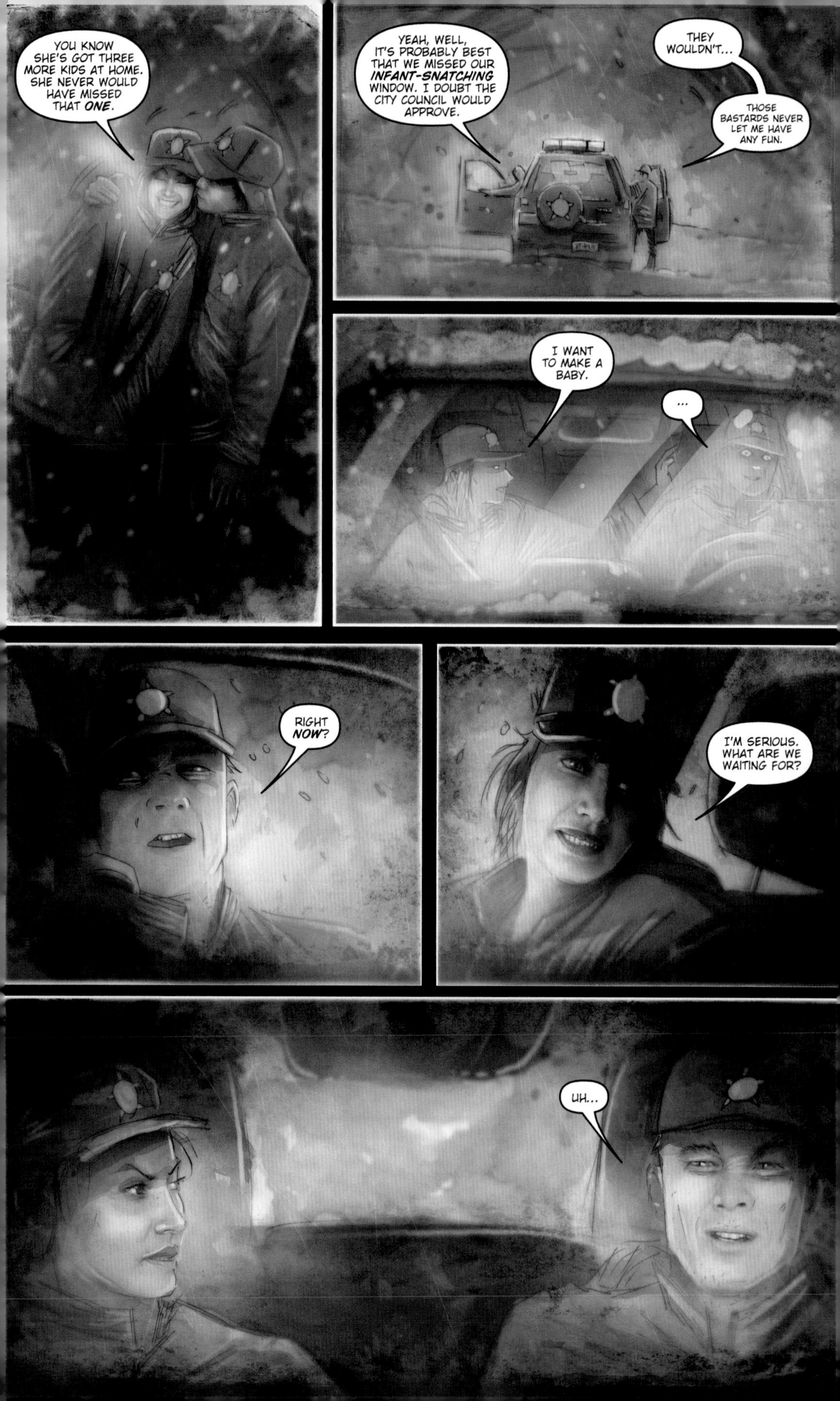
YOU KNOW SHE'S GOT THREE MORE KIDS AT HOME. SHE NEVER WOULD HAVE MISSED THAT ONE.
YEAH, WELL, IT'S PROBABLY BEST THAT WE MISSED OUR INFANT-SNATCHING WINDOW. I DOUBT THE CITY COUNCIL WOULD APPROVE.
THEY WOULDN'T...
THOSE BASTARDS NEVER LET ME HAVE ANY FUN.
I WANT TO MAKE A BABY.
...
RIGHT NOW?
I'M SERIOUS. WHAT ARE WE WAITING FOR?
UH...

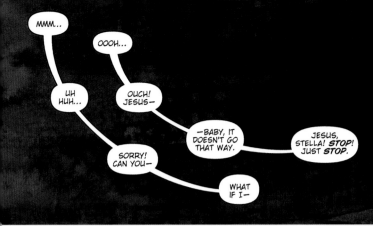

MMM...

OOOH...

UH HUH...

OUCH! JESUS—

SORRY! CAN YOU—

—BABY, IT DOESN'T GO THAT WAY.

WHAT IF I—

JESUS, STELLA! *STOP!* JUST *STOP.*

I'M SORRY.

ME, TOO.

LOOK, ONE DAY YOU ARE GOING TO MAKE AN *AMAZING* MOTHER TO A SMALL ARMY OF LITTLE MONSTERS. I PROMISE YOU THAT. BUT *RIGHT NOW...*

IF WE DO THIS RIGHT NOW, WE'RE GONNA GET *STUCK.* RIGHT HERE IN BARROW, LOOKING AFTER THESE SAME PEOPLE FOR THE *REST OF OUR LIVES.*

YOU *LOVE* BARROW!

YEAH, I DO, BUT... I'M JUST THINKING MAYBE IT'S TIME TO CONSIDER THE *POSSIBILITY* THAT THERE MIGHT BE SOMETHING ELSE OUT THERE FOR US. AN EASIER LIFE THAN MY OLD MAN'S...

WHAT KIND OF LIFE? WHERE?

I DON'T KNOW YET...

SOMEPLACE *SUNNY...*

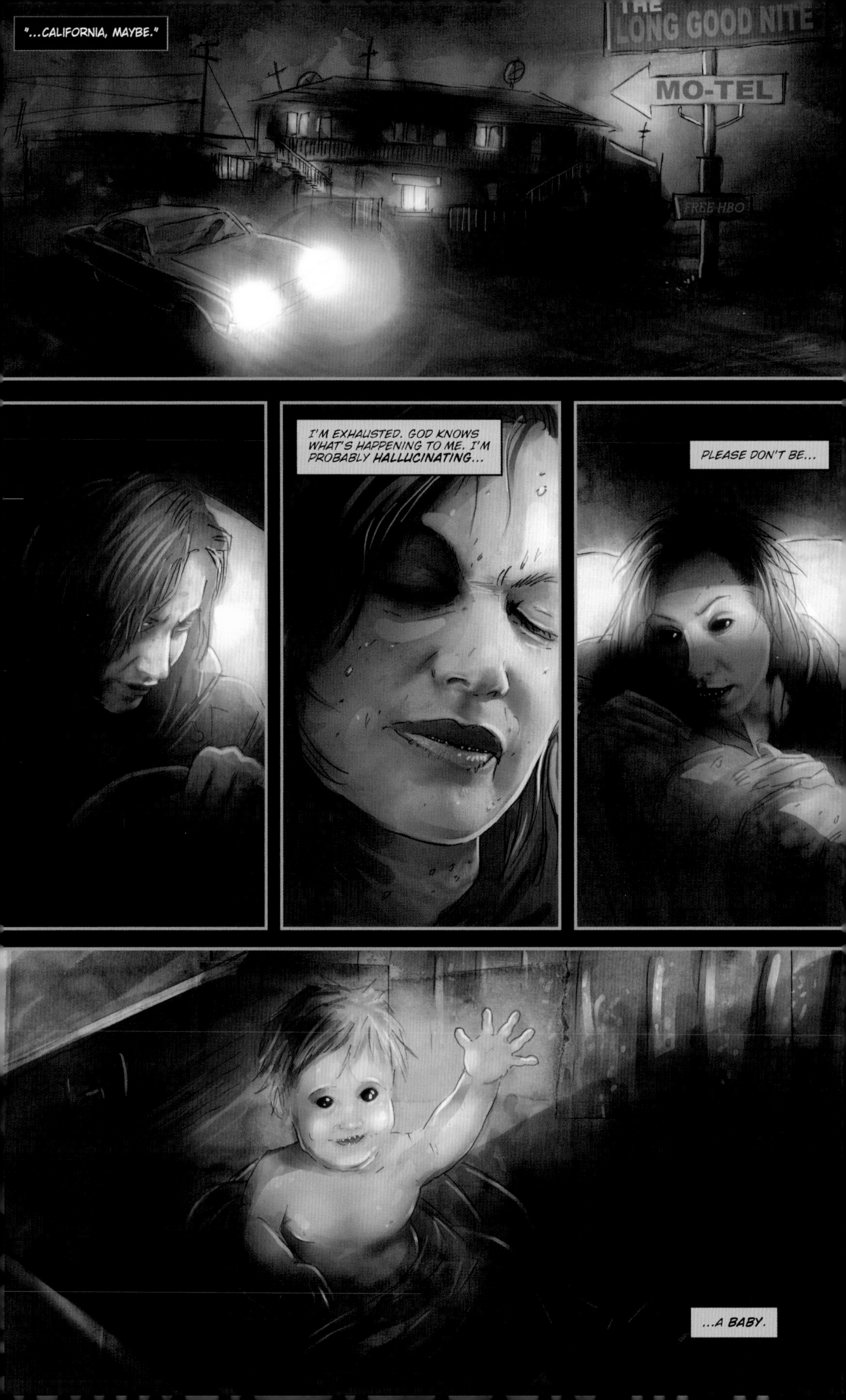
"...CALIFORNIA, MAYBE."
THE LONG GOOD NITE
MO-TEL
FREE HBO
I'M EXHAUSTED. GOD KNOWS WHAT'S HAPPENING TO ME. I'M PROBABLY HALLUCINATING...
PLEASE DON'T BE...
...A BABY.

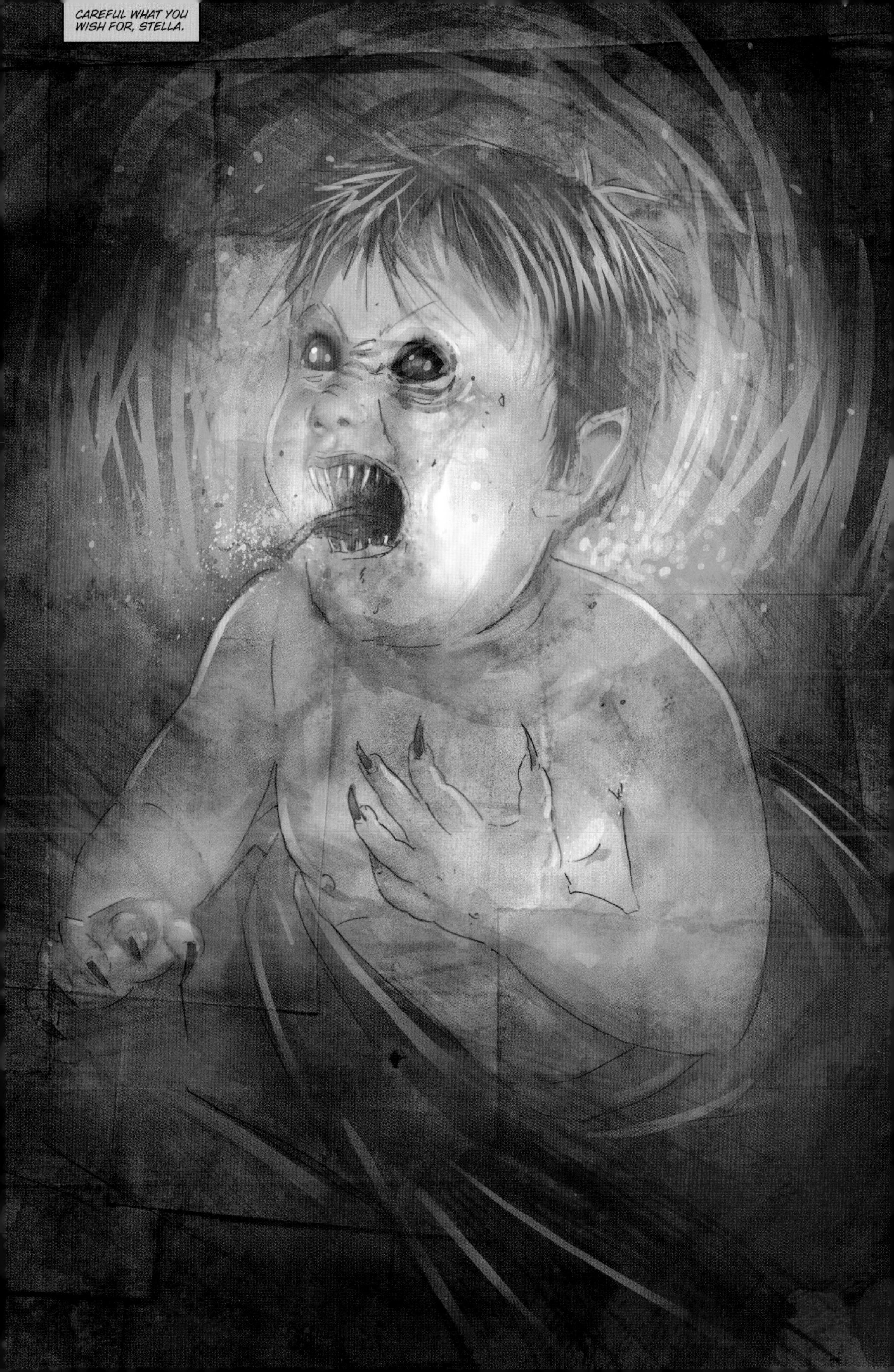
CAREFUL WHAT YOU WISH FOR, STELLA.

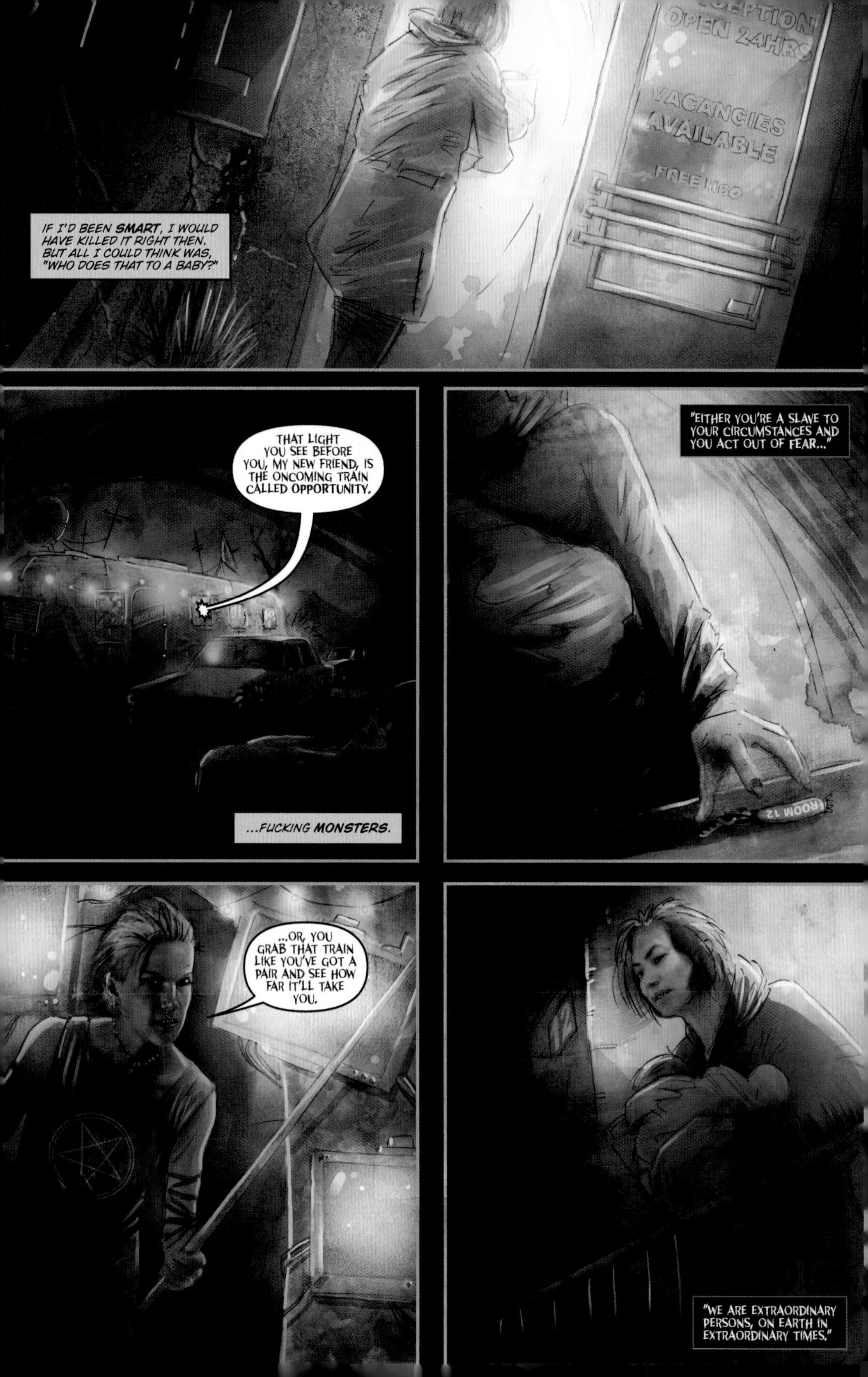
OPEN 24HRS
VACANCIES AVAILABLE
FREE HBO
IF I'D BEEN **SMART**, I WOULD HAVE KILLED IT RIGHT THEN. BUT ALL I COULD THINK WAS, "WHO DOES THAT TO A BABY?"
THAT LIGHT YOU SEE BEFORE YOU, MY NEW FRIEND, IS THE ONCOMING TRAIN CALLED **OPPORTUNITY.**
...FUCKING **MONSTERS.**
"EITHER YOU'RE A SLAVE TO YOUR CIRCUMSTANCES AND YOU ACT OUT OF **FEAR**..."
ROOM 12
...OR, YOU GRAB THAT TRAIN LIKE YOU'VE GOT A PAIR AND SEE HOW FAR IT'LL TAKE YOU.
12
"WE ARE EXTRAORDINARY PERSONS, ON EARTH IN EXTRAORDINARY TIMES."

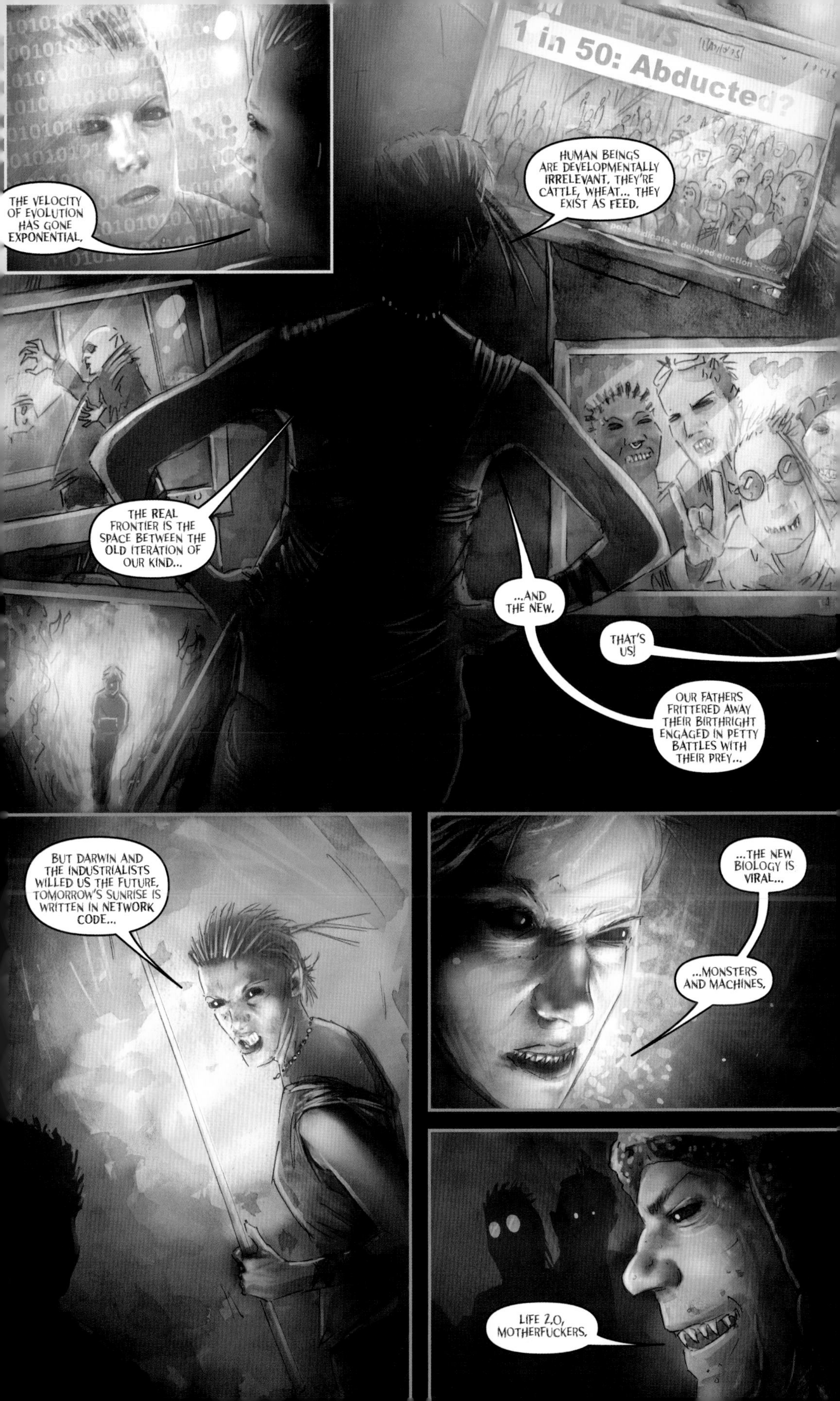
THE VELOCITY OF EVOLUTION HAS GONE EXPONENTIAL.
1 in 50: Abducted?
HUMAN BEINGS ARE DEVELOPMENTALLY IRRELEVANT. THEY'RE CATTLE, WHEAT... THEY EXIST AS FEED.
THE REAL FRONTIER IS THE SPACE BETWEEN THE OLD ITERATION OF OUR KIND...
...AND THE NEW.
THAT'S US!
OUR FATHERS FRITTERED AWAY THEIR BIRTHRIGHT ENGAGED IN PETTY BATTLES WITH THEIR PREY...
BUT DARWIN AND THE INDUSTRIALISTS WILLED US THE FUTURE. TOMORROW'S SUNRISE IS WRITTEN IN NETWORK CODE...
...THE NEW BIOLOGY IS VIRAL...
...MONSTERS AND MACHINES.
LIFE 2.0, MOTHERFUCKERS.

...NEW BLOOD!

THE OLD GUARD PAID FOR ITS LACK OF IMAGINATION WITH ITS LIFE.

WE REQUIRE LEADERSHIP, DIRECTION...

BUT—

—TRADITION DEMANDS THAT THE ELDEST AMONG US RULE.

SO HOW DO WE RECONCILE THE OLD WITH THE NEW?

HISTORY PROVIDES A MODEL, MY FRIENDS...

THE OLDEST IS THE YOUNGEST.

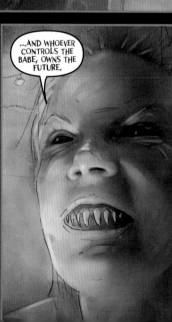

PROTECTED BY OUR KIND FOR MILLENNIA, THIS KID IS OLDER THAN ALL OF US PUT TOGETHER, PATIENT ZERO OF THE NEXT EVOLUTIONARY LEAP...

...AND WHOEVER CONTROLS THE BABE, OWNS THE FUTURE.

WE'VE FOUND OURSELVES A GODDAMNED CHILD KING.

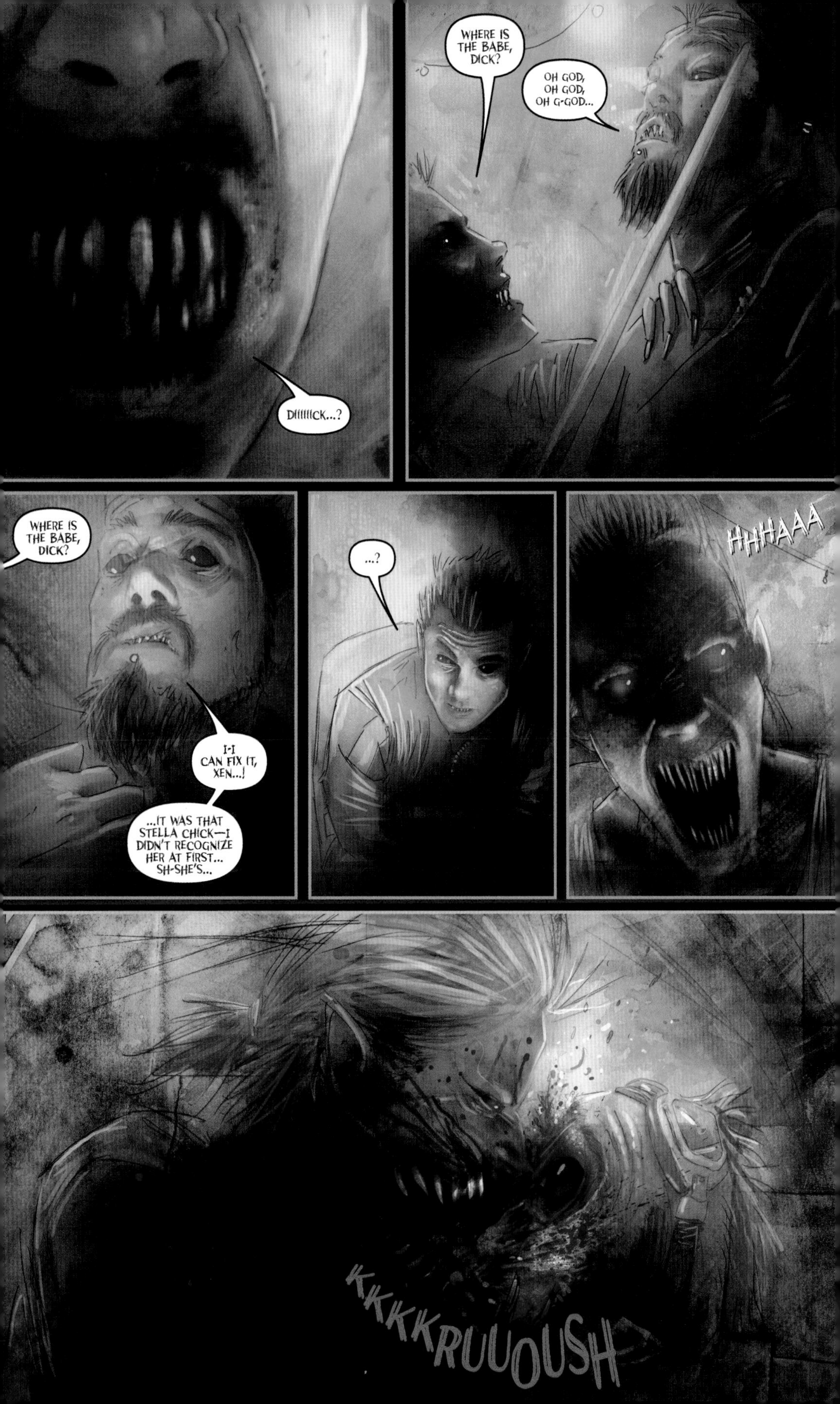
DIIIIIICK...?
WHERE IS THE BABE, DICK?
OH GOD, OH GOD, OH G-GOD...
WHERE IS THE BABE, DICK?
I-I CAN FIX IT, XEN...!
...IT WAS THAT STELLA CHICK—I DIDN'T RECOGNIZE HER AT FIRST... SH-SHE'S...
...?
HHHAAA
KKKKRUUUOUSH

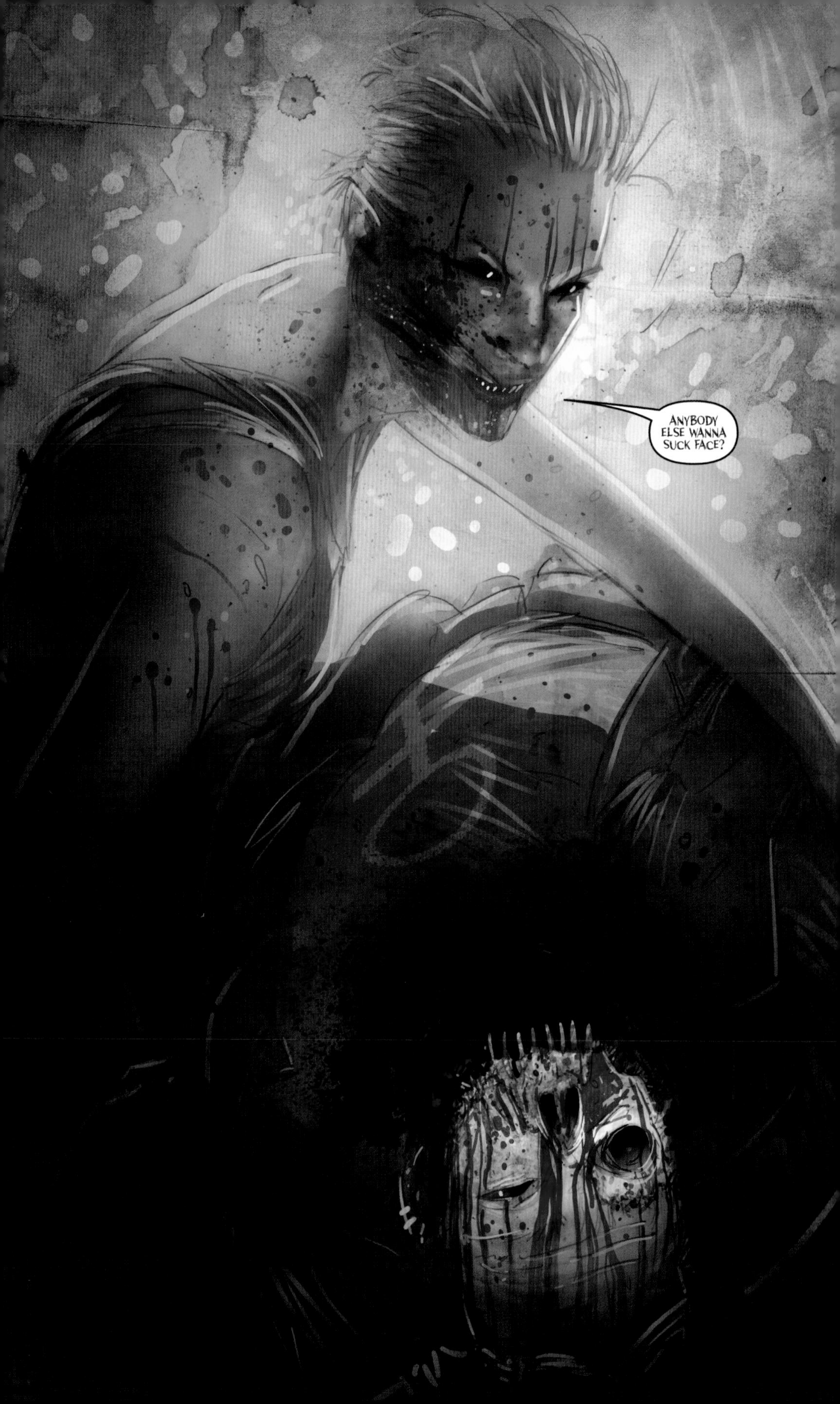
ANYBODY ELSE WANNA SUCK FACE?

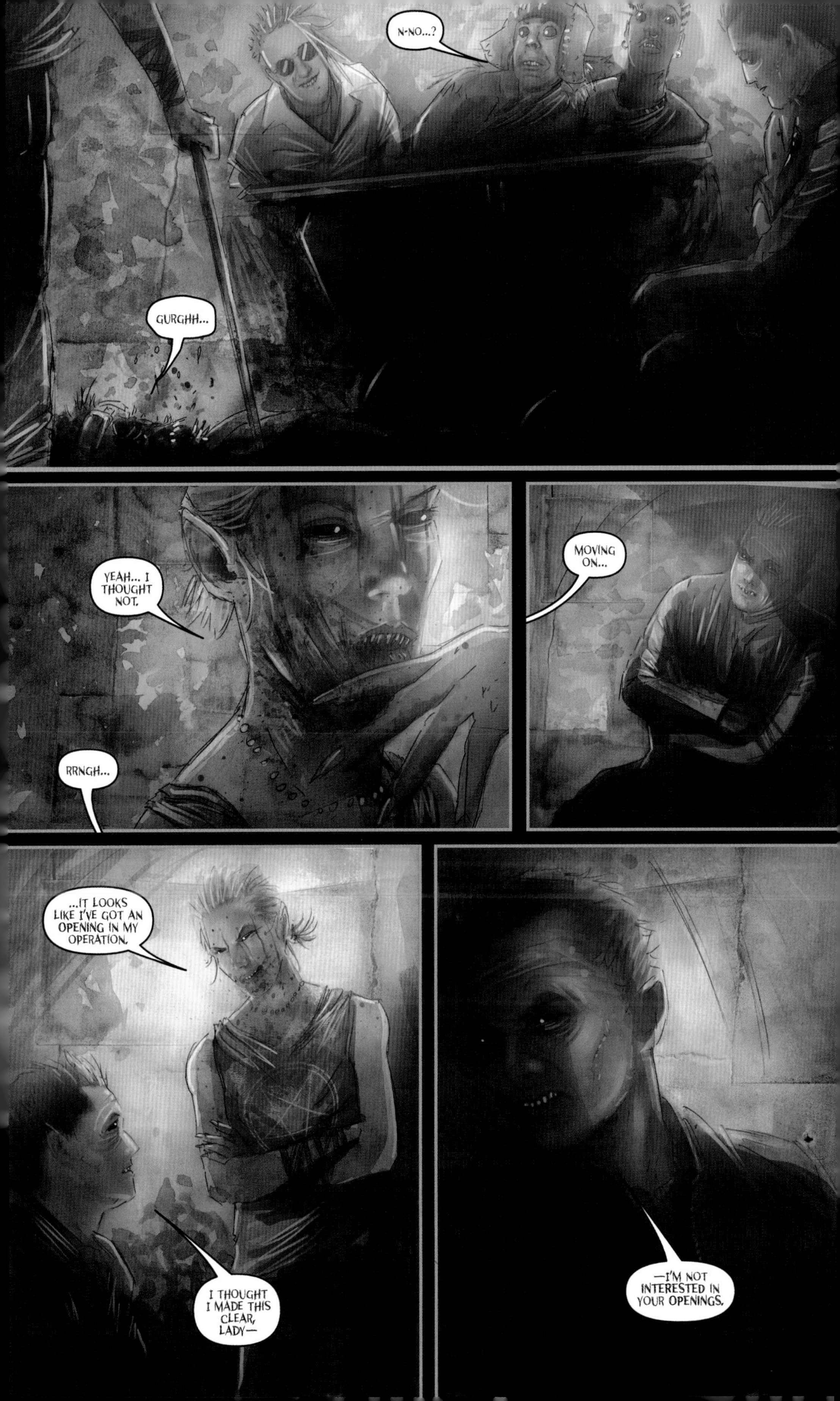

N-NO...?
GURGHH...
YEAH... I THOUGHT NOT.
RRNGH...
MOVING ON...
...IT LOOKS LIKE I'VE GOT AN OPENING IN MY OPERATION.
I THOUGHT I MADE THIS CLEAR, LADY—
—I'M NOT INTERESTED IN YOUR OPENINGS.

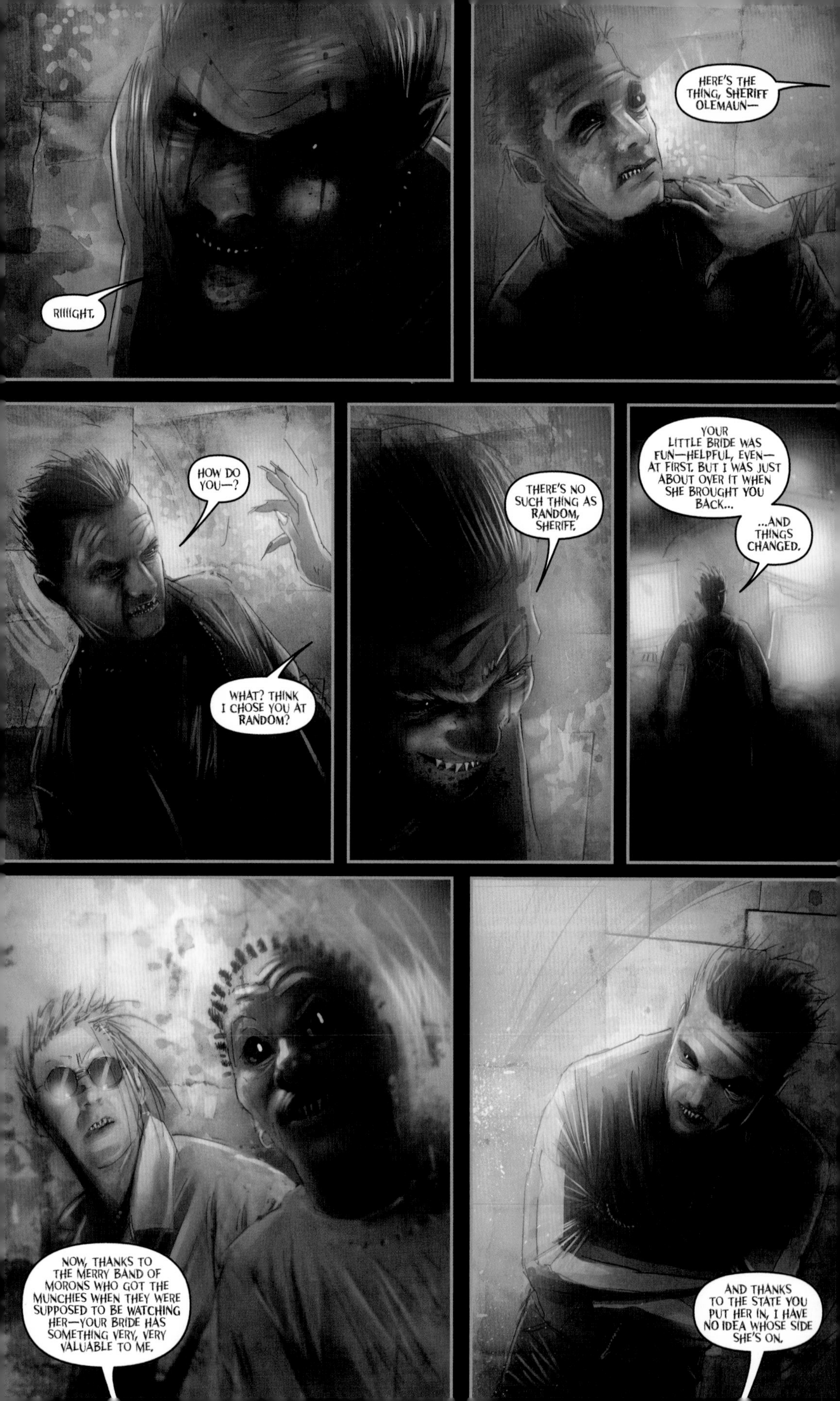
RIIIIGHT.
HERE'S THE THING, SHERIFF OLEMAUN—
HOW DO YOU—?
WHAT? THINK I CHOSE YOU AT RANDOM?
THERE'S NO SUCH THING AS RANDOM, SHERIFF.
YOUR LITTLE BRIDE WAS FUN—HELPFUL, EVEN—AT FIRST. BUT I WAS JUST ABOUT OVER IT WHEN SHE BROUGHT YOU BACK...
...AND THINGS CHANGED.
NOW, THANKS TO THE MERRY BAND OF MORONS WHO GOT THE MUNCHIES WHEN THEY WERE SUPPOSED TO BE WATCHING HER—YOUR BRIDE HAS SOMETHING VERY, VERY VALUABLE TO ME.
AND THANKS TO THE STATE YOU PUT HER IN, I HAVE NO IDEA WHOSE SIDE SHE'S ON.

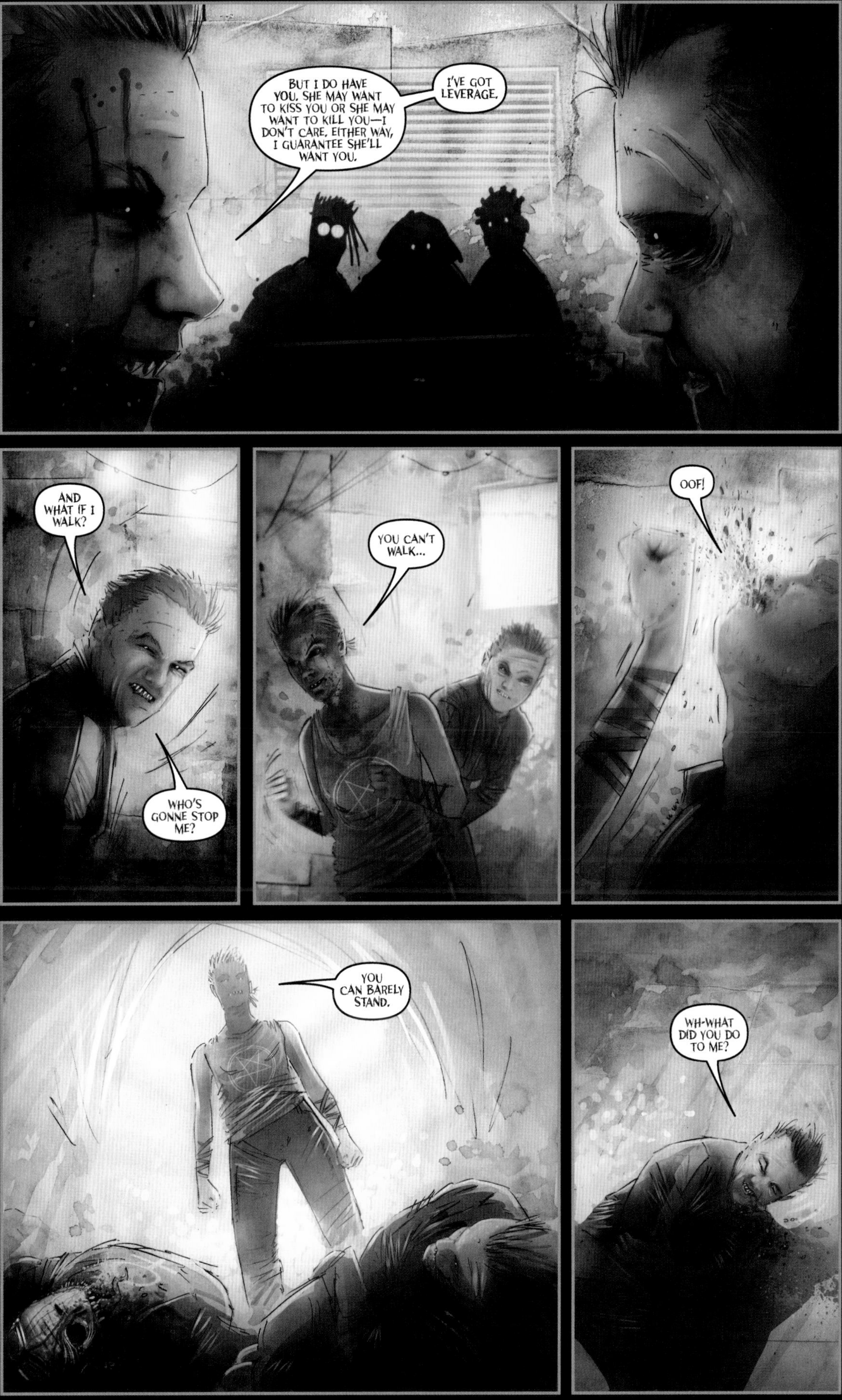
BUT I DO HAVE YOU. SHE MAY WANT TO KISS YOU OR SHE MAY WANT TO KILL YOU—I DON'T CARE. EITHER WAY, I GUARANTEE SHE'LL WANT YOU.
I'VE GOT LEVERAGE.
AND WHAT IF I WALK?
WHO'S GONNE STOP ME?
YOU CAN'T WALK...
OOF!
YOU CAN BARELY STAND.
WH-WHAT DID YOU DO TO ME?

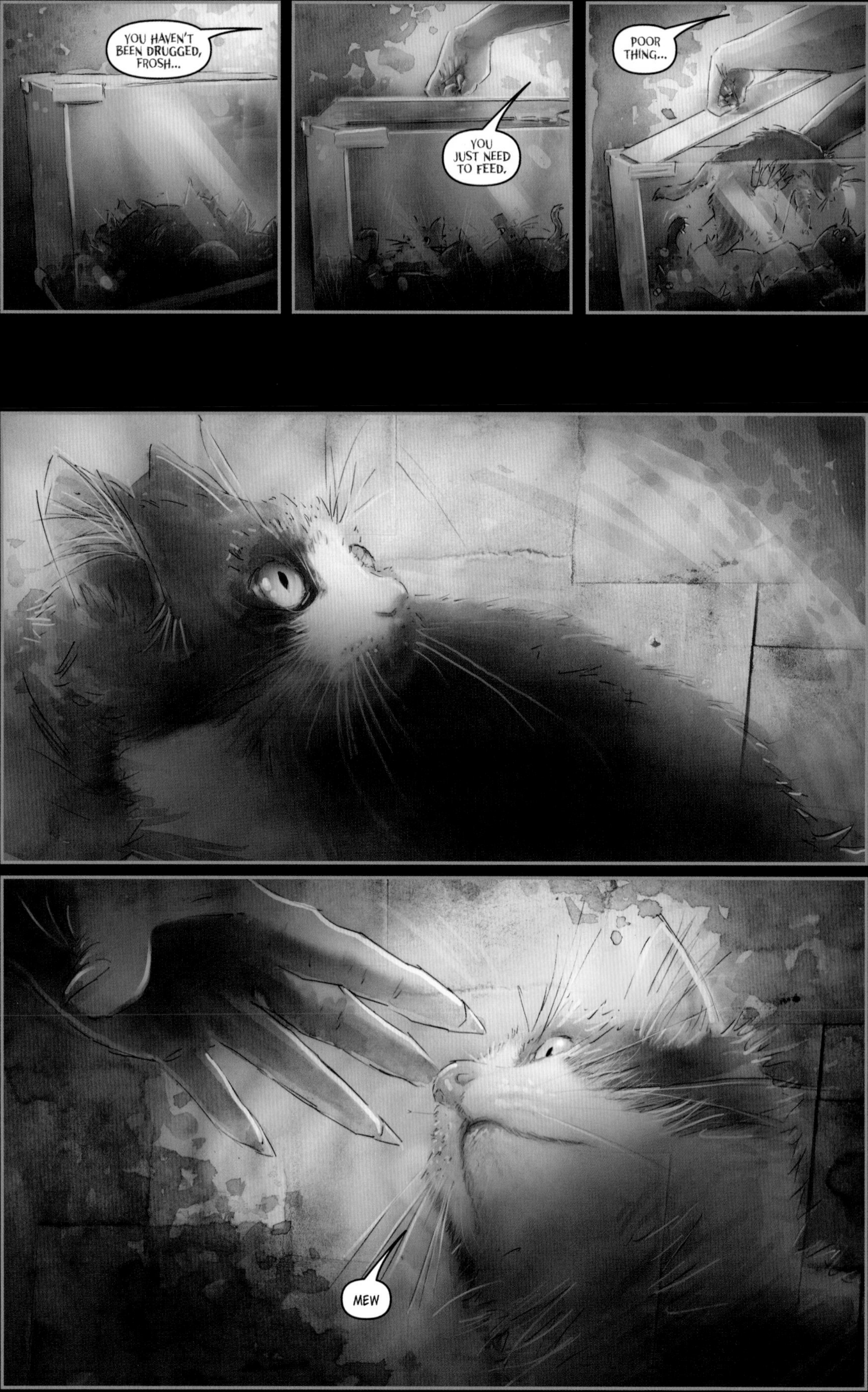
YOU HAVEN'T BEEN DRUGGED, FROSH...
YOU JUST NEED TO FEED.
POOR THING...
MEW

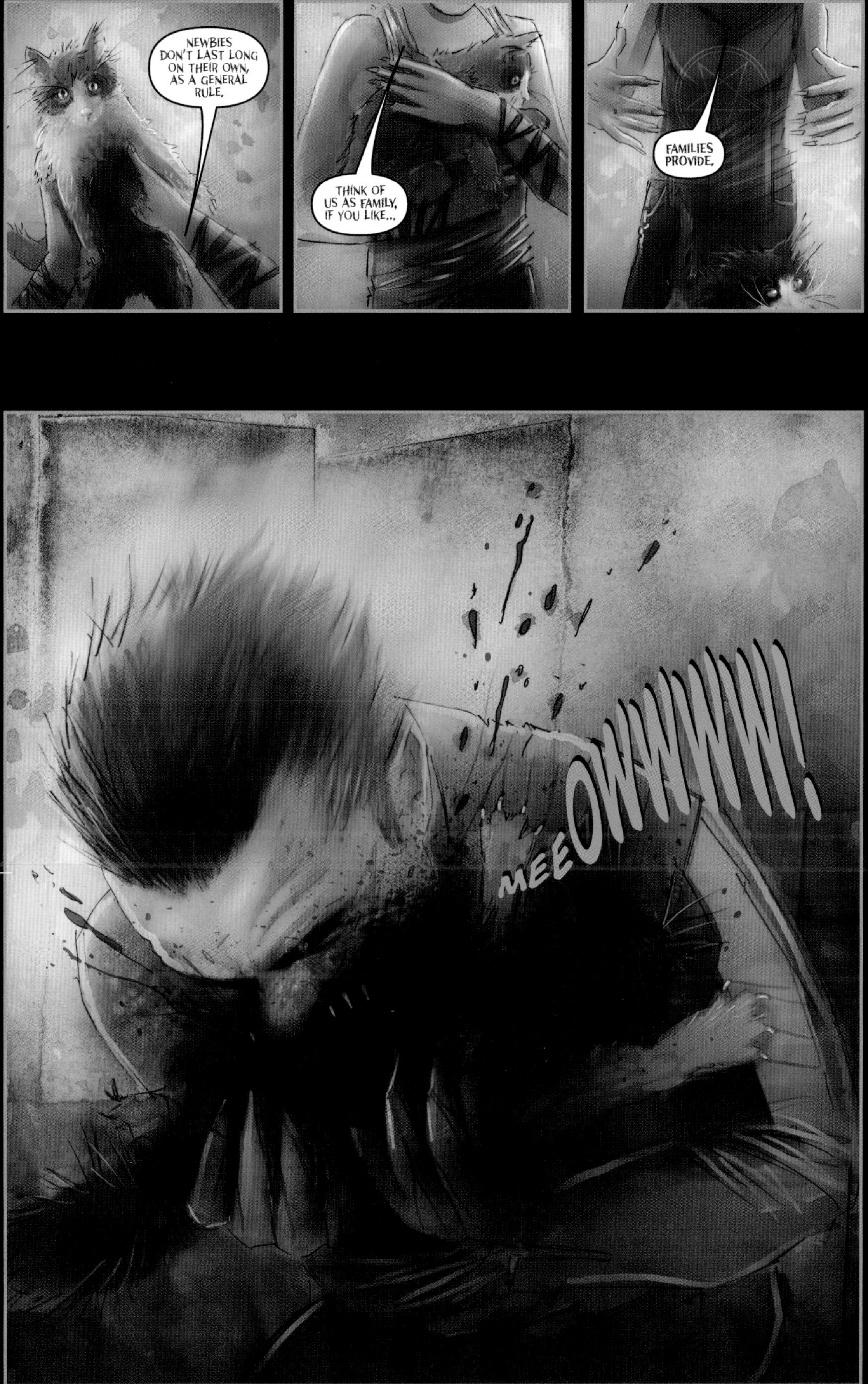
NEWBIES DON'T LAST LONG ON THEIR OWN, AS A GENERAL RULE,
THINK OF US AS FAMILY, IF YOU LIKE...
FAMILIES PROVIDE.
MEEOWWWW!

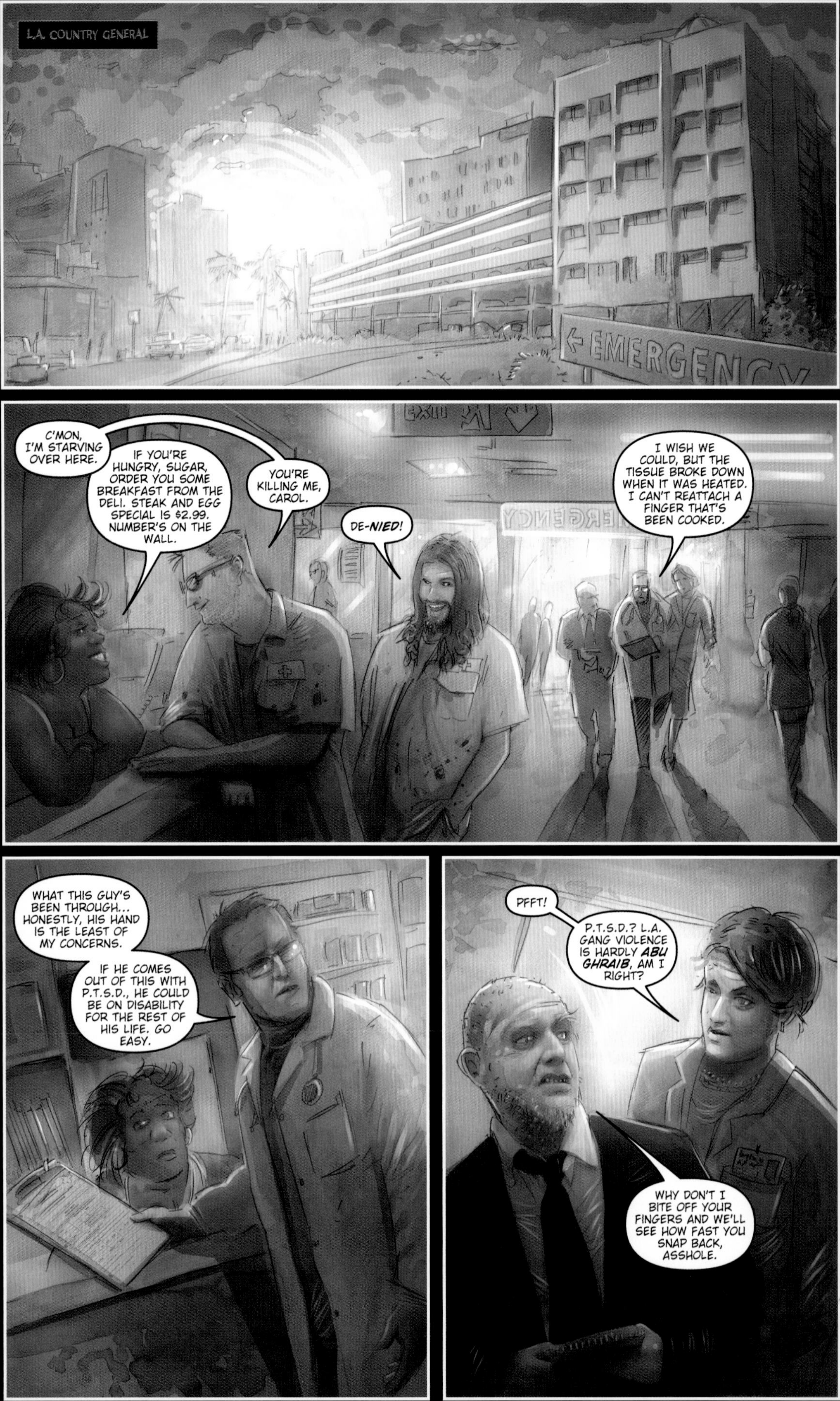
L.A. COUNTRY GENERAL
EMERGENCY
C'MON, I'M STARVING OVER HERE.
IF YOU'RE HUNGRY, SUGAR, ORDER YOU SOME BREAKFAST FROM THE DELI. STEAK AND EGG SPECIAL IS $2.99. NUMBER'S ON THE WALL.
YOU'RE KILLING ME, CAROL.
DE-NIED!
I WISH WE COULD, BUT THE TISSUE BROKE DOWN WHEN IT WAS HEATED. I CAN'T REATTACH A FINGER THAT'S BEEN COOKED.
WHAT THIS GUY'S BEEN THROUGH... HONESTLY, HIS HAND IS THE LEAST OF MY CONCERNS.
IF HE COMES OUT OF THIS WITH P.T.S.D., HE COULD BE ON DISABILITY FOR THE REST OF HIS LIFE. GO EASY.
PFFT!
P.T.S.D.? L.A. GANG VIOLENCE IS HARDLY ABU GHRAIB, AM I RIGHT?
WHY DON'T I BITE OFF YOUR FINGERS AND WE'LL SEE HOW FAST YOU SNAP BACK, ASSHOLE.

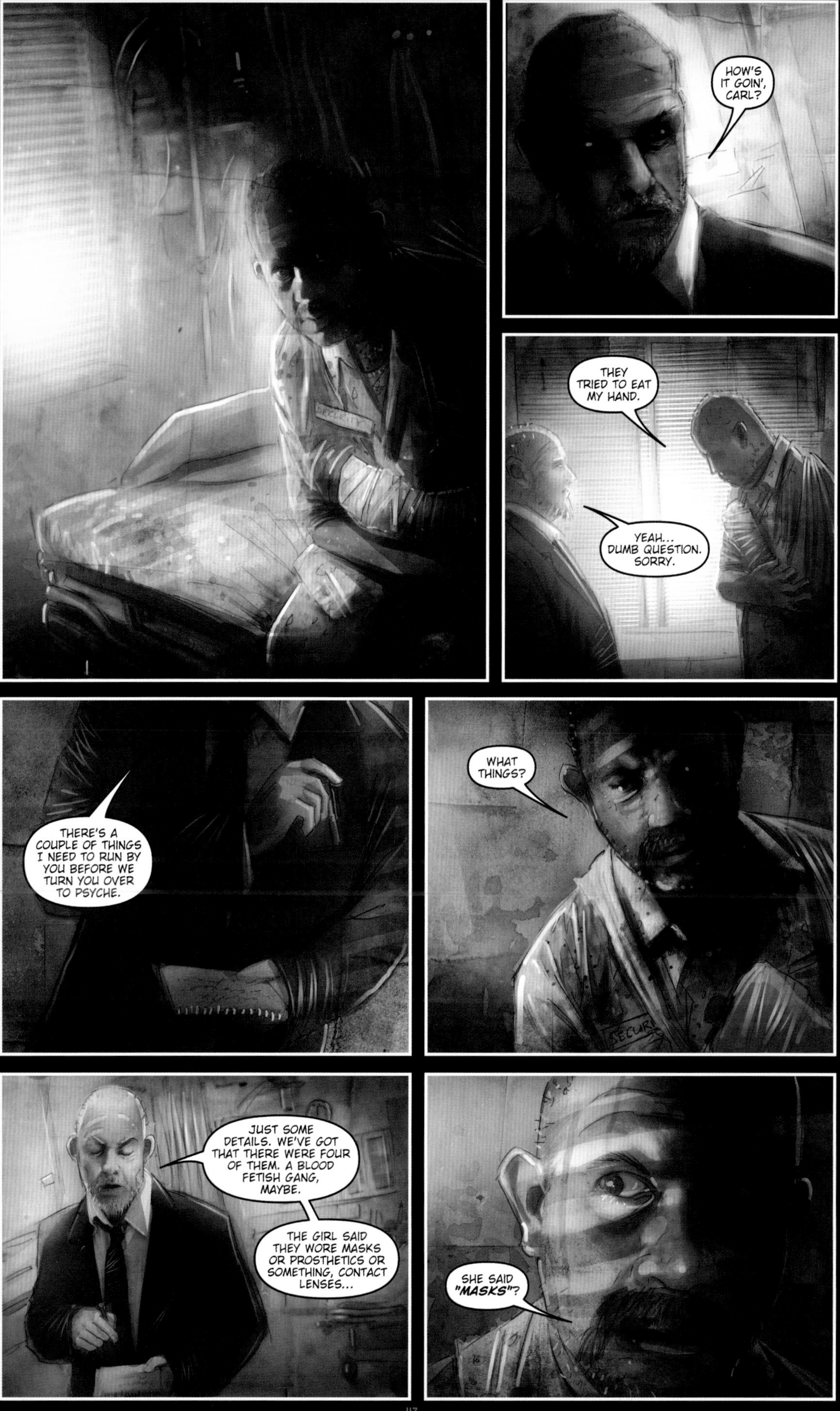
HOW'S IT GOIN', CARL?
THEY TRIED TO EAT MY HAND.
YEAH... DUMB QUESTION. SORRY.
THERE'S A COUPLE OF THINGS I NEED TO RUN BY YOU BEFORE WE TURN YOU OVER TO PSYCHE.
WHAT THINGS?
JUST SOME DETAILS. WE'VE GOT THAT THERE WERE FOUR OF THEM. A BLOOD FETISH GANG, MAYBE.
THE GIRL SAID THEY WORE MASKS OR PROSTHETICS OR SOMETHING, CONTACT LENSES...
SHE SAID *"MASKS"*?

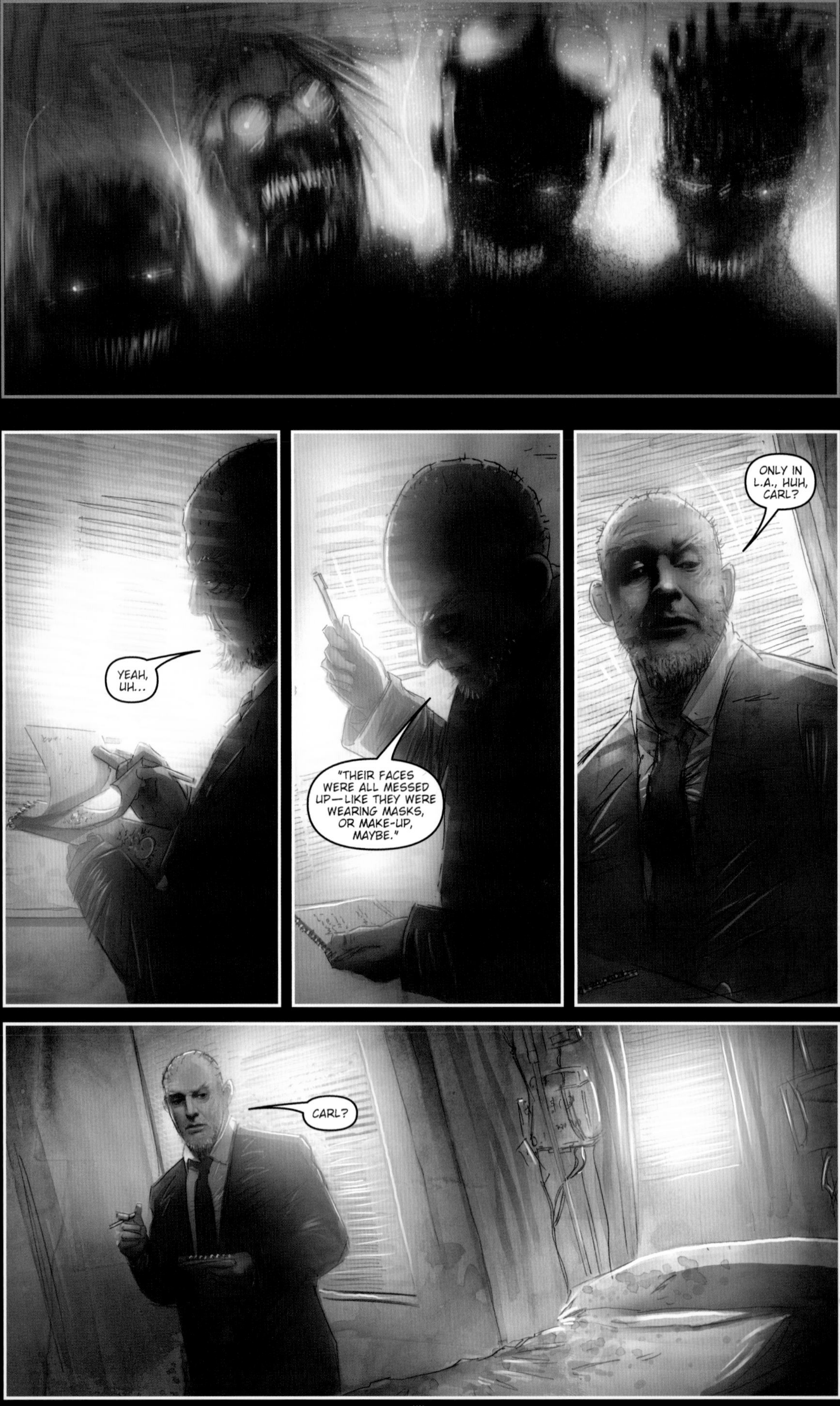
YEAH, UH...
"THEIR FACES WERE ALL MESSED UP—LIKE THEY WERE WEARING MASKS, OR MAKE-UP, MAYBE."
ONLY IN L.A., HUH, CARL?
CARL?

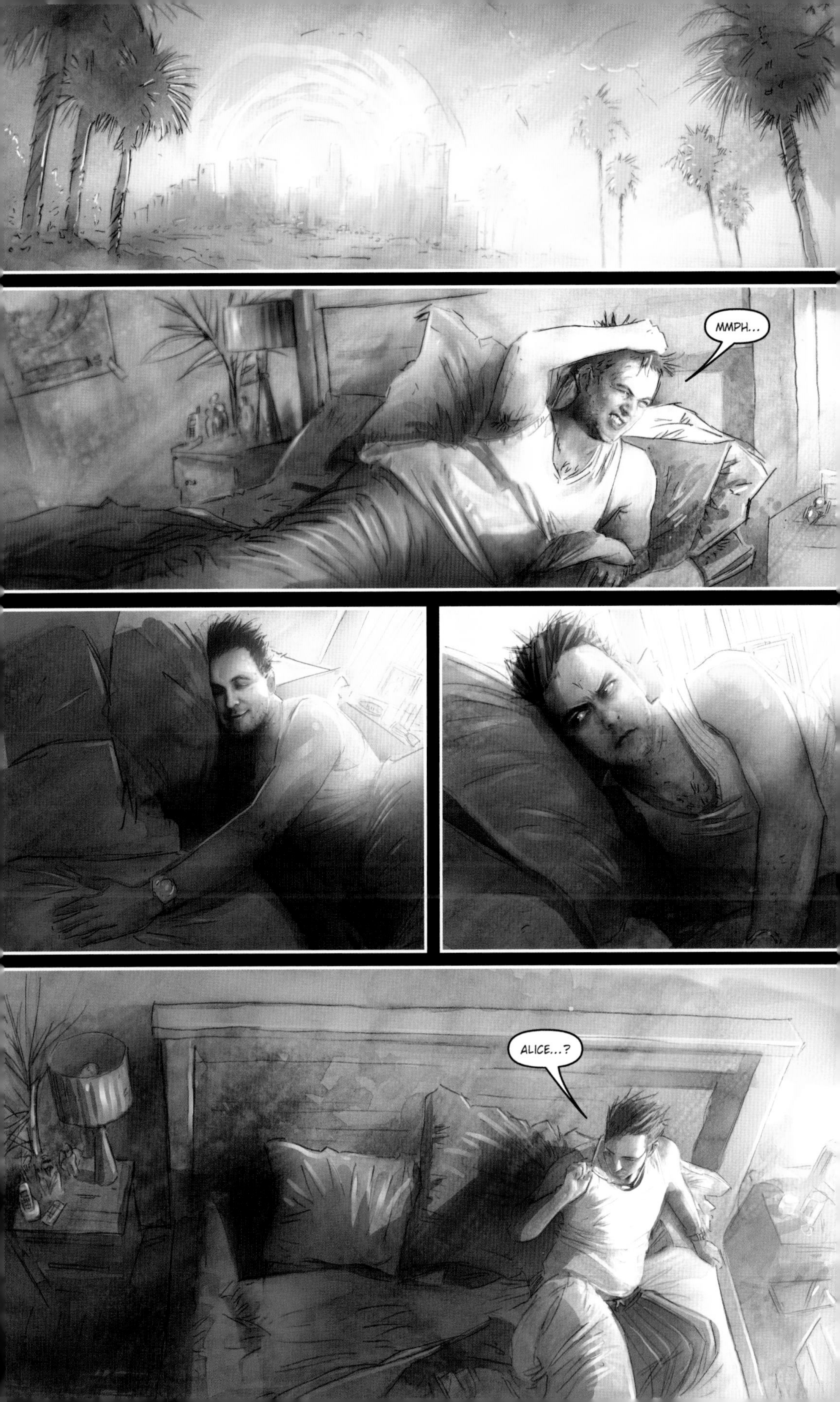
MMPH...
ALICE...?

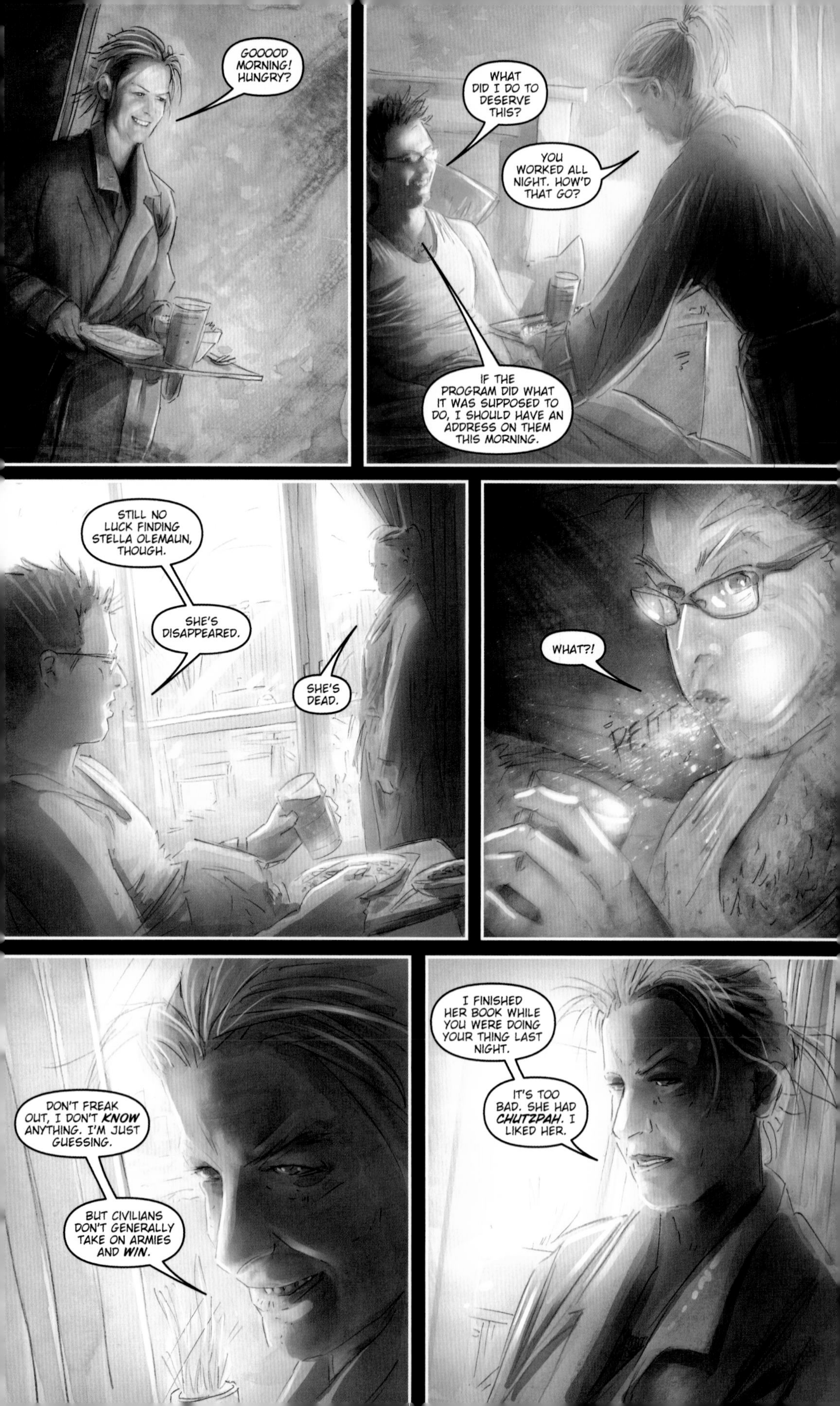

GOOOOD MORNING! HUNGRY?
WHAT DID I DO TO DESERVE THIS?
YOU WORKED ALL NIGHT. HOW'D THAT GO?
IF THE PROGRAM DID WHAT IT WAS SUPPOSED TO DO, I SHOULD HAVE AN ADDRESS ON THEM THIS MORNING.
STILL NO LUCK FINDING STELLA OLEMAUN, THOUGH.
SHE'S DISAPPEARED.
SHE'S DEAD.
WHAT?!
DON'T FREAK OUT, I DON'T ***KNOW*** ANYTHING. I'M JUST GUESSING.
BUT CIVILIANS DON'T GENERALLY TAKE ON ARMIES AND ***WIN***.
I FINISHED HER BOOK WHILE YOU WERE DOING YOUR THING LAST NIGHT.
IT'S TOO BAD. SHE HAD ***CHUTZPAH***. I LIKED HER.

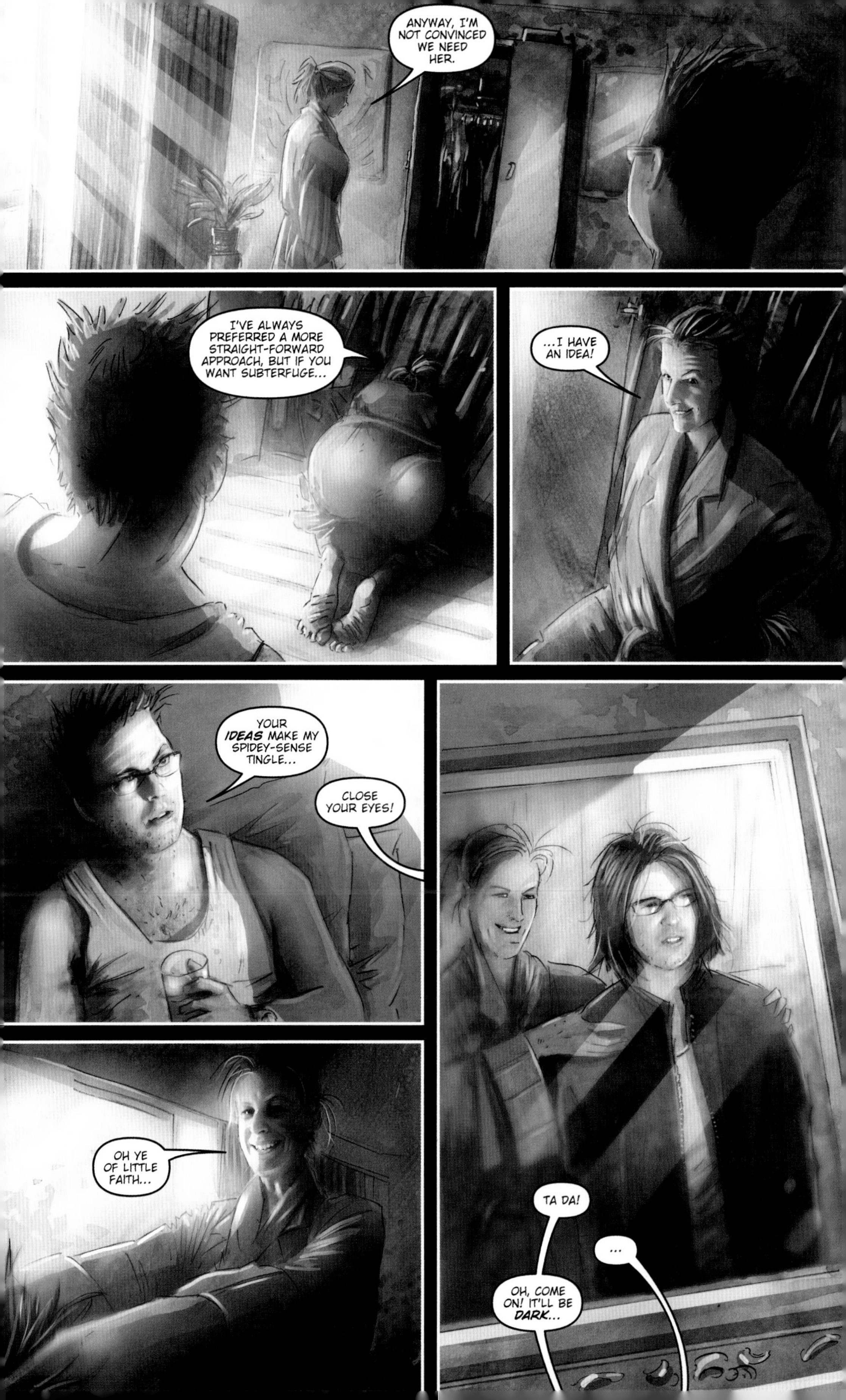
ANYWAY, I'M NOT CONVINCED WE NEED HER.
I'VE ALWAYS PREFERRED A MORE STRAIGHT-FORWARD APPROACH, BUT IF YOU WANT SUBTERFUGE...
...I HAVE AN IDEA!
YOUR *IDEAS* MAKE MY SPIDEY-SENSE TINGLE...
CLOSE YOUR EYES!
OH YE OF LITTLE FAITH...
TA DA!
...
OH, COME ON! IT'LL BE *DARK*...

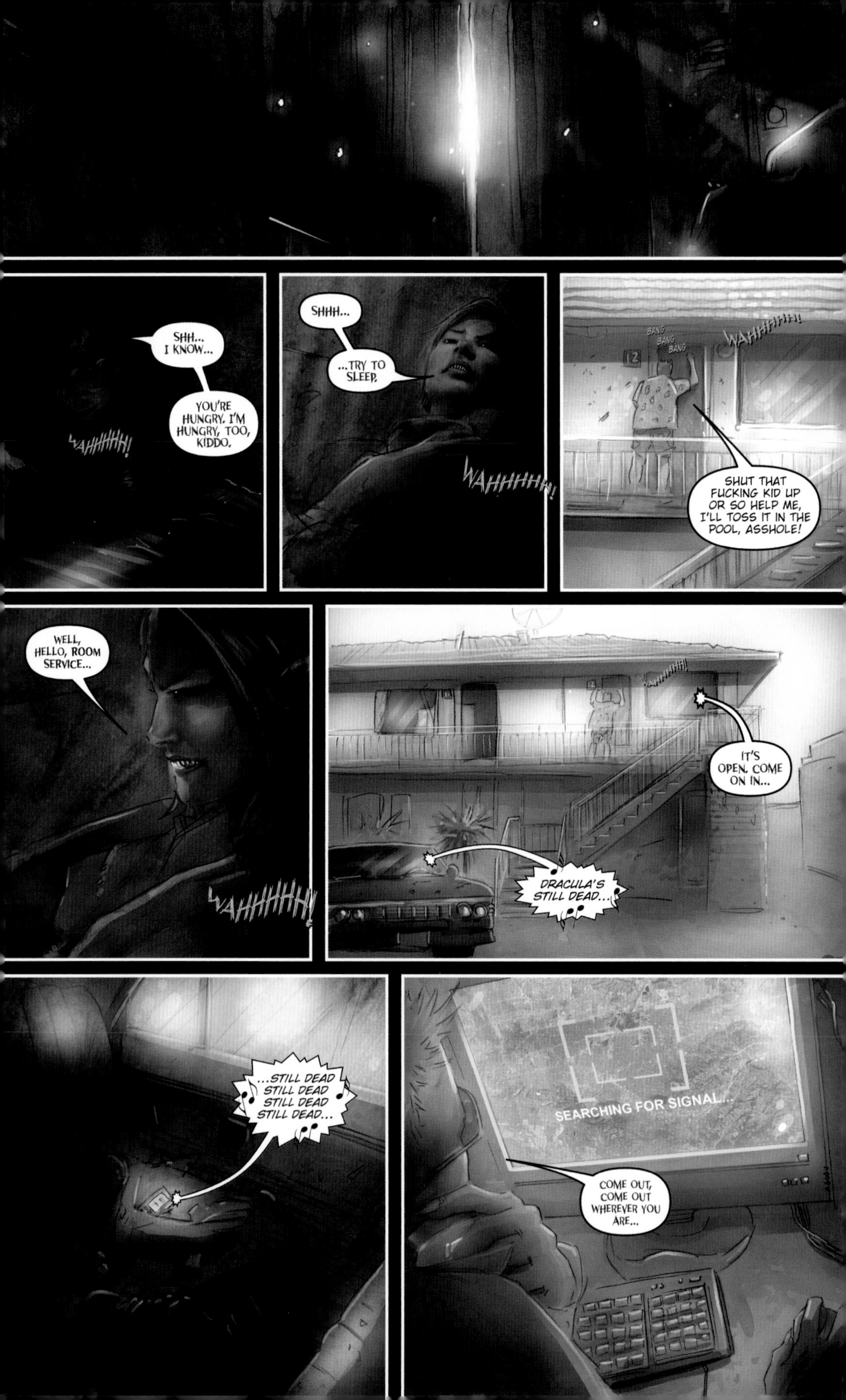
SHH... I KNOW...
YOU'RE HUNGRY. I'M HUNGRY, TOO, KIDDO.
WAHHHHH!
SHHH...
...TRY TO SLEEP.
WAHHHHHH!
BANG BANG BANG
WAHHHHHH!
SHUT THAT FUCKING KID UP OR SO HELP ME, I'LL TOSS IT IN THE POOL, ASSHOLE!
WELL, HELLO, ROOM SERVICE...
WAHHHHHH!
WAHHHHH!
IT'S OPEN. COME ON IN...
DRACULA'S STILL DEAD...
...STILL DEAD STILL DEAD STILL DEAD STILL DEAD...
SEARCHING FOR SIGNAL...
COME OUT, COME OUT WHEREVER YOU ARE...

OMNIA MUTANTUR, NOS ET MUTAMUR IN ILLIS...

...ALL THINGS CHANGE, AND WE CHANGE WITH THEM.

Chapter 3

IT WEARS ON A BODY, THIS *CONSTANT EVOLUTION*.

TIME *GIVETH*...

...AND, FOR NO PARTICULAR REASON, TIME *TAKETH AWAY*.

ONE DAY WE WAKE TO FIND WE NO LONGER *RECOGNIZE* THE WORLD AROUND US.

WE ARE RELICS, WALKING *GHOSTS*.

WE CAN *GRIEVE*, OR WE CAN *ADAPT*.

WE CAN CHANGE...

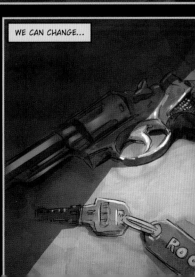

...OR *DIE*.

WE CAN MAKE THAT CHOICE.

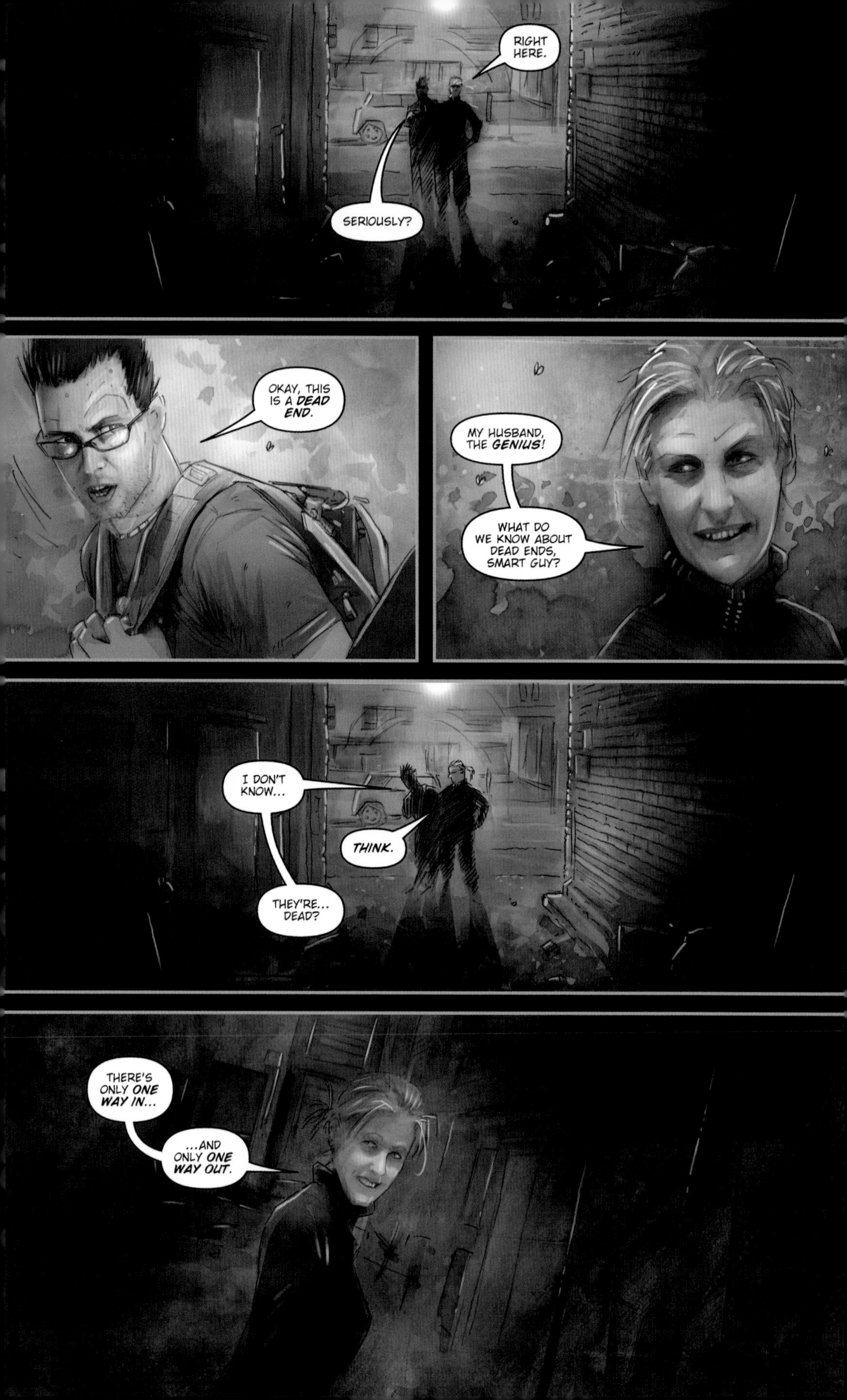
RIGHT HERE.
SERIOUSLY?
OKAY, THIS IS A DEAD END.
MY HUSBAND, THE GENIUS!
WHAT DO WE KNOW ABOUT DEAD ENDS, SMART GUY?
I DON'T KNOW...
THINK.
THEY'RE... DEAD?
THERE'S ONLY ONE WAY IN...
...AND ONLY ONE WAY OUT.

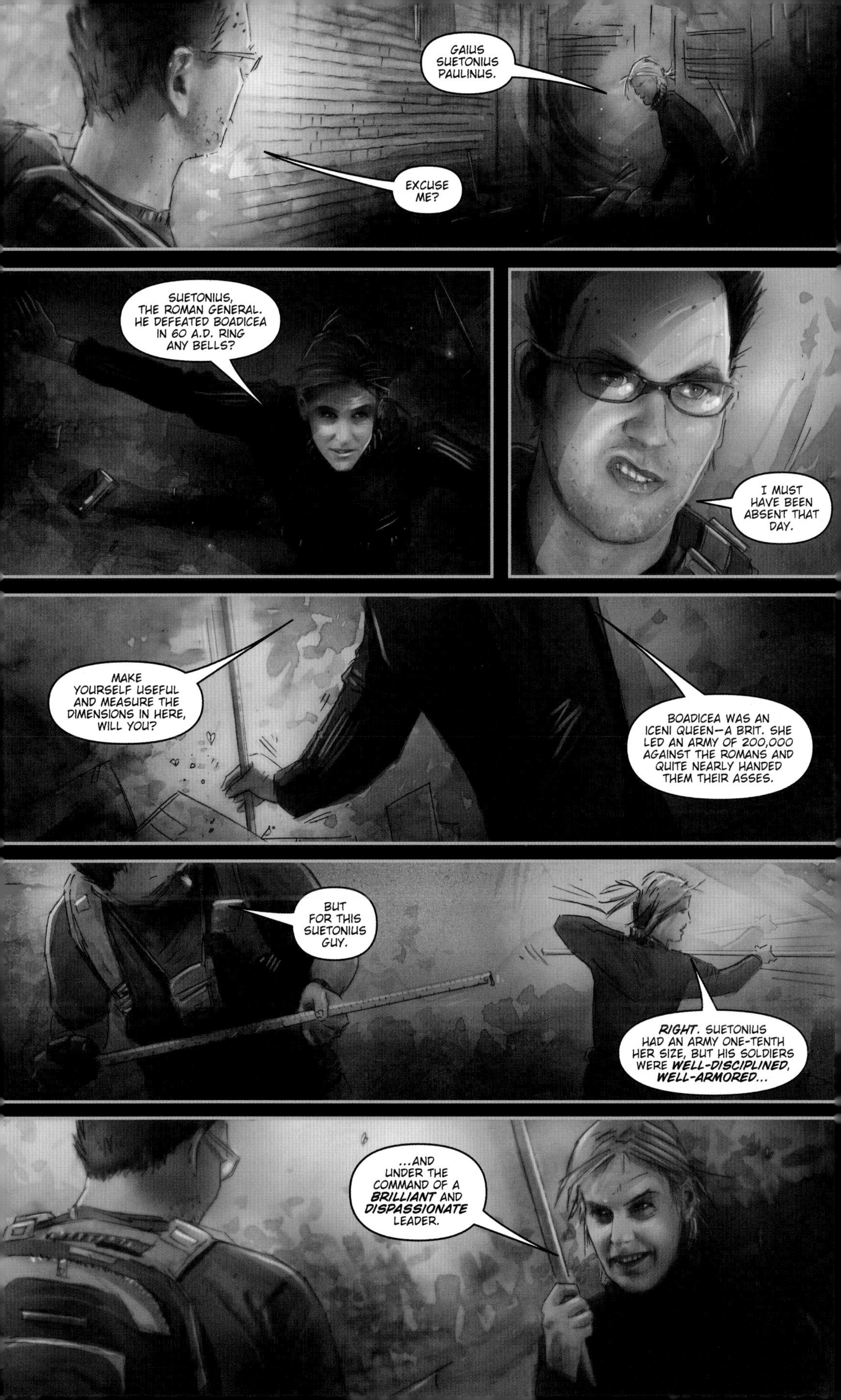
GAIUS SUETONIUS PAULINUS.
EXCUSE ME?
SUETONIUS, THE ROMAN GENERAL. HE DEFEATED BOADICEA IN 60 A.D. RING ANY BELLS?
I MUST HAVE BEEN ABSENT THAT DAY.
MAKE YOURSELF USEFUL AND MEASURE THE DIMENSIONS IN HERE, WILL YOU?
BOADICEA WAS AN ICENI QUEEN—A BRIT. SHE LED AN ARMY OF 200,000 AGAINST THE ROMANS AND QUITE NEARLY HANDED THEM THEIR ASSES.
BUT FOR THIS SUETONIUS GUY.
RIGHT. SUETONIUS HAD AN ARMY ONE-TENTH HER SIZE, BUT HIS SOLDIERS WERE WELL-DISCIPLINED, WELL-ARMORED...
...AND UNDER THE COMMAND OF A BRILLIANT AND DISPASSIONATE LEADER.

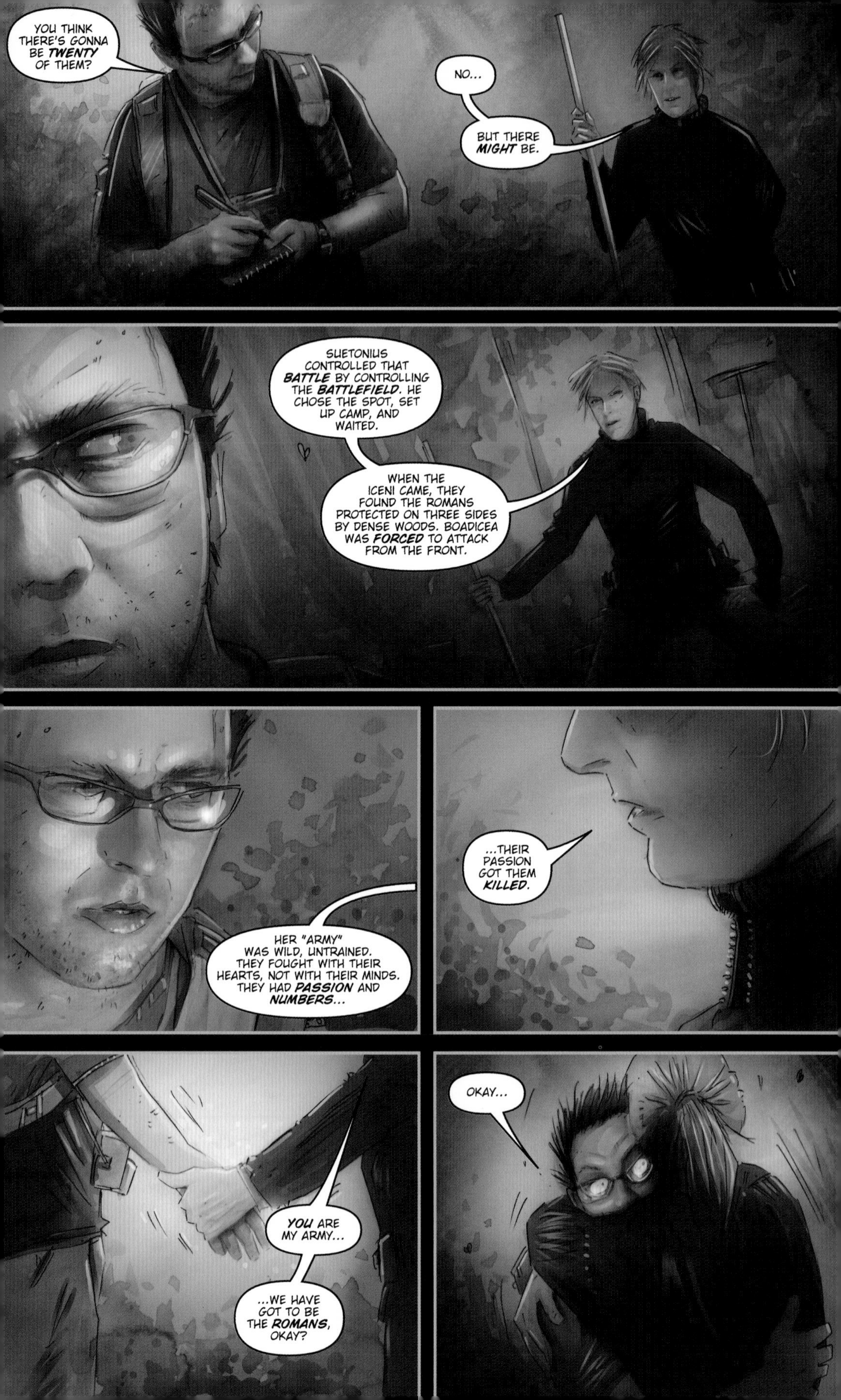
YOU THINK THERE'S GONNA BE *TWENTY* OF THEM?
NO...
BUT THERE *MIGHT* BE.
SUETONIUS CONTROLLED THAT *BATTLE* BY CONTROLLING THE *BATTLEFIELD*. HE CHOSE THE SPOT, SET UP CAMP, AND WAITED.
WHEN THE ICENI CAME, THEY FOUND THE ROMANS PROTECTED ON THREE SIDES BY DENSE WOODS. BOADICEA WAS *FORCED* TO ATTACK FROM THE FRONT.
HER "ARMY" WAS WILD, UNTRAINED. THEY FOUGHT WITH THEIR HEARTS, NOT WITH THEIR MINDS. THEY HAD *PASSION* AND *NUMBERS*...
...THEIR PASSION GOT THEM *KILLED*.
YOU ARE MY ARMY...
...WE HAVE GOT TO BE THE *ROMANS*, OKAY?
OKAY...

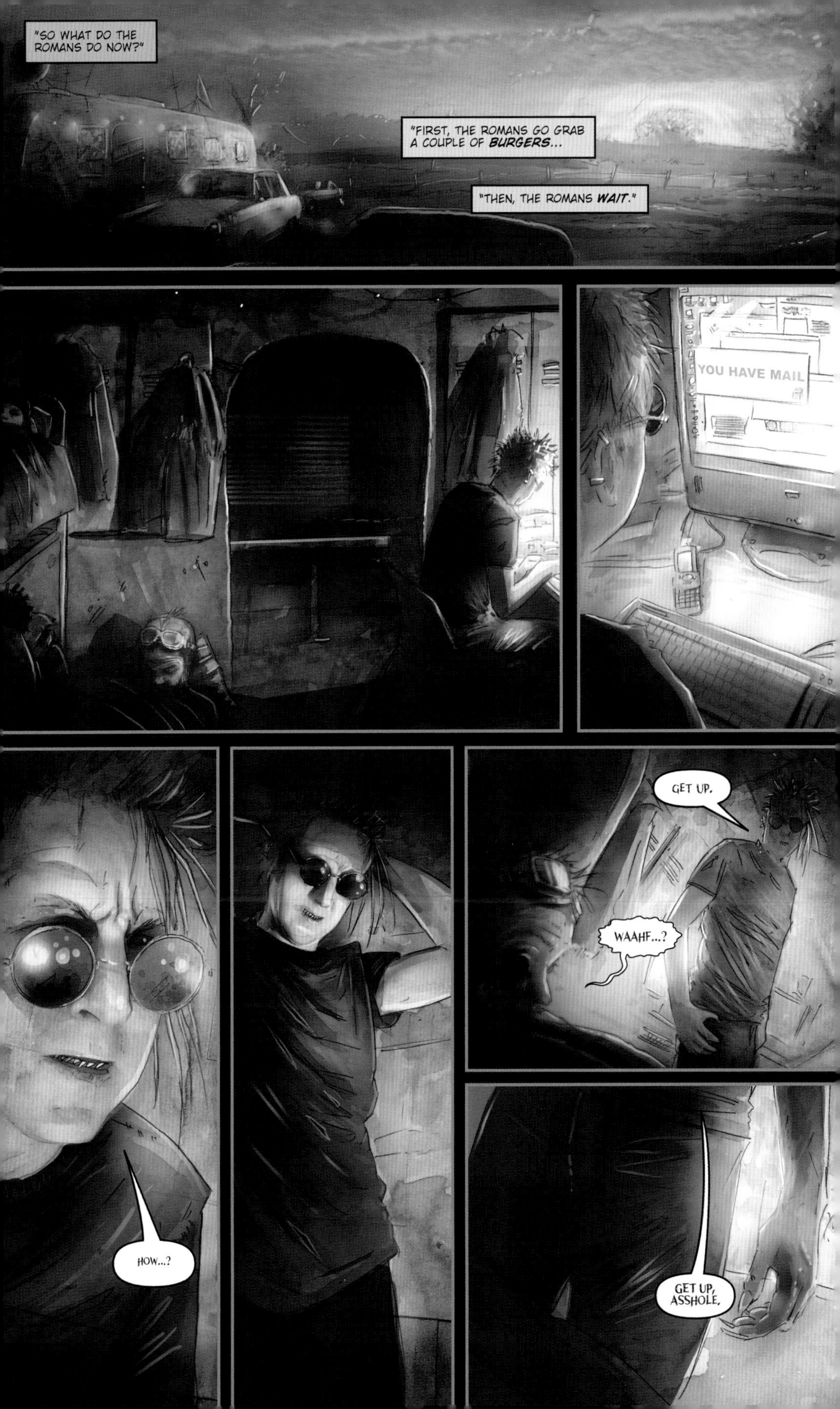
"SO WHAT DO THE ROMANS DO NOW?"
"FIRST, THE ROMANS GO GRAB A COUPLE OF **BURGERS**...
"THEN, THE ROMANS **WAIT**."
YOU HAVE MAIL
HOW...?
GET UP.
WAAHF...?
GET UP, ASSHOLE.

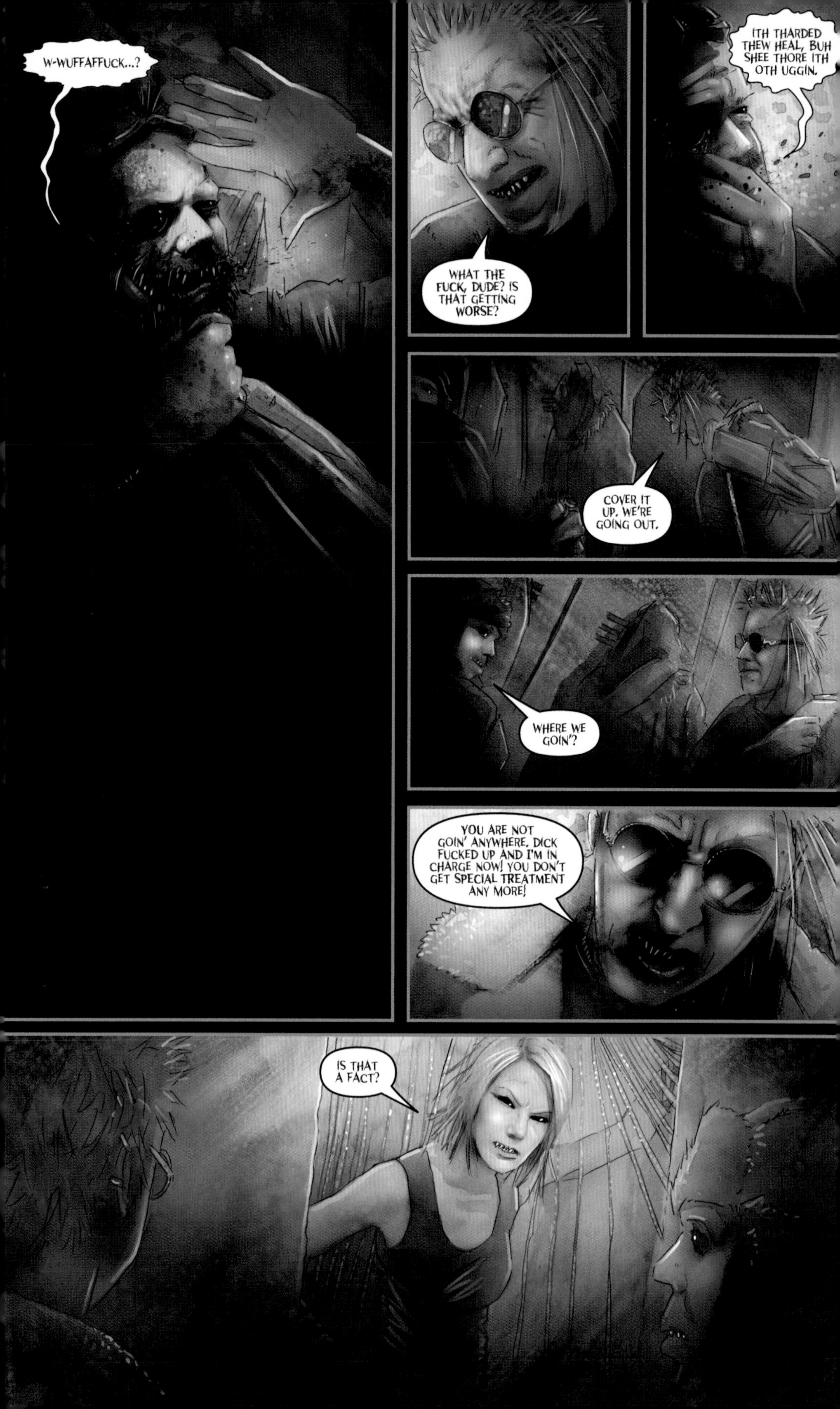
W-WUFFAFFUCK...?
WHAT THE FUCK, DUDE? IS THAT GETTING WORSE?
ITH THARDED THEW HEAL, BUH SHEE THORE ITH OTH UGGIN.
COVER IT UP. WE'RE GOING OUT.
WHERE WE GOIN'?
YOU ARE NOT GOIN' ANYWHERE. DICK FUCKED UP AND I'M IN CHARGE NOW! YOU DON'T GET SPECIAL TREATMENT ANY MORE!
IS THAT A FACT?

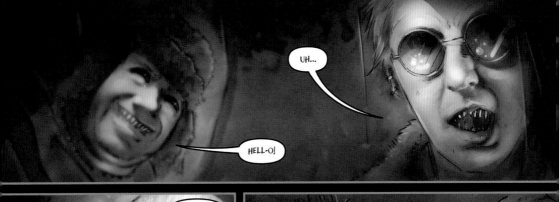

UH...

HELL-O!

WHERE YOU GOIN'?

UH...

WHERE, TODD?

DANNY'S.

THE DINER?

UH-HUH.

...

TAKE THE GENIUS, OLEMAUN, TOO.

GREAT, WE'LL HAVE A LITTLE TIME TO GET TO KNOW EACH OTHER.

GOODY.

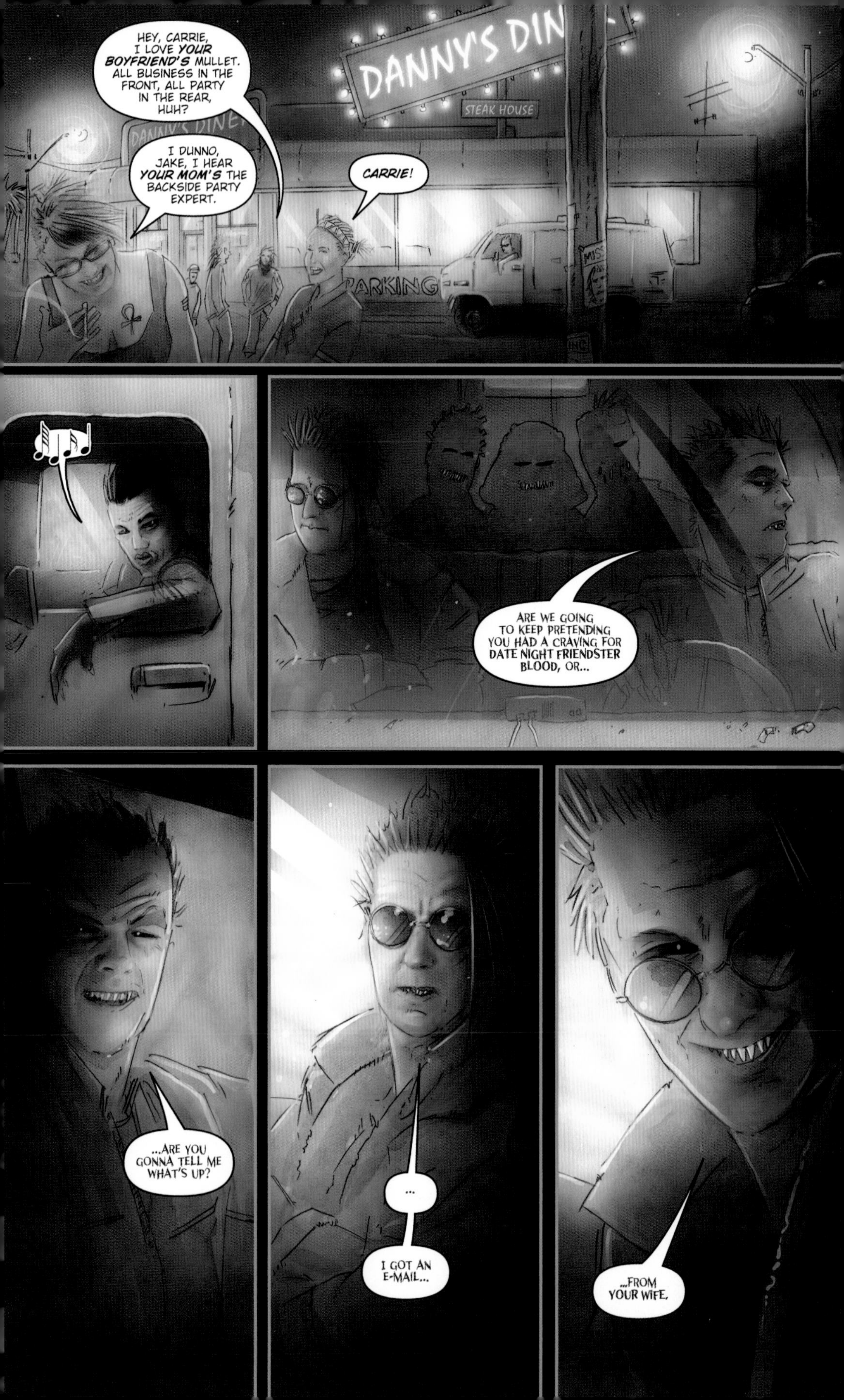

DANNY'S DIN
STEAK HOUSE
HEY, CARRIE, I LOVE YOUR BOYFRIEND'S MULLET. ALL BUSINESS IN THE FRONT, ALL PARTY IN THE REAR, HUH?
I DUNNO, JAKE, I HEAR YOUR MOM'S THE BACKSIDE PARTY EXPERT.
CARRIE!
PARKING
ARE WE GOING TO KEEP PRETENDING YOU HAD A CRAVING FOR DATE NIGHT FRIENDSTER BLOOD, OR...
...ARE YOU GONNA TELL ME WHAT'S UP?
...
I GOT AN E-MAIL...
...FROM YOUR WIFE.

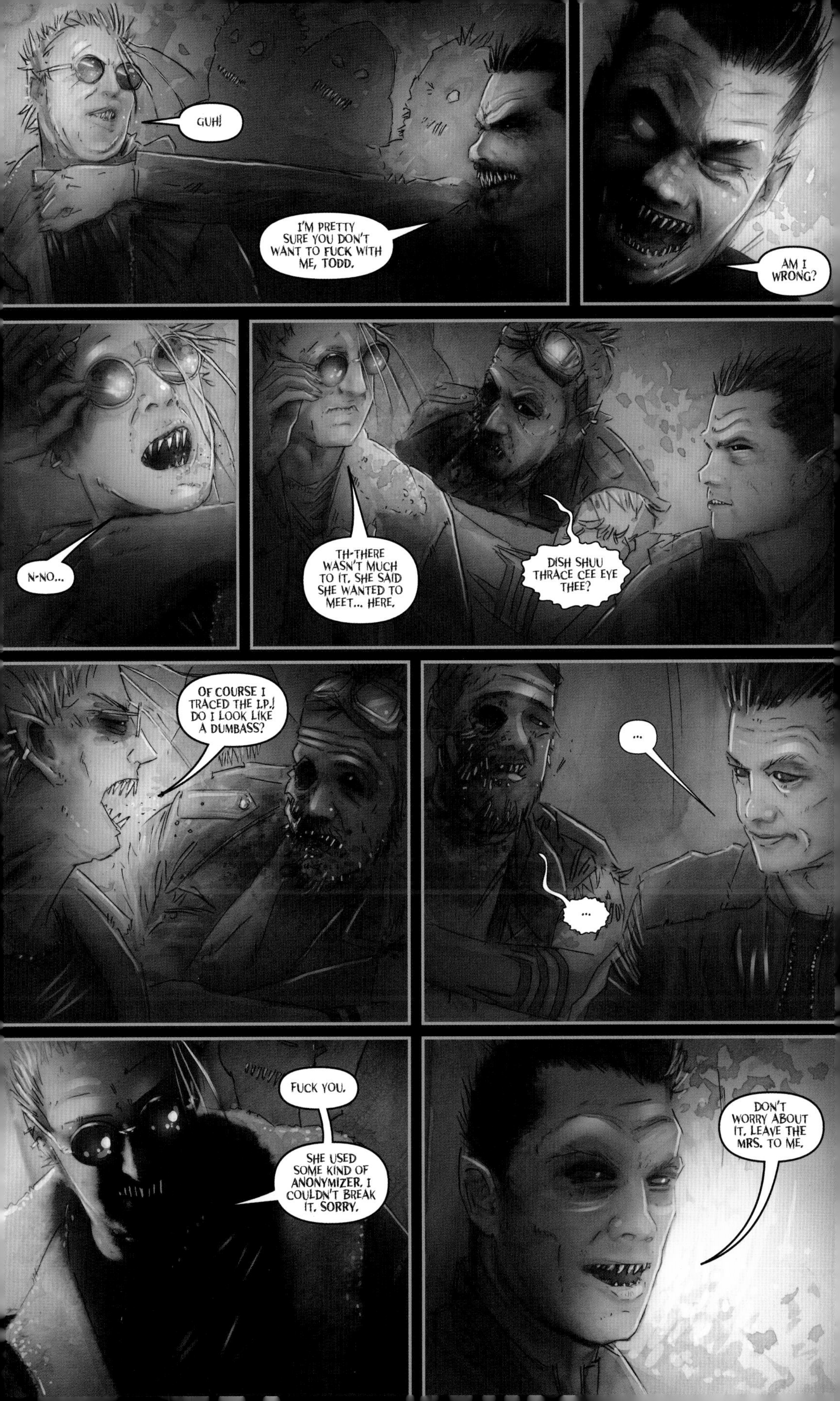
GUH!
I'M PRETTY SURE YOU DON'T WANT TO FUCK WITH ME, TODD.
AM I WRONG?
N-NO...
TH-THERE WASN'T MUCH TO IT. SHE SAID SHE WANTED TO MEET... HERE.
DISH SHUU THRACE CEE EYE THEE?
OF COURSE I TRACED THE I.P.! DO I LOOK LIKE A DUMBASS?
...
...
FUCK YOU.
SHE USED SOME KIND OF ANONYMIZER. I COULDN'T BREAK IT. SORRY.
DON'T WORRY ABOUT IT. LEAVE THE MRS. TO ME.

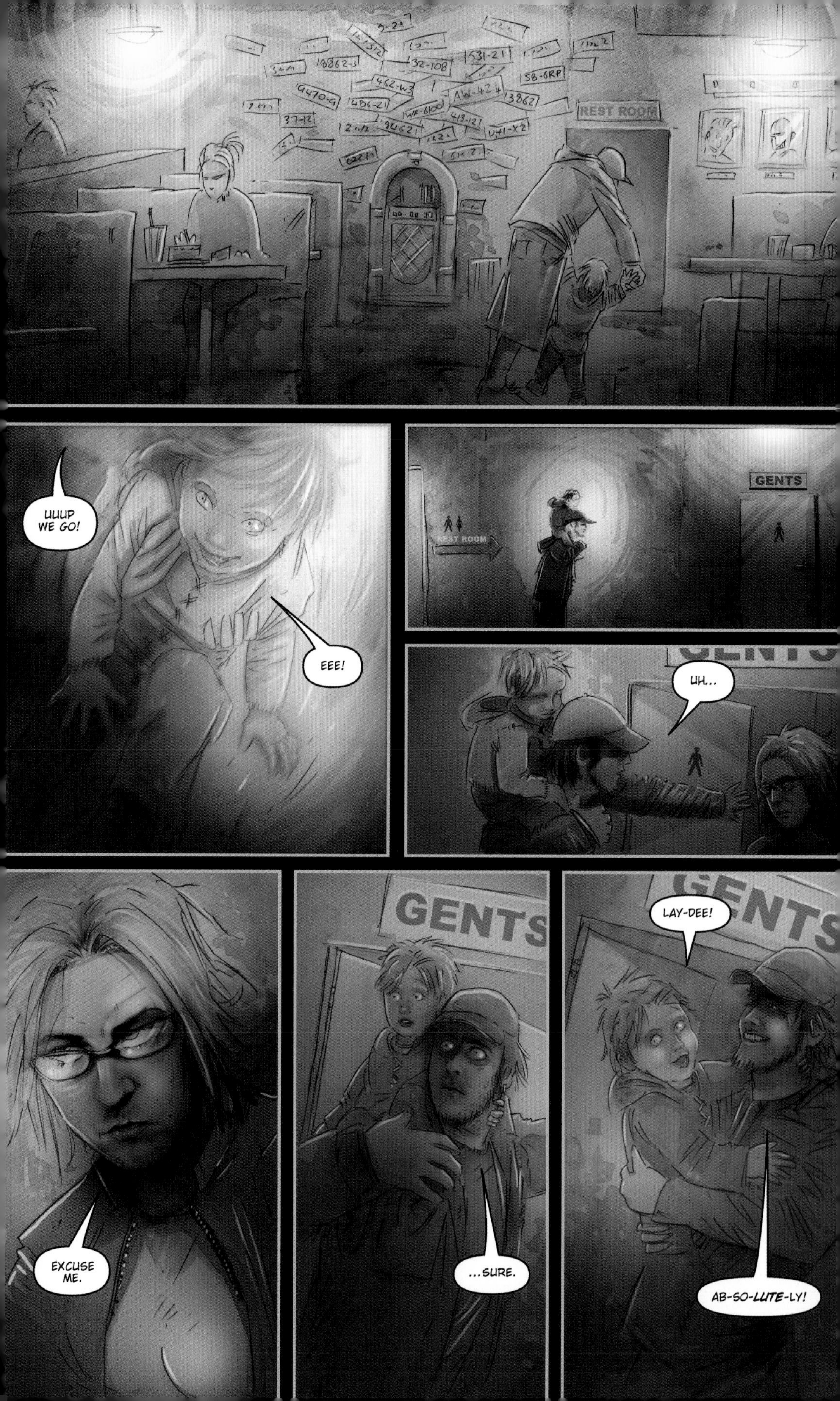
REST ROOM
UUUP WE GO!
EEE!
GENTS
REST ROOM
UH...
EXCUSE ME.
GENTS
...SURE.
LAY-DEE!
AB-SO-**LUTE**-LY!

HELLOOOO, NURSE!

ALL RIGHT. YOU *DO* REALIZE THAT ABSOLUTELY *NO ONE* IS GOING TO BE FOOLED BY THIS, DON'T YOU?

I DISAGREE.

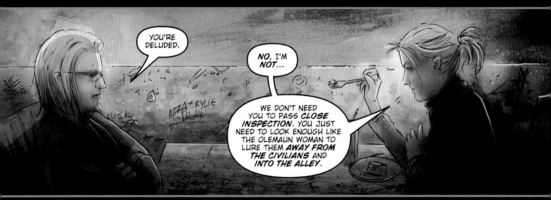

YOU'RE DELUDED.

NO, I'M *NOT...*

WE DON'T NEED YOU TO PASS *CLOSE INSPECTION*. YOU JUST NEED TO LOOK ENOUGH LIKE THE OLEMAUN WOMAN TO LURE THEM *AWAY FROM THE CIVILIANS* AND *INTO THE ALLEY.*

AT WHICH POINT, YOU SITUATE YOURSELF BEHIND ME AND *DO NOT ENGAGE THE BITERS.*

WHATEVER *USED* TO BE HUMAN INSIDE THEM, THEY'VE GIVEN UP TO THE SICKNESS. THIS ISN'T *MURDER*—IT'S *EUTHANASIA.* ARE WE CLEAR?

YEAH.

I'M SCARED.

ME, TOO.

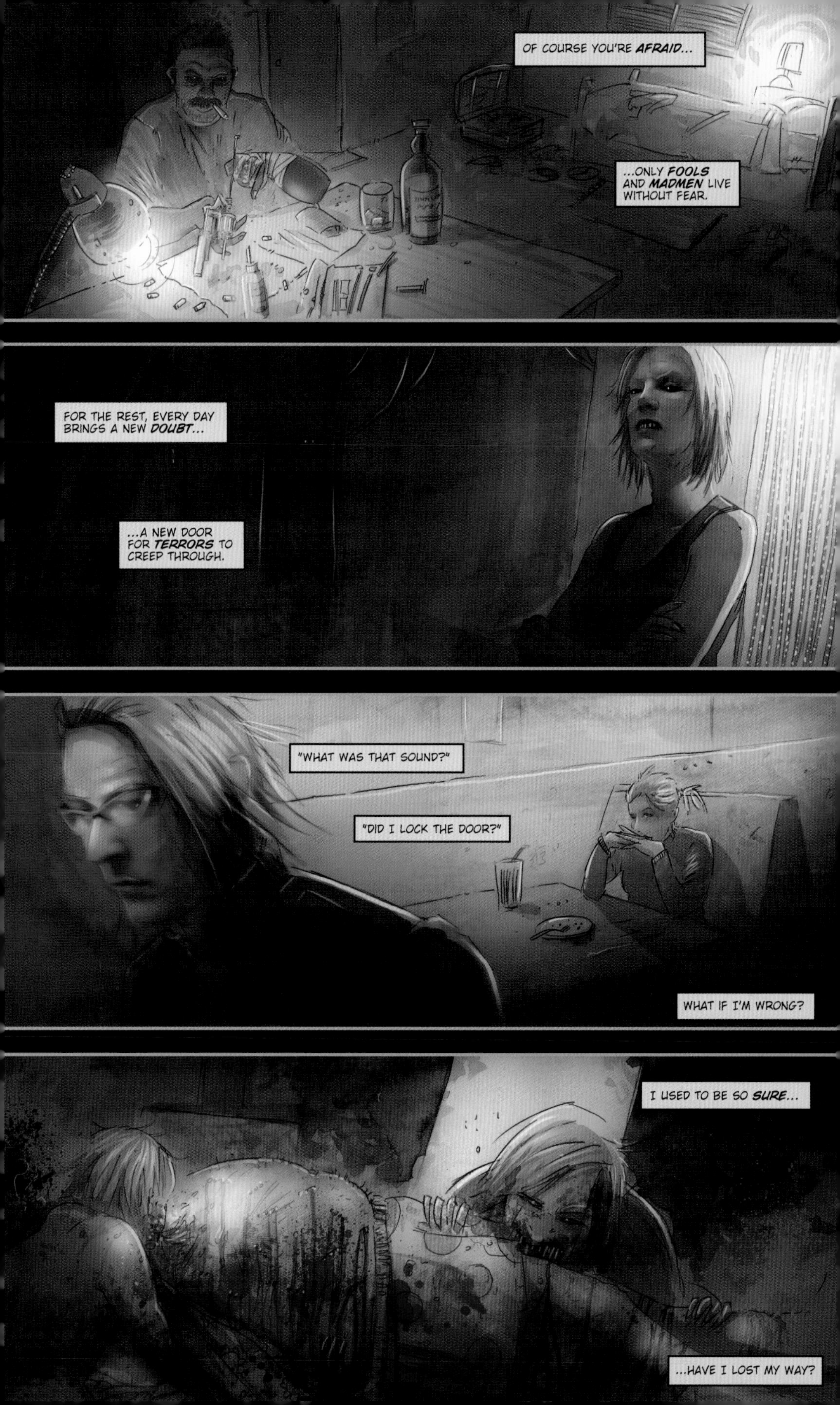
OF COURSE YOU'RE AFRAID...
...ONLY FOOLS AND MADMEN LIVE WITHOUT FEAR.
FOR THE REST, EVERY DAY BRINGS A NEW DOUBT...
...A NEW DOOR FOR TERRORS TO CREEP THROUGH.
"WHAT WAS THAT SOUND?"
"DID I LOCK THE DOOR?"
WHAT IF I'M WRONG?
I USED TO BE SO SURE...
...HAVE I LOST MY WAY?

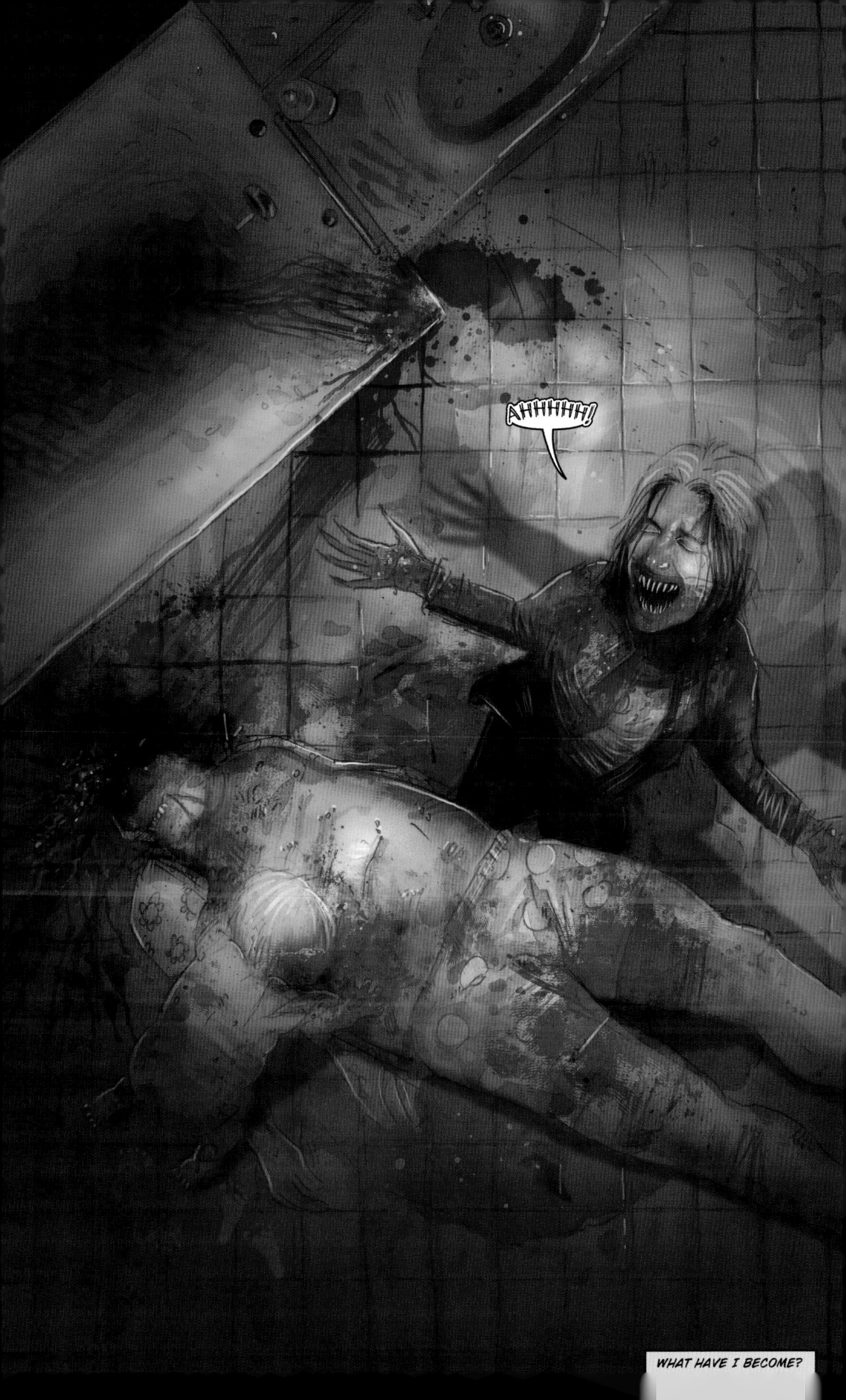
AHHHHHH!
WHAT HAVE I BECOME?

THE TRICK IS NOT TO LET THE FEAR MAKE YOU FORGET *WHO YOU ARE*...

...OR *WHY YOU'RE HERE.*

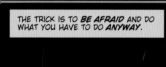

THE TRICK IS TO *BE AFRAID* AND DO WHAT YOU HAVE TO DO *ANYWAY.*

DANNY'S DINER
10-2AM WEEKLY

...

THAT WAS A DUDE.

PARKING AT REAR

NOW, NOW. WHERE'S YOUR SENSE OF ADVENTURE? WHEN A MYSTERIOUS LADY INVITES YOU TO FOLLOW HER AROUND A DARK CORNER...

...YOU GO.

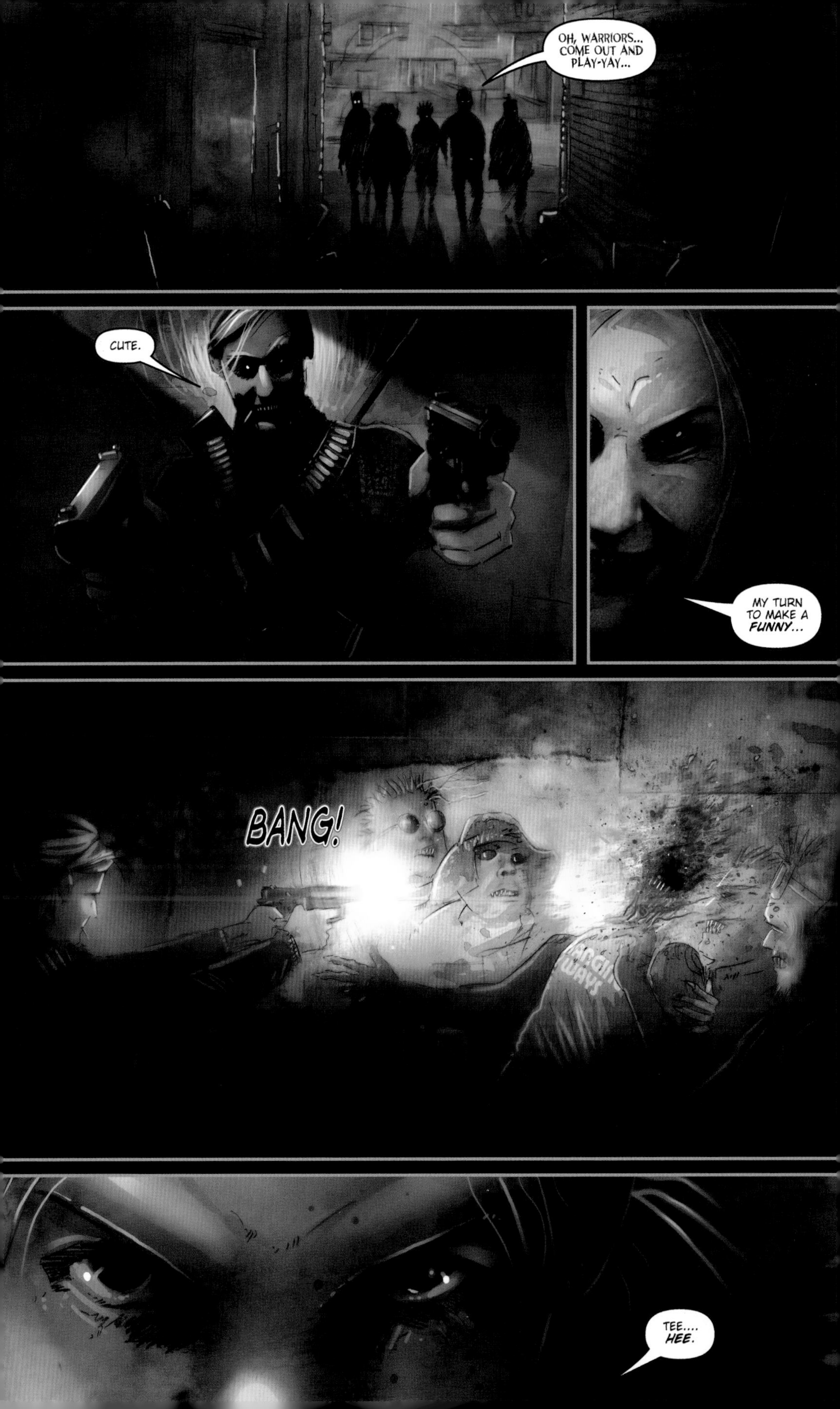

OH, WARRIORS... COME OUT AND PLAY-YAY...
CUTE.
MY TURN TO MAKE A *FUNNY*...
BANG!
TEE.... *HEE*.

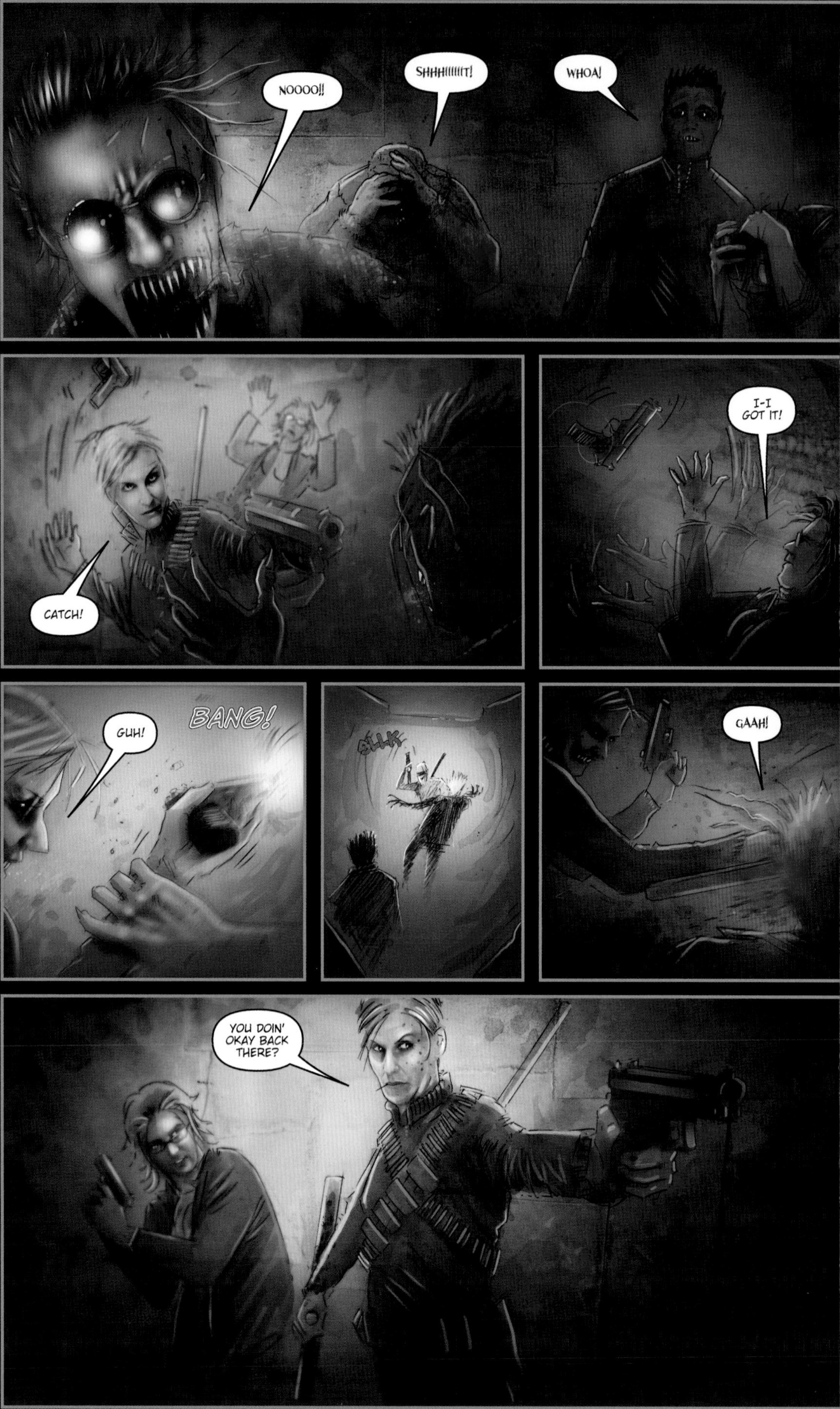
NOOOO!!
SHHHIIIIIIT!
WHOA!
CATCH!
I-I GOT IT!
GUH!
BANG!
GLLK
GAAH!
YOU DOIN' OKAY BACK THERE?

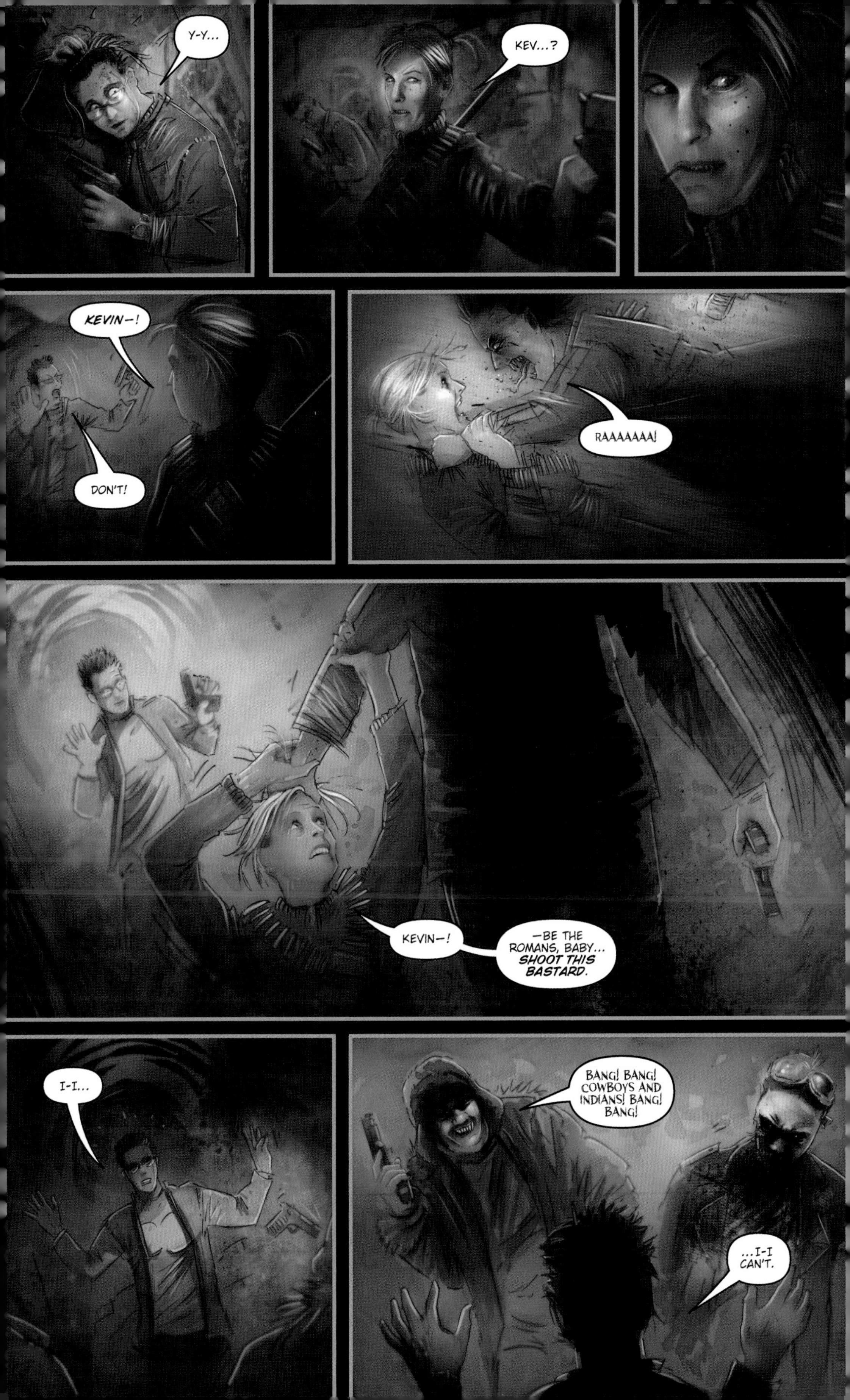
Y-Y...
KEV...?
KEVIN--!
DON'T!
RAAAAAAA!
KEVIN--!
--BE THE ROMANS, BABY... SHOOT THIS BASTARD.
I-I...
BANG! BANG! COWBOYS AND INDIANS! BANG! BANG!
...I-I CAN'T.

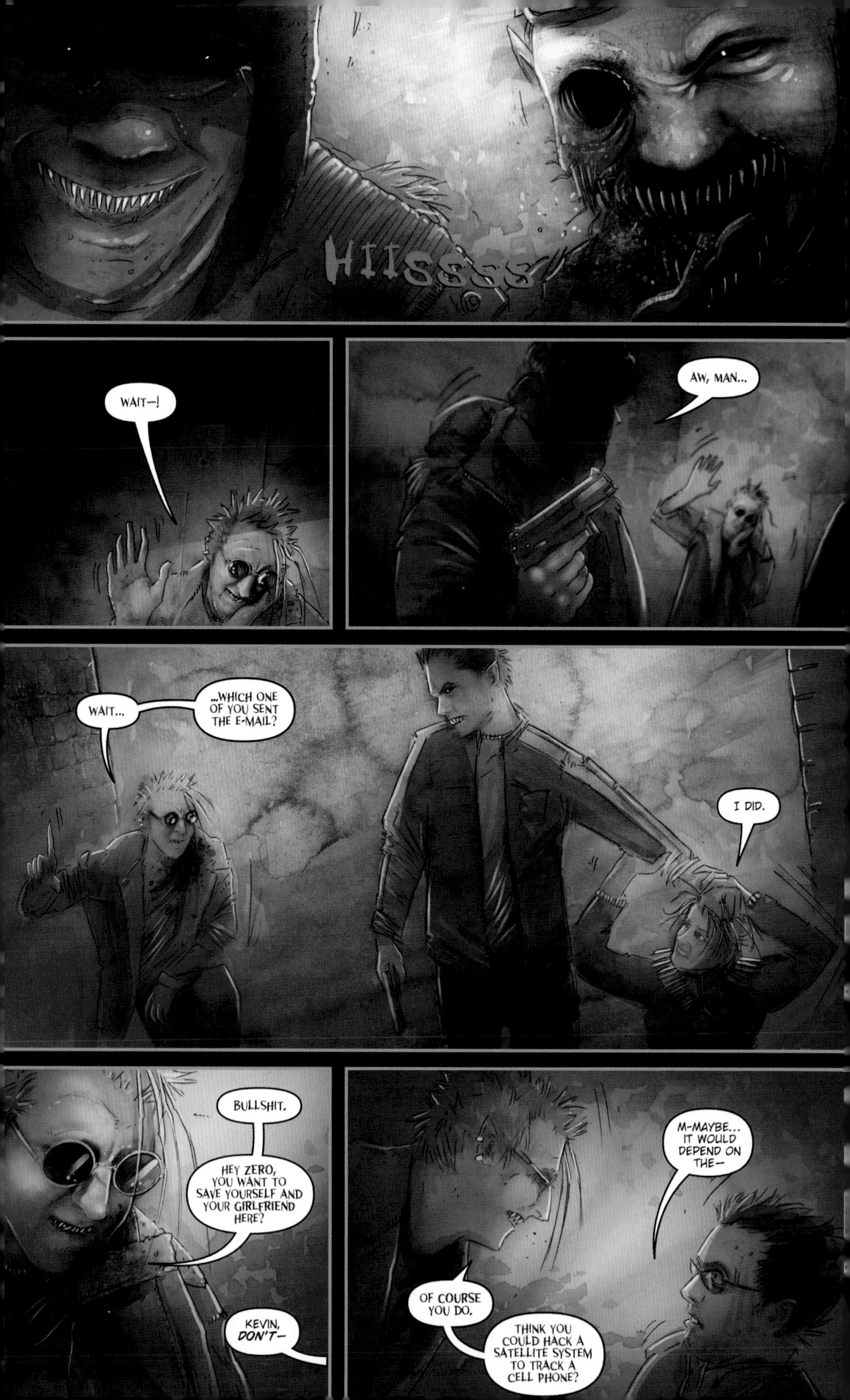
HIISSSS
WAIT—!
AW, MAN...
WAIT...
...WHICH ONE OF YOU SENT THE E-MAIL?
I DID.
BULLSHIT.
HEY ZERO, YOU WANT TO SAVE YOURSELF AND YOUR GIRLFRIEND HERE?
KEVIN, DON'T—
M-MAYBE... IT WOULD DEPEND ON THE—
OF COURSE YOU DO.
THINK YOU COULD HACK A SATELLITE SYSTEM TO TRACK A CELL PHONE?

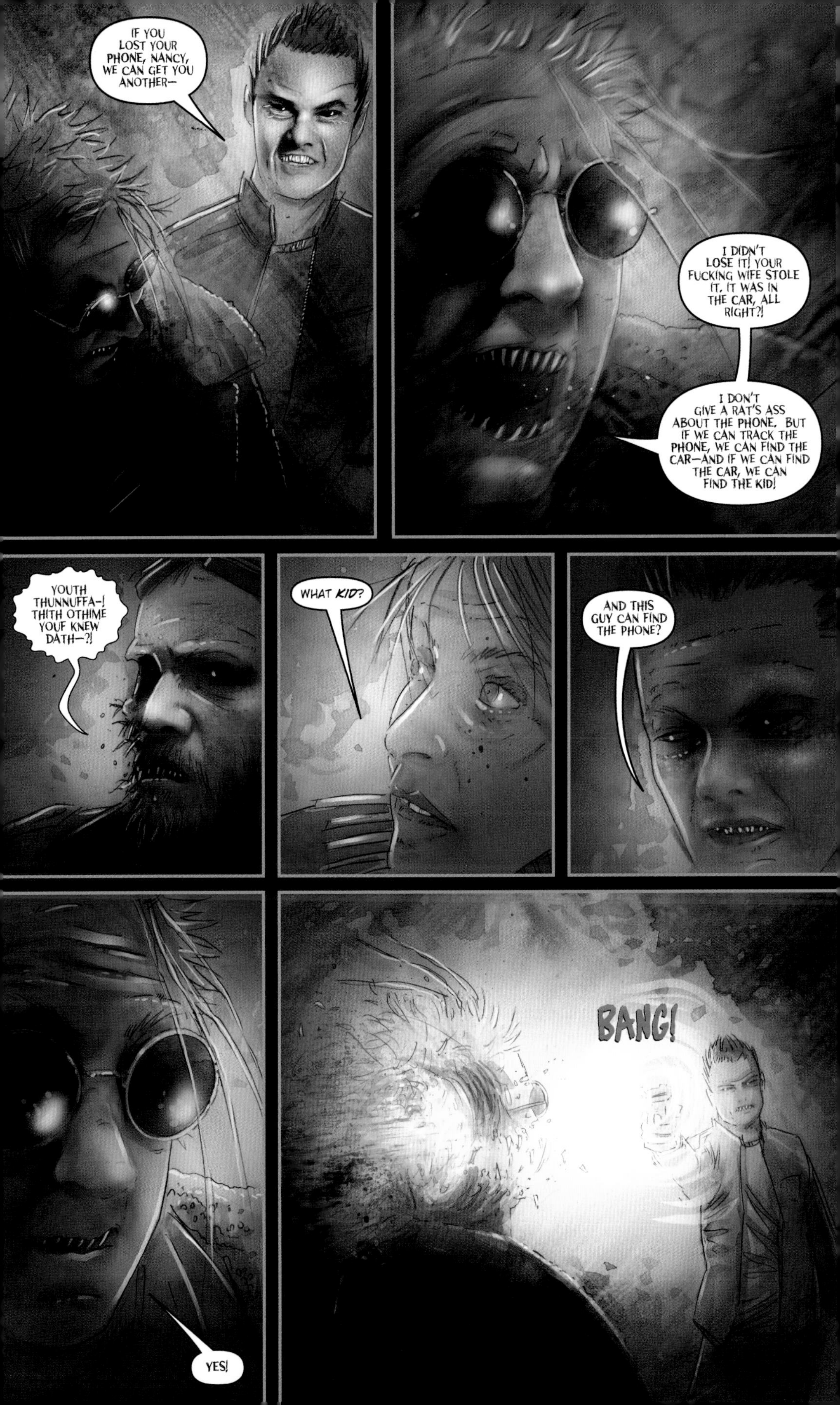
IF YOU LOST YOUR PHONE, NANCY, WE CAN GET YOU ANOTHER—
I DIDN'T LOSE IT! YOUR FUCKING WIFE STOLE IT. IT WAS IN THE CAR, ALL RIGHT?!
I DON'T GIVE A RAT'S ASS ABOUT THE PHONE. BUT IF WE CAN TRACK THE PHONE, WE CAN FIND THE CAR—AND IF WE CAN FIND THE CAR, WE CAN FIND THE KID!
YOUTH THUNNUFFA-! THITH OTHIME YOUF KNEW DATH—?!
WHAT KID?
AND THIS GUY CAN FIND THE PHONE?
YES!
BANG!

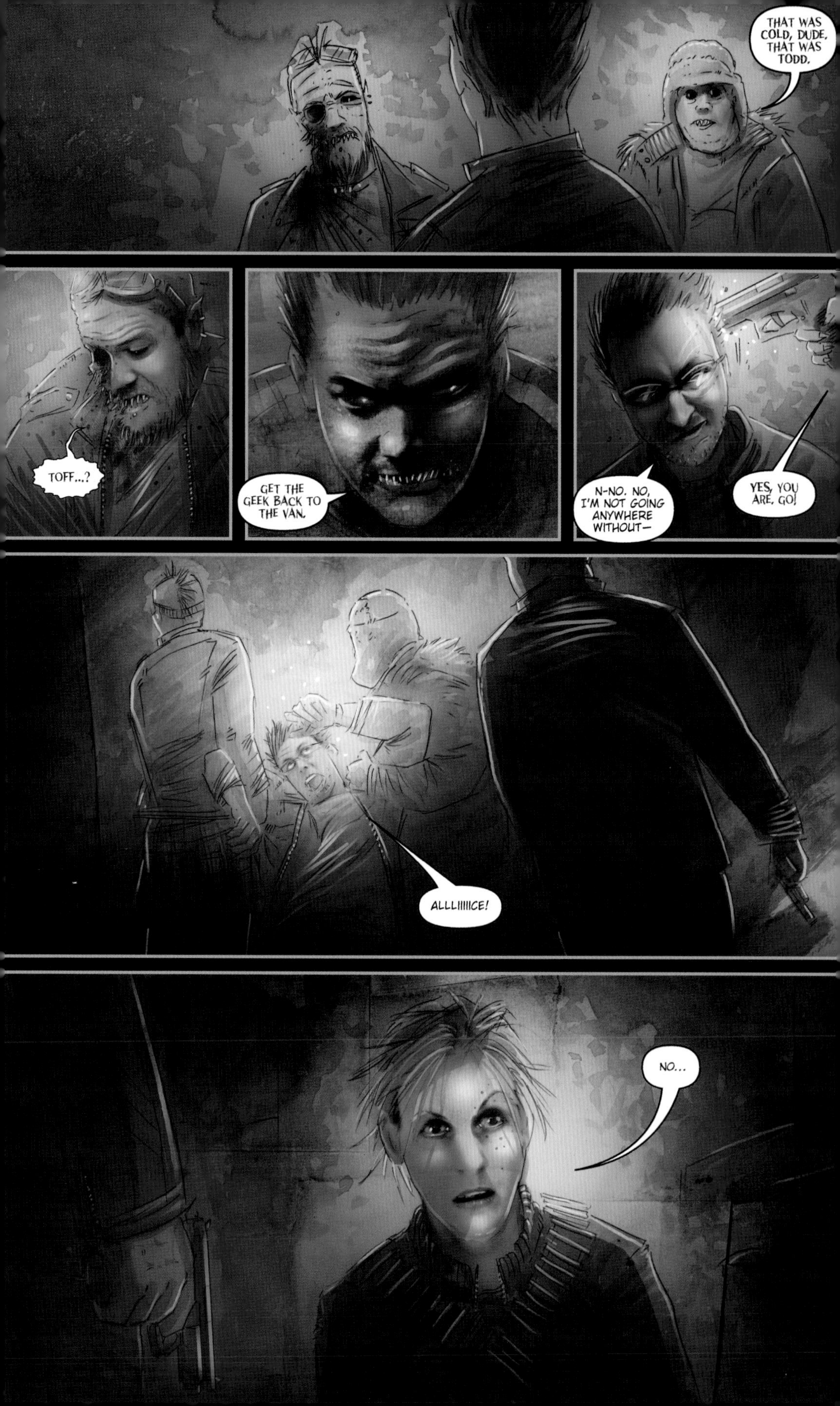
THAT WAS COLD, DUDE, THAT WAS TODD.
TOFF...?
GET THE GEEK BACK TO THE VAN.
N-NO. NO, I'M NOT GOING ANYWHERE WITHOUT—
YES, YOU ARE. GO!
ALLLIIIIICE!
NO...

HISSSS

IT DOESN'T MATTER WHAT *THEY* DO TO YOU... IT MATTERS HOW *YOU* REACT.

YOU CAN CHOOSE TO FACE YOUR DEATH WITH A *WARRIOR'S GRACE*...

TO SET ASIDE *FEAR* AND *FURY* AND BE GRATEFUL THAT YOU KNEW *LOVE*...

IF YOU CAN DO *THAT*, THEN EVEN IF THEY KILL YOU...

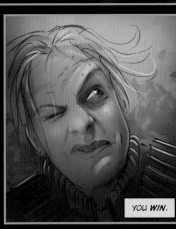

YOU *WIN*.

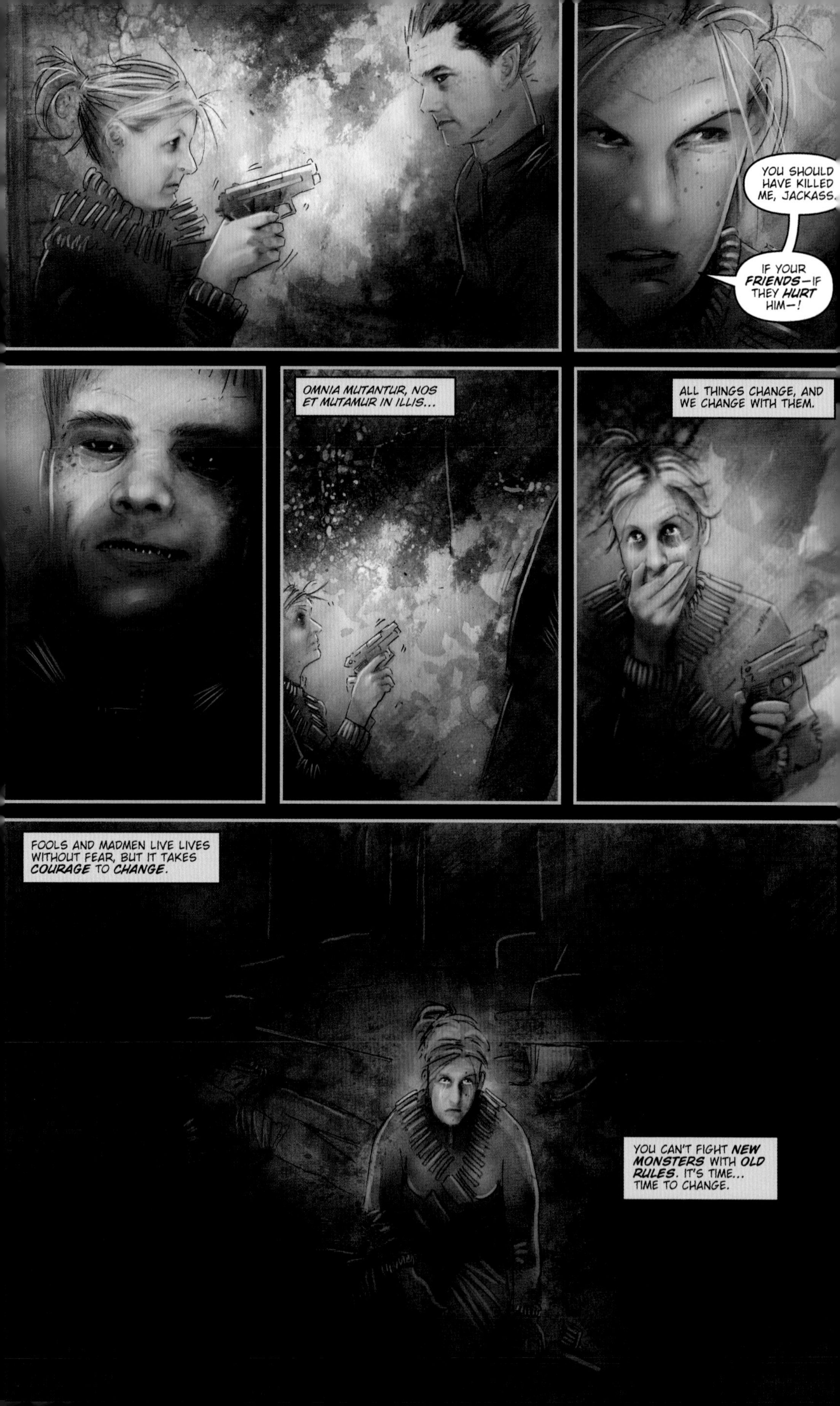

YOU SHOULD HAVE KILLED ME, JACKASS.
IF YOUR FRIENDS—IF THEY HURT HIM—!
OMNIA MUTANTUR, NOS ET MUTAMUR IN ILLIS...
ALL THINGS CHANGE, AND WE CHANGE WITH THEM.
FOOLS AND MADMEN LIVE LIVES WITHOUT FEAR, BUT IT TAKES COURAGE TO CHANGE.
YOU CAN'T FIGHT NEW MONSTERS WITH OLD RULES. IT'S TIME... TIME TO CHANGE.

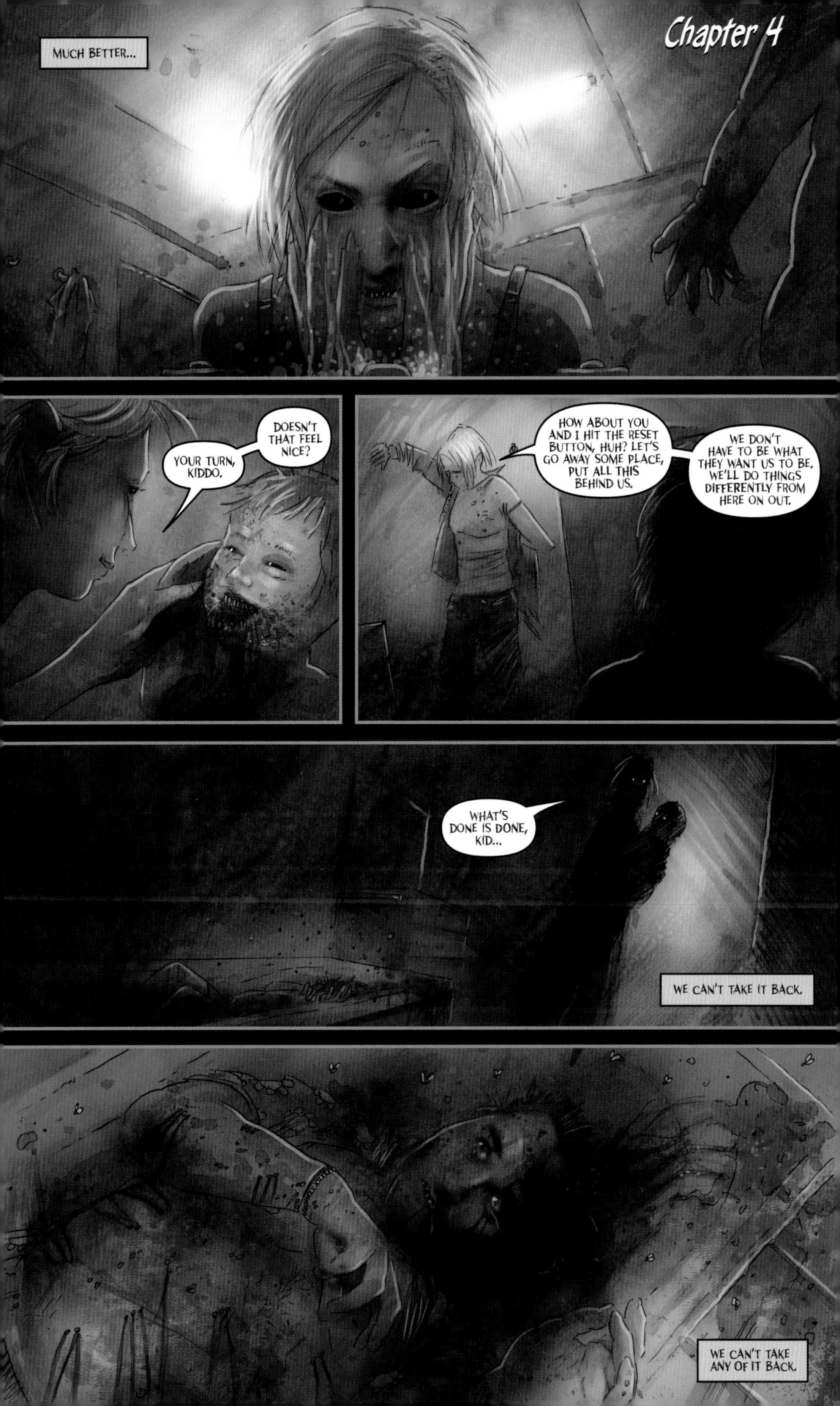

Chapter 4
MUCH BETTER...
YOUR TURN, KIDDO.
DOESN'T THAT FEEL NICE?
HOW ABOUT YOU AND I HIT THE RESET BUTTON, HUH? LET'S GO AWAY SOME PLACE, PUT ALL THIS BEHIND US.
WE DON'T HAVE TO BE WHAT THEY WANT US TO BE, WE'LL DO THINGS DIFFERENTLY FROM HERE ON OUT.
WHAT'S DONE IS DONE, KID...
WE CAN'T TAKE IT BACK.
WE CAN'T TAKE ANY OF IT BACK.

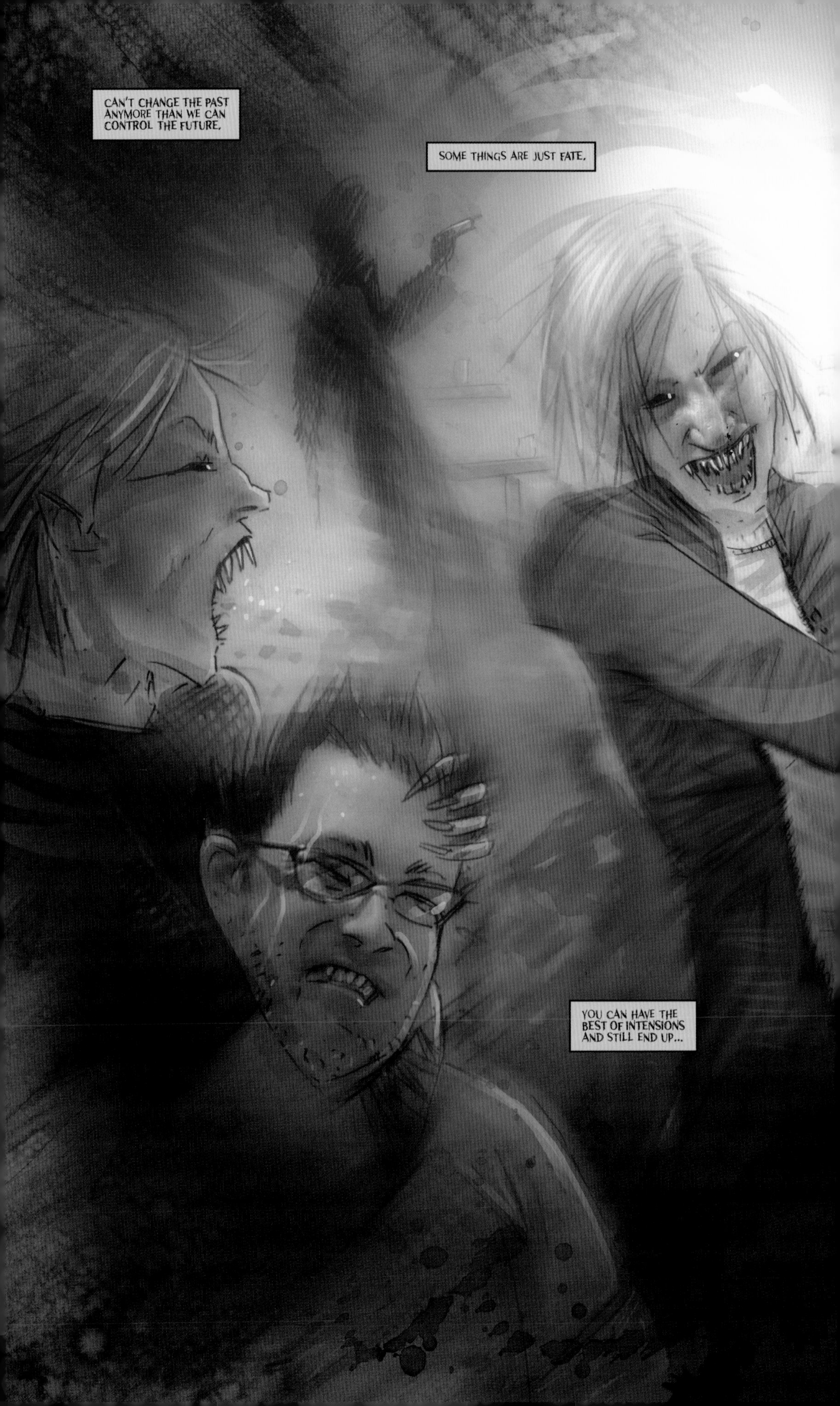
CAN'T CHANGE THE PAST ANYMORE THAN WE CAN CONTROL THE FUTURE.
SOME THINGS ARE JUST FATE.
YOU CAN HAVE THE BEST OF INTENSIONS AND STILL END UP...

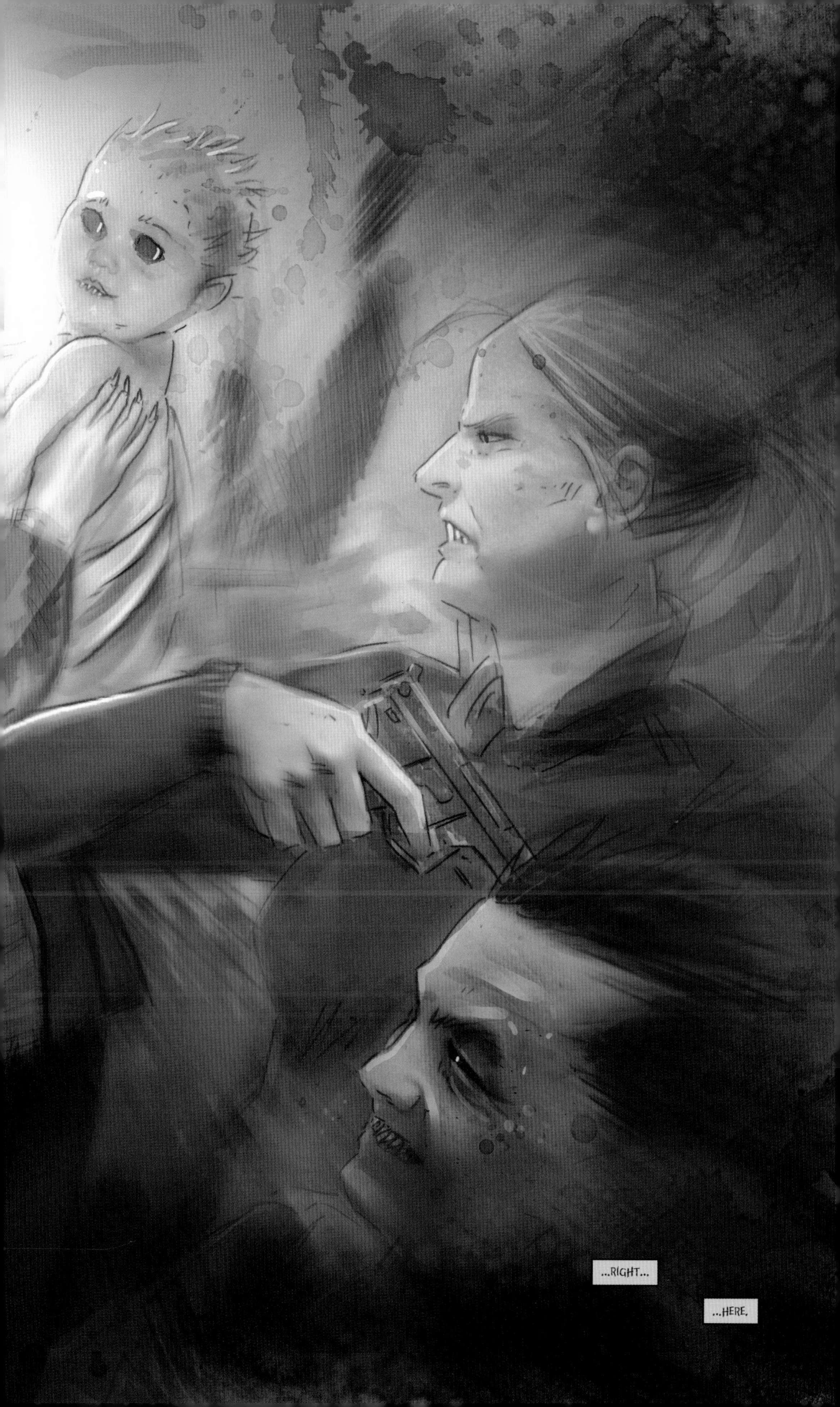
...RIGHT...
...HERE.

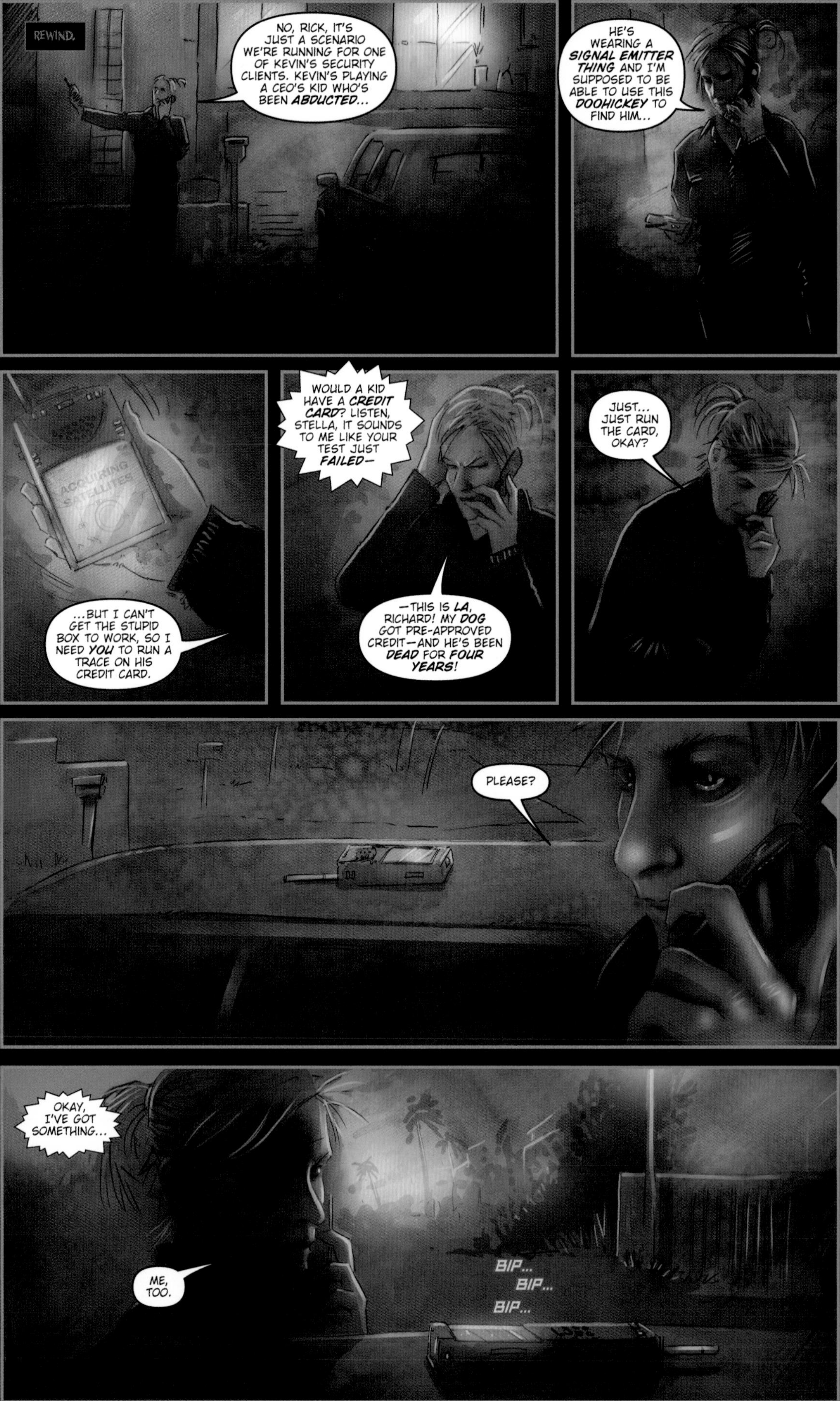
REWIND.
NO, RICK, IT'S JUST A SCENARIO WE'RE RUNNING FOR ONE OF KEVIN'S SECURITY CLIENTS. KEVIN'S PLAYING A CEO'S KID WHO'S BEEN ABDUCTED...
HE'S WEARING A SIGNAL EMITTER THING AND I'M SUPPOSED TO BE ABLE TO USE THIS DOOHICKEY TO FIND HIM...
ACQUIRING SATELLITES
...BUT I CAN'T GET THE STUPID BOX TO WORK, SO I NEED YOU TO RUN A TRACE ON HIS CREDIT CARD.
WOULD A KID HAVE A CREDIT CARD? LISTEN, STELLA, IT SOUNDS TO ME LIKE YOUR TEST JUST FAILED—
—THIS IS LA, RICHARD! MY DOG GOT PRE-APPROVED CREDIT—AND HE'S BEEN DEAD FOR FOUR YEARS!
JUST... JUST RUN THE CARD, OKAY?
PLEASE?
OKAY, I'VE GOT SOMETHING...
ME, TOO.
BIP...
BIP...
BIP...

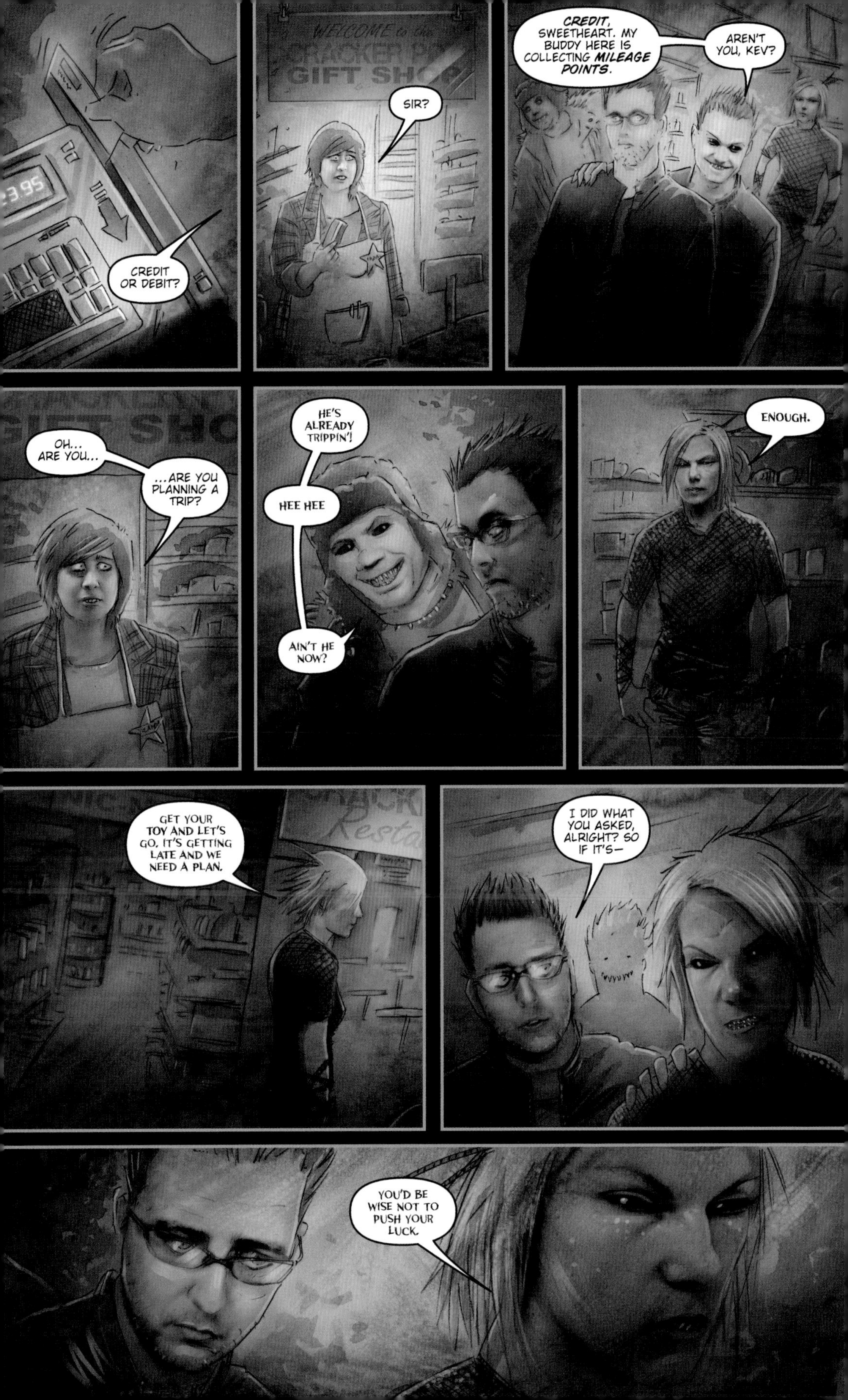
CREDIT OR DEBIT?
SIR?
CREDIT, SWEETHEART. MY BUDDY HERE IS COLLECTING MILEAGE POINTS.
AREN'T YOU, KEV?
OH... ARE YOU...
...ARE YOU PLANNING A TRIP?
HE'S ALREADY TRIPPIN'!
HEE HEE
AIN'T HE NOW?
ENOUGH.
GET YOUR TOY AND LET'S GO. IT'S GETTING LATE AND WE NEED A PLAN.
I DID WHAT YOU ASKED, ALRIGHT? SO IF IT'S—
YOU'D BE WISE NOT TO PUSH YOUR LUCK.

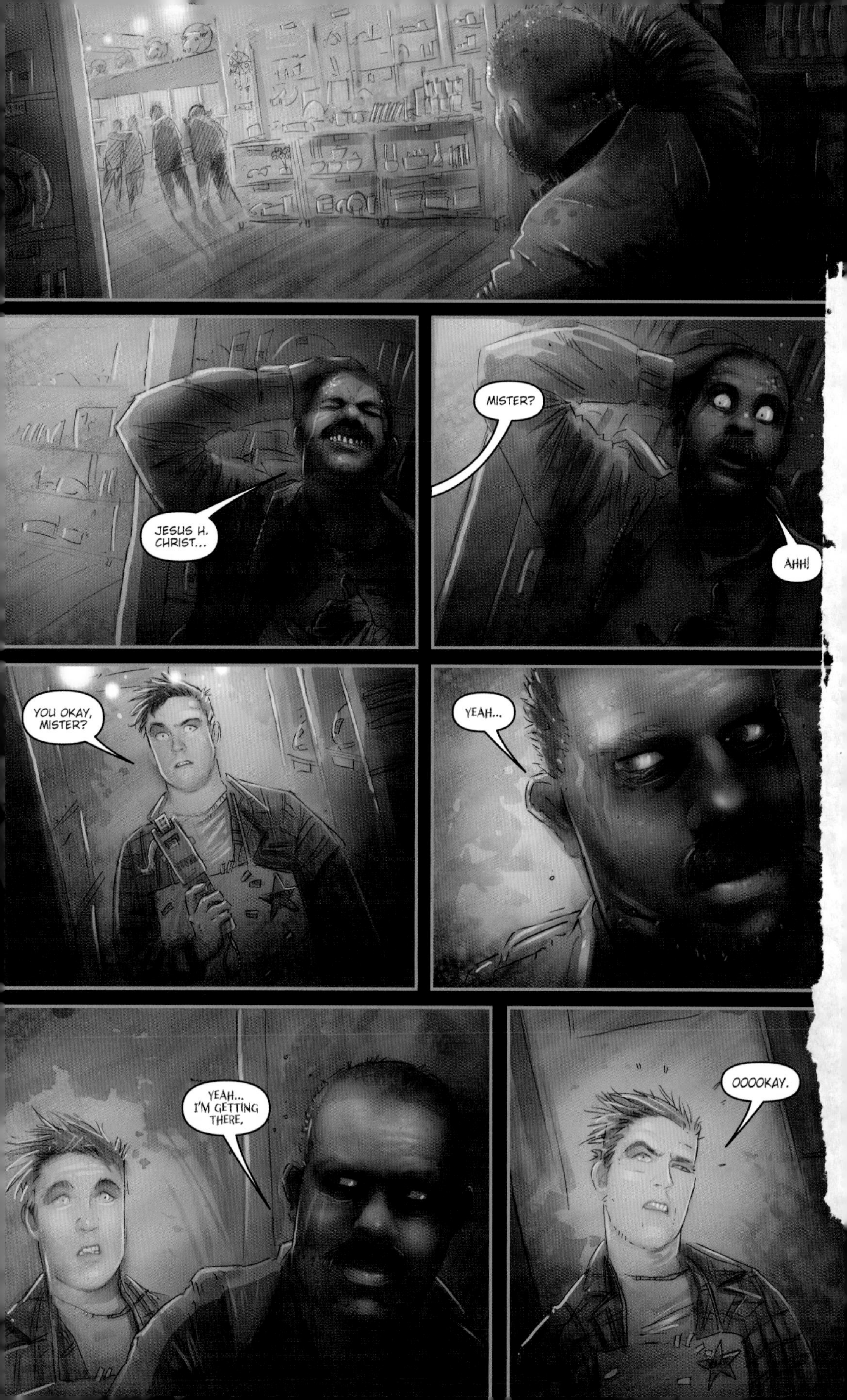
JESUS H. CHRIST...
MISTER?
AHH!
YOU OKAY, MISTER?
YEAH...
YEAH... I'M GETTING THERE.
OOOOKAY.

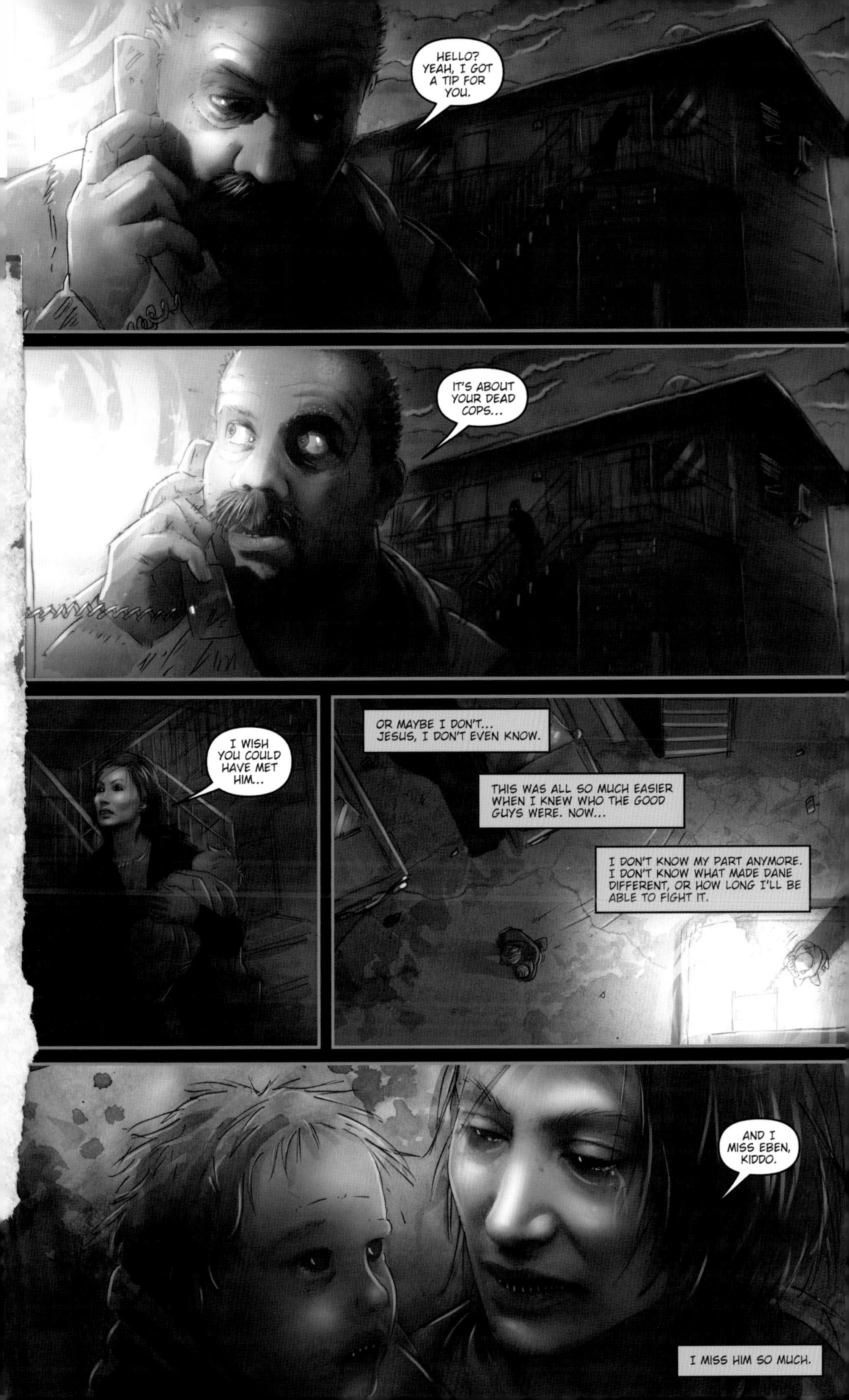
HELLO? YEAH, I GOT A TIP FOR YOU.
IT'S ABOUT YOUR DEAD COPS...
I WISH YOU COULD HAVE MET HIM...
OR MAYBE I DON'T... JESUS, I DON'T EVEN KNOW.
THIS WAS ALL SO MUCH EASIER WHEN I KNEW WHO THE GOOD GUYS WERE. NOW...
I DON'T KNOW MY PART ANYMORE. I DON'T KNOW WHAT MADE DANE DIFFERENT, OR HOW LONG I'LL BE ABLE TO FIGHT IT.
AND I MISS EBEN, KIDDO.
I MISS HIM SO MUCH.

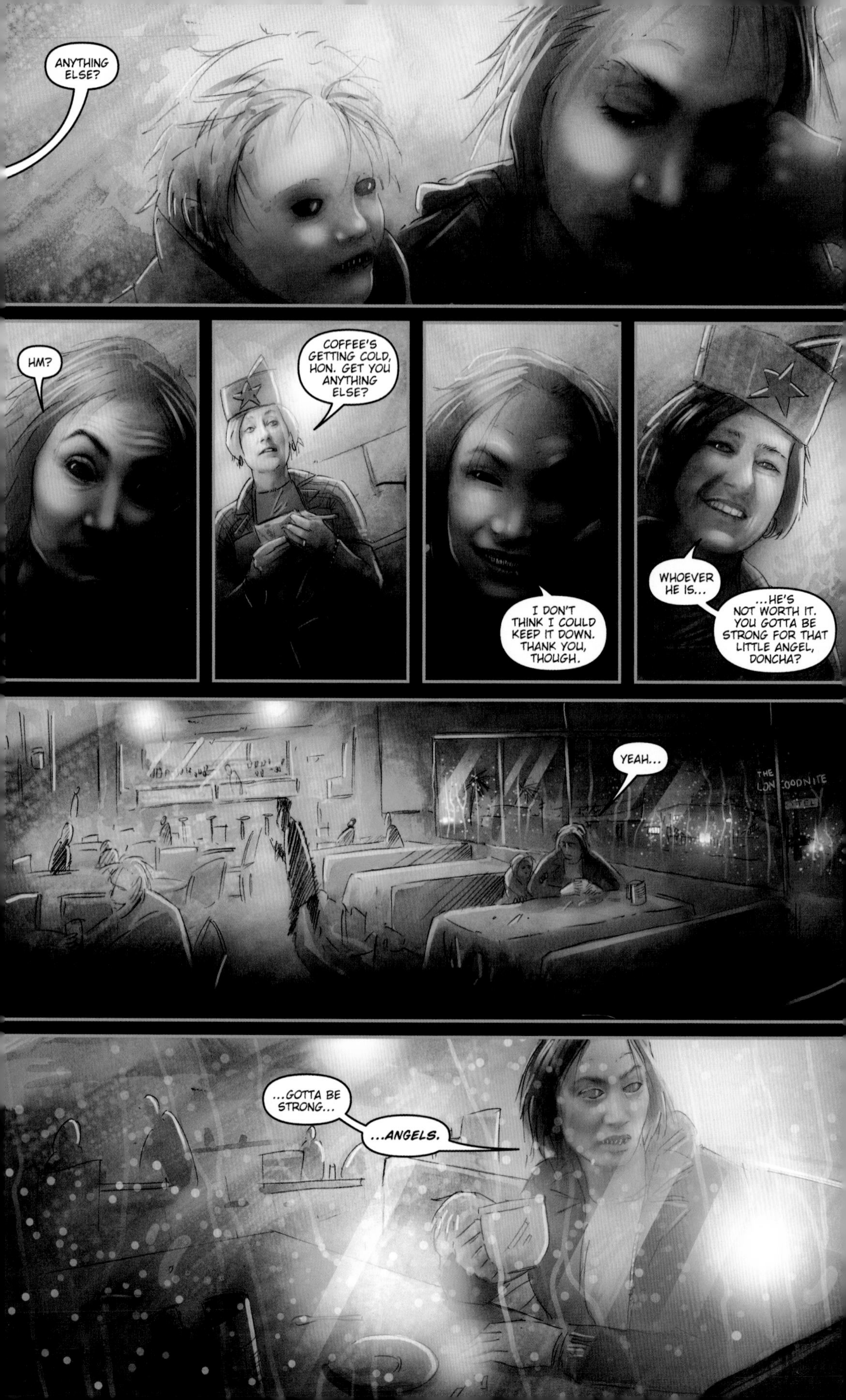
ANYTHING ELSE?
HM?
COFFEE'S GETTING COLD, HON. GET YOU ANYTHING ELSE?
I DON'T THINK I COULD KEEP IT DOWN. THANK YOU, THOUGH.
WHOEVER HE IS...
...HE'S NOT WORTH IT. YOU GOTTA BE STRONG FOR THAT LITTLE ANGEL, DONCHA?
YEAH...
...GOTTA BE STRONG...
...ANGELS.

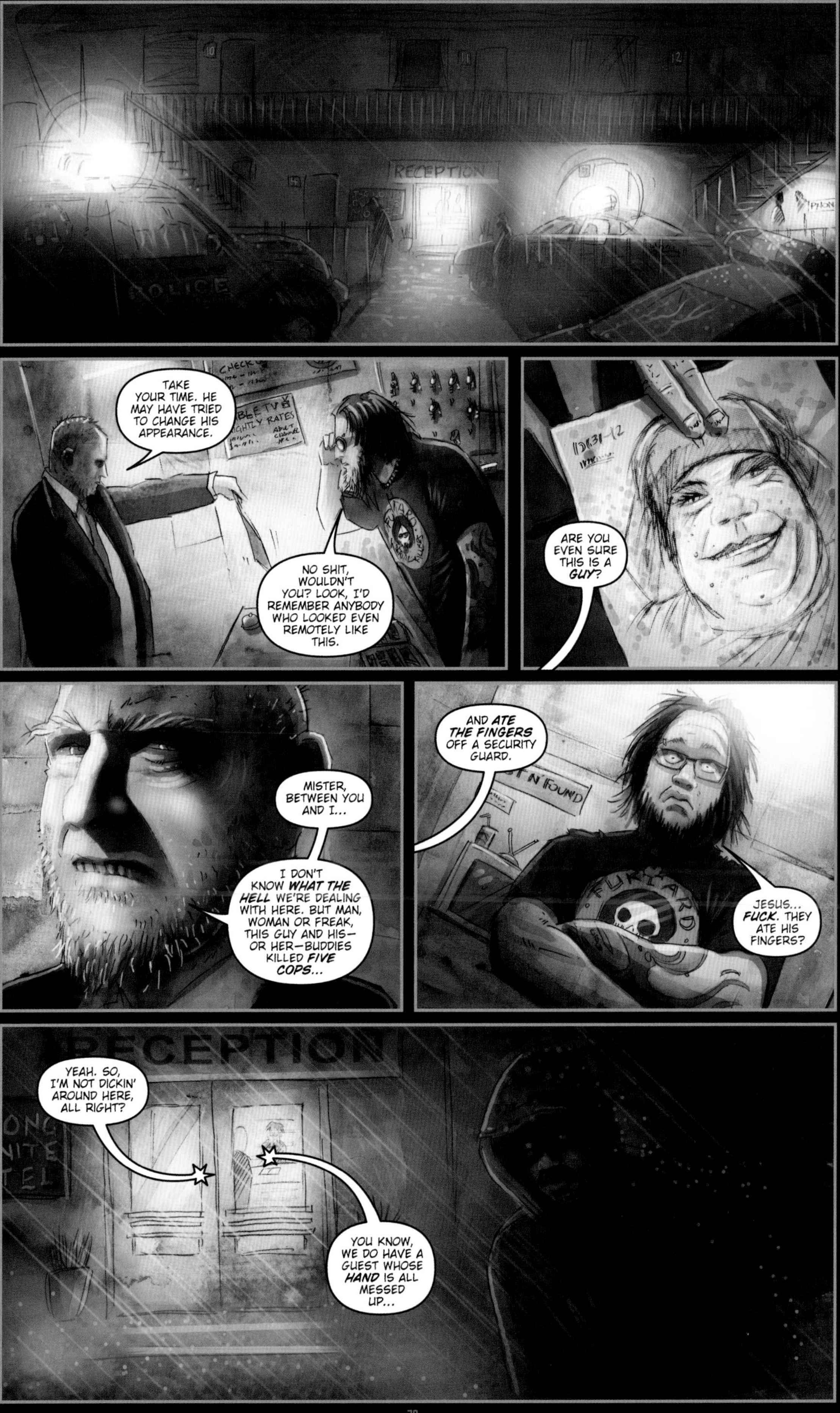
RECEPTION
POLICE
TAKE YOUR TIME. HE MAY HAVE TRIED TO CHANGE HIS APPEARANCE.
NO SHIT, WOULDN'T YOU? LOOK, I'D REMEMBER ANYBODY WHO LOOKED EVEN REMOTELY LIKE THIS.
ARE YOU EVEN SURE THIS IS A *GUY*?
MISTER, BETWEEN YOU AND I...
I DON'T KNOW *WHAT THE HELL* WE'RE DEALING WITH HERE. BUT MAN, WOMAN OR FREAK, THIS GUY AND HIS—OR HER—BUDDIES KILLED *FIVE COPS*...
AND *ATE THE FINGERS* OFF A SECURITY GUARD.
JESUS... *FUCK*. THEY ATE HIS FINGERS?
RECEPTION
YEAH. SO, I'M NOT DICKIN' AROUND HERE, ALL RIGHT?
YOU KNOW, WE DO HAVE A GUEST WHOSE *HAND* IS ALL MESSED UP...

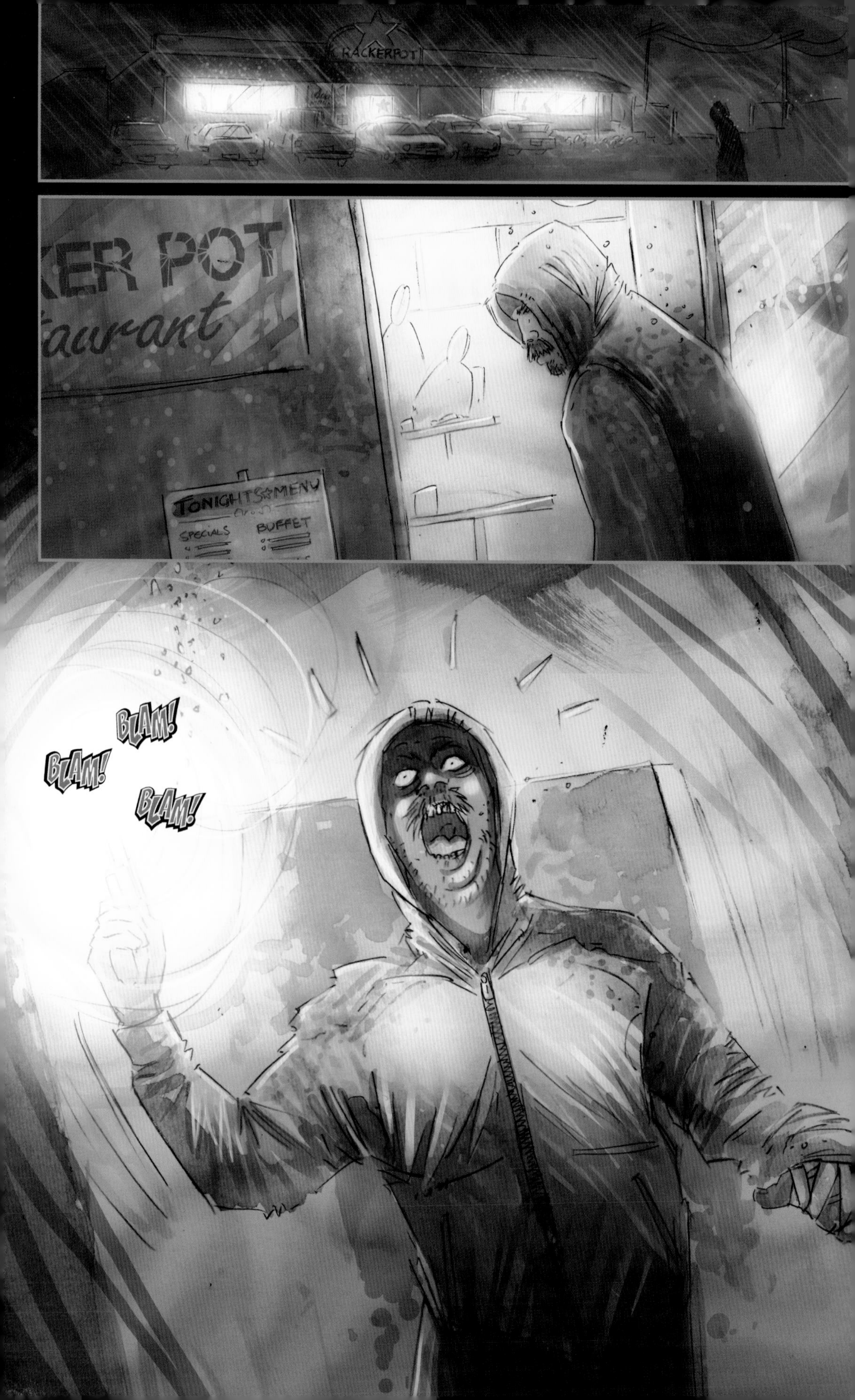

CRACKERPOT
KER POT
taurant
TONIGHTS MENU
SPECIALS
BUFFET
BLAM!
BLAM!
BLAM!

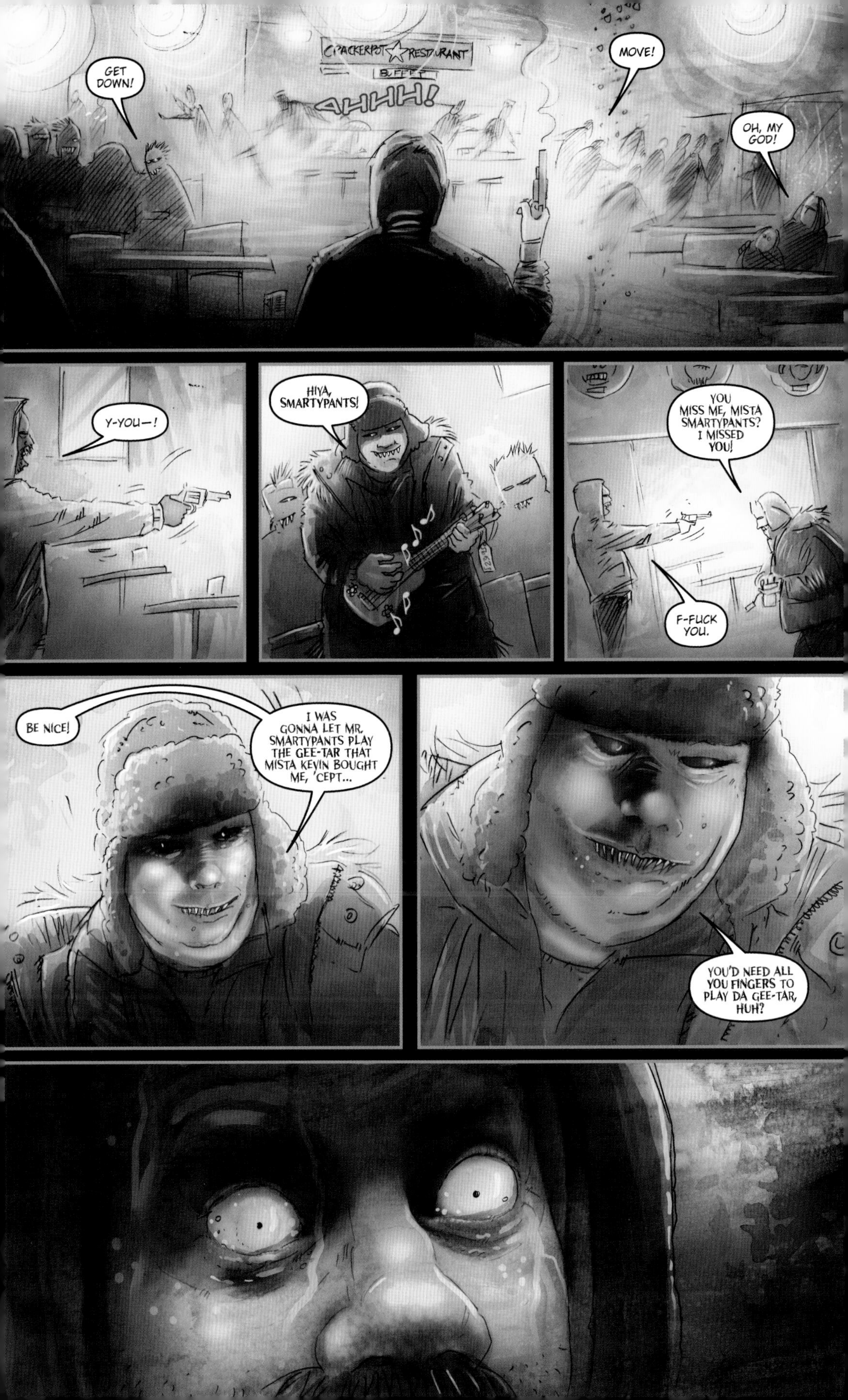
CRACKERPOT RESTAURANT
BUFFET
GET DOWN!
AHHH!
MOVE!
OH, MY GOD!
Y-YOU—!
HIYA, SMARTYPANTS!
YOU MISS ME, MISTA SMARTYPANTS? I MISSED YOU!
F-FUCK YOU.
BE NICE!
I WAS GONNA LET MR. SMARTYPANTS PLAY THE GEE-TAR THAT MISTA KEVIN BOUGHT ME, 'CEPT...
YOU'D NEED ALL YOU FINGERS TO PLAY DA GEE-TAR, HUH?

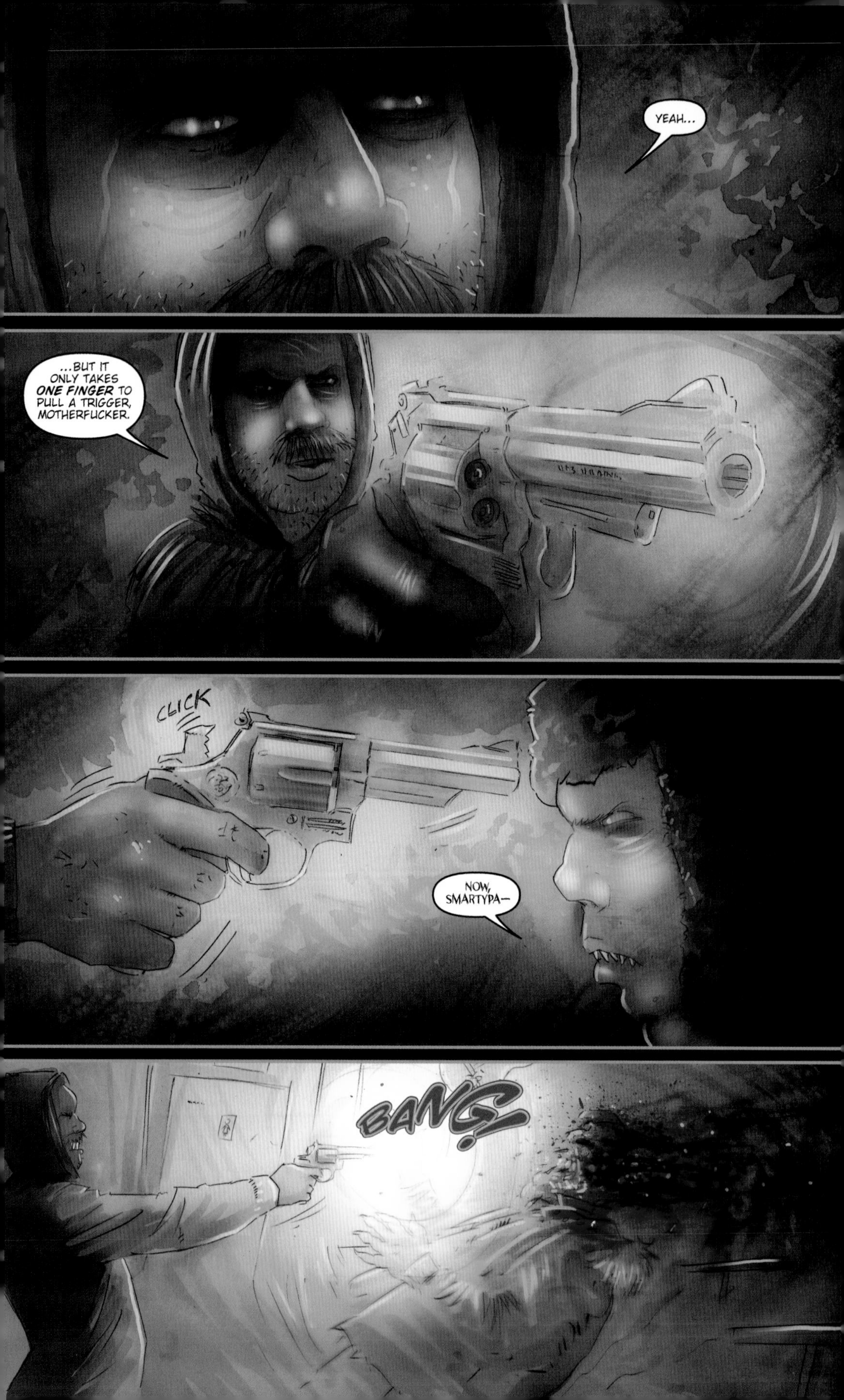
YEAH...
...BUT IT ONLY TAKES ONE FINGER TO PULL A TRIGGER, MOTHERFUCKER.
CLICK
NOW, SMARTYPA—
BANG!

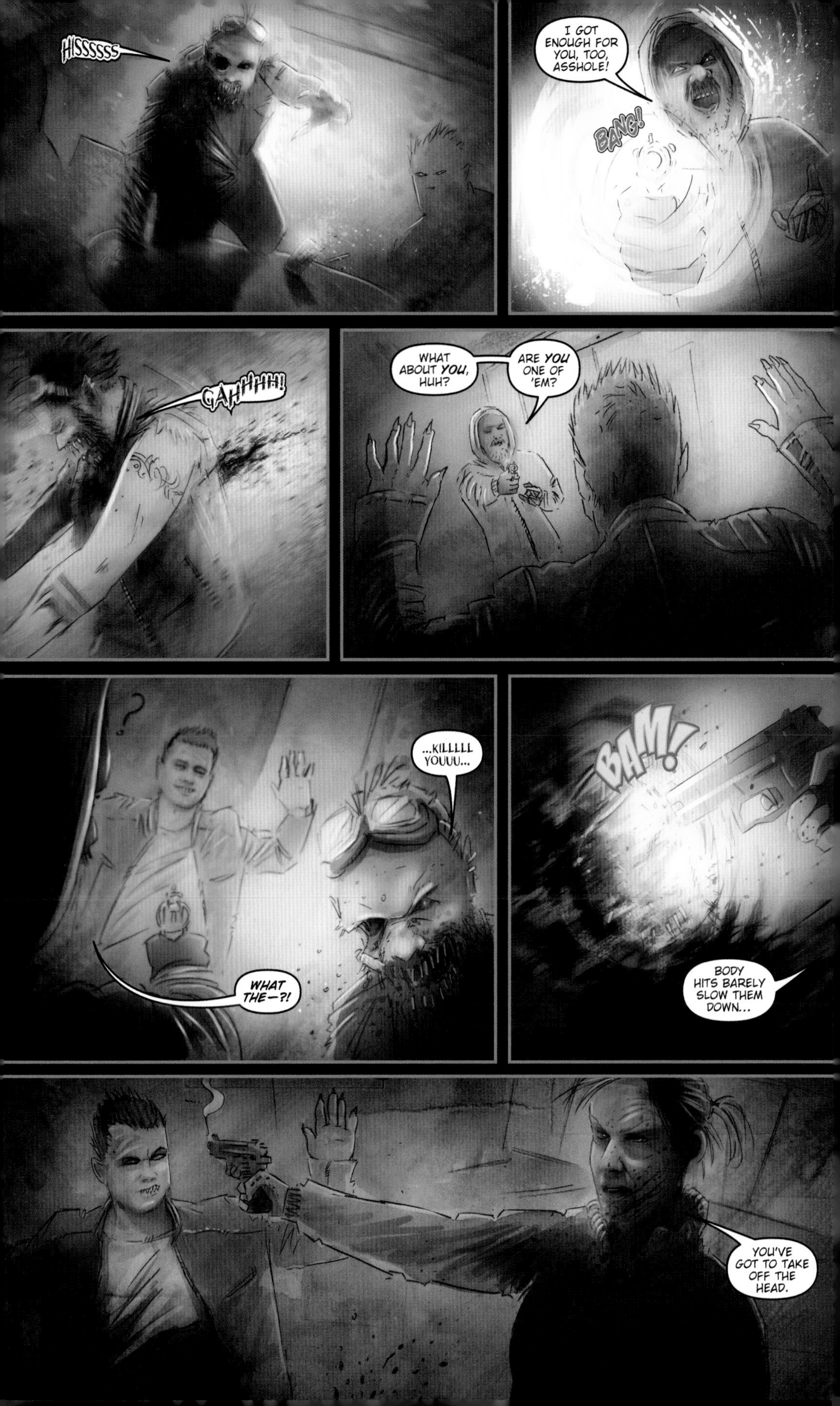
HISSSSSS
I GOT ENOUGH FOR YOU, TOO, ASSHOLE!
BANG!
GAHHHH!
WHAT ABOUT YOU, HUH?
ARE YOU ONE OF 'EM?
?
...KILLLLL YOUUU...
WHAT THE—?!
BAM!
BODY HITS BARELY SLOW THEM DOWN...
YOU'VE GOT TO TAKE OFF THE HEAD.

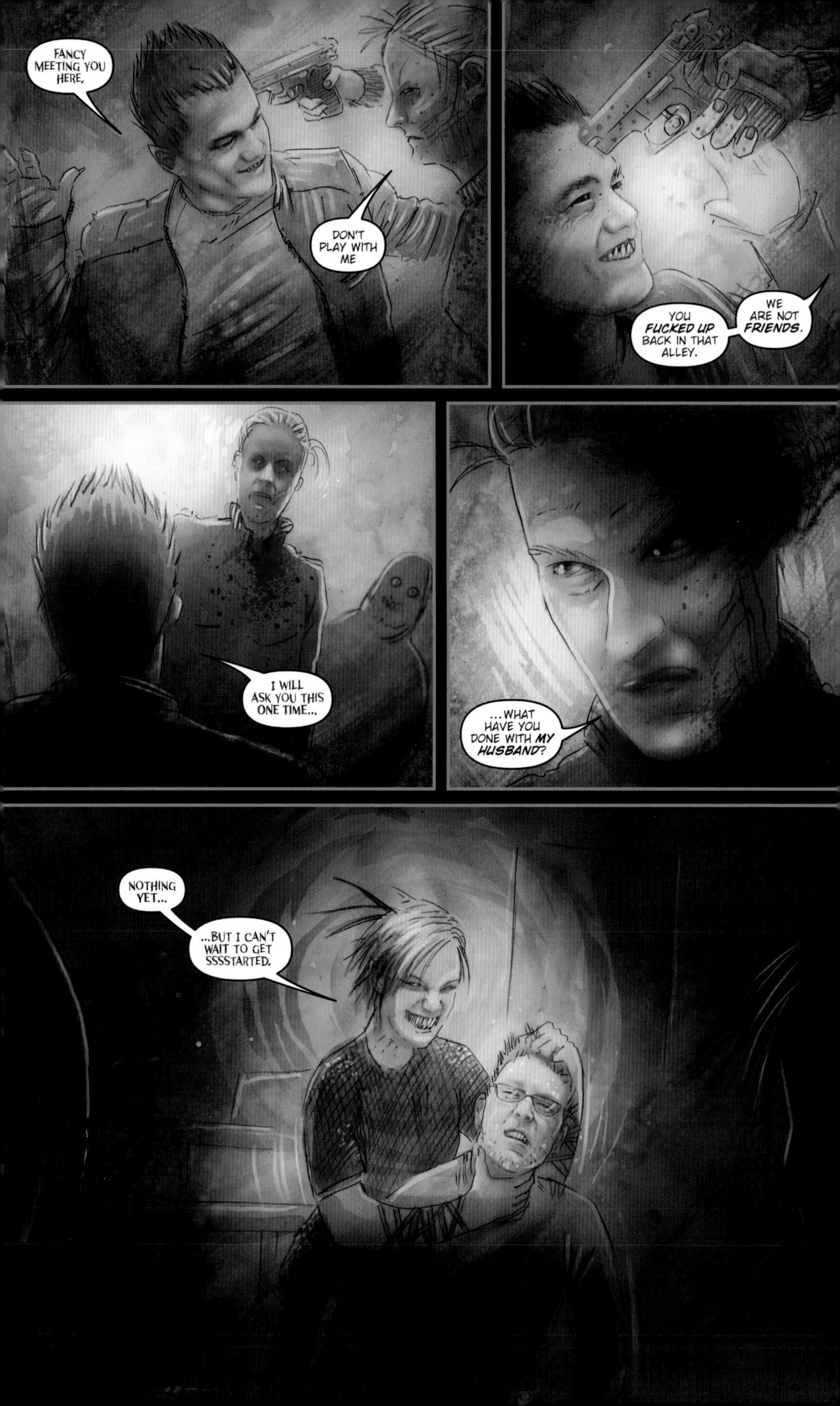

FANCY MEETING YOU HERE.
DON'T PLAY WITH ME
YOU FUCKED UP BACK IN THAT ALLEY.
WE ARE NOT FRIENDS.
I WILL ASK YOU THIS ONE TIME...
...WHAT HAVE YOU DONE WITH MY HUSBAND?
NOTHING YET...
...BUT I CAN'T WAIT TO GET SSSSTARTED.

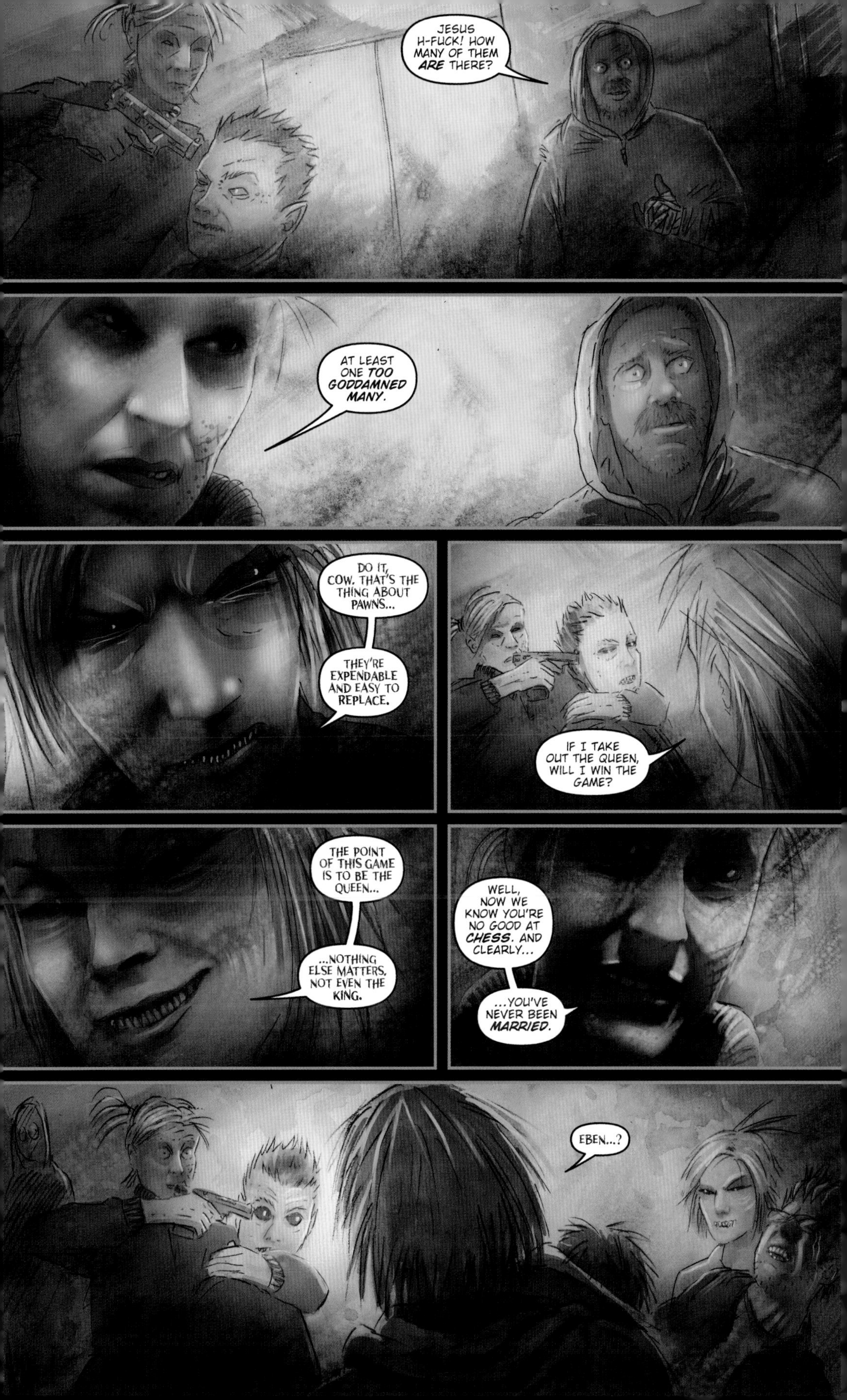
JESUS H-FUCK! HOW MANY OF THEM ARE THERE?
AT LEAST ONE TOO GODDAMNED MANY.
DO IT, COW. THAT'S THE THING ABOUT PAWNS...
THEY'RE EXPENDABLE AND EASY TO REPLACE.
IF I TAKE OUT THE QUEEN, WILL I WIN THE GAME?
THE POINT OF THIS GAME IS TO BE THE QUEEN...
...NOTHING ELSE MATTERS, NOT EVEN THE KING.
WELL, NOW WE KNOW YOU'RE NO GOOD AT CHESS. AND CLEARLY...
...YOU'VE NEVER BEEN MARRIED.
EBEN...?

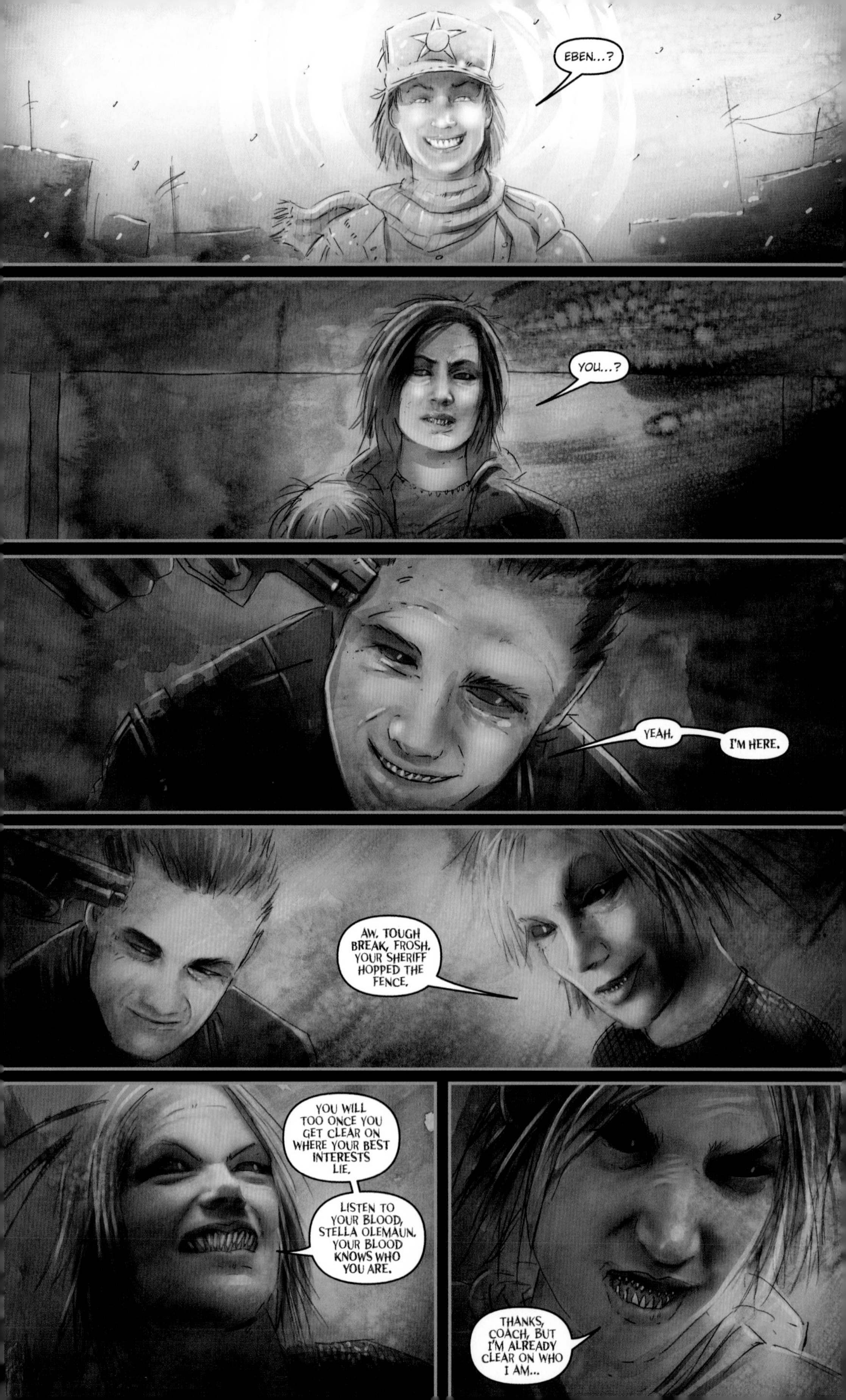
EBEN...?
YOU...?
YEAH.
I'M HERE.
AW. TOUGH BREAK, FROSH. YOUR SHERIFF HOPPED THE FENCE.
YOU WILL TOO ONCE YOU GET CLEAR ON WHERE YOUR BEST INTERESTS LIE.
LISTEN TO YOUR BLOOD, STELLA OLEMAUN. YOUR BLOOD KNOWS WHO YOU ARE.
THANKS, COACH, BUT I'M ALREADY CLEAR ON WHO I AM...

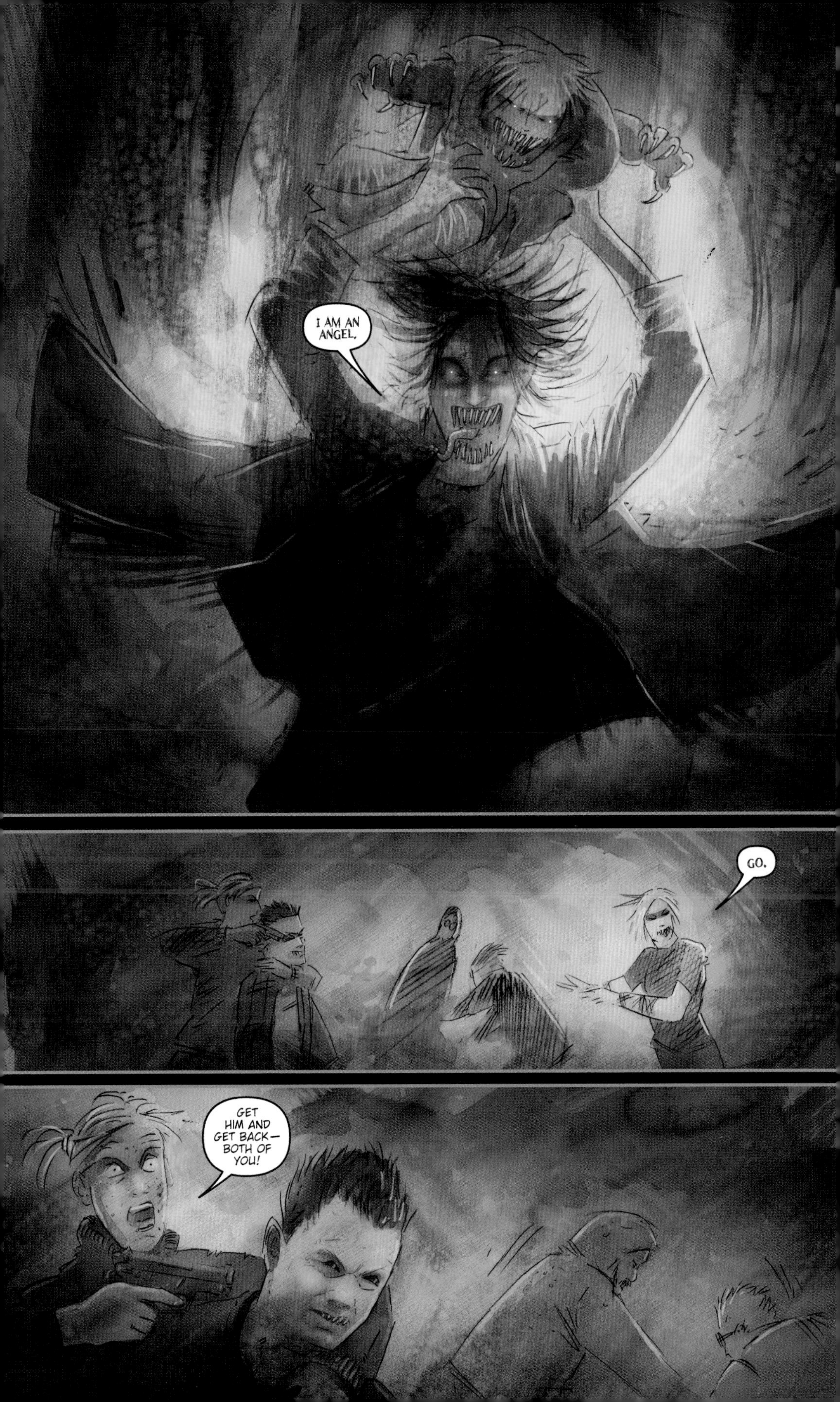
I AM AN ANGEL,
GO.
GET HIM AND GET BACK— BOTH OF YOU!

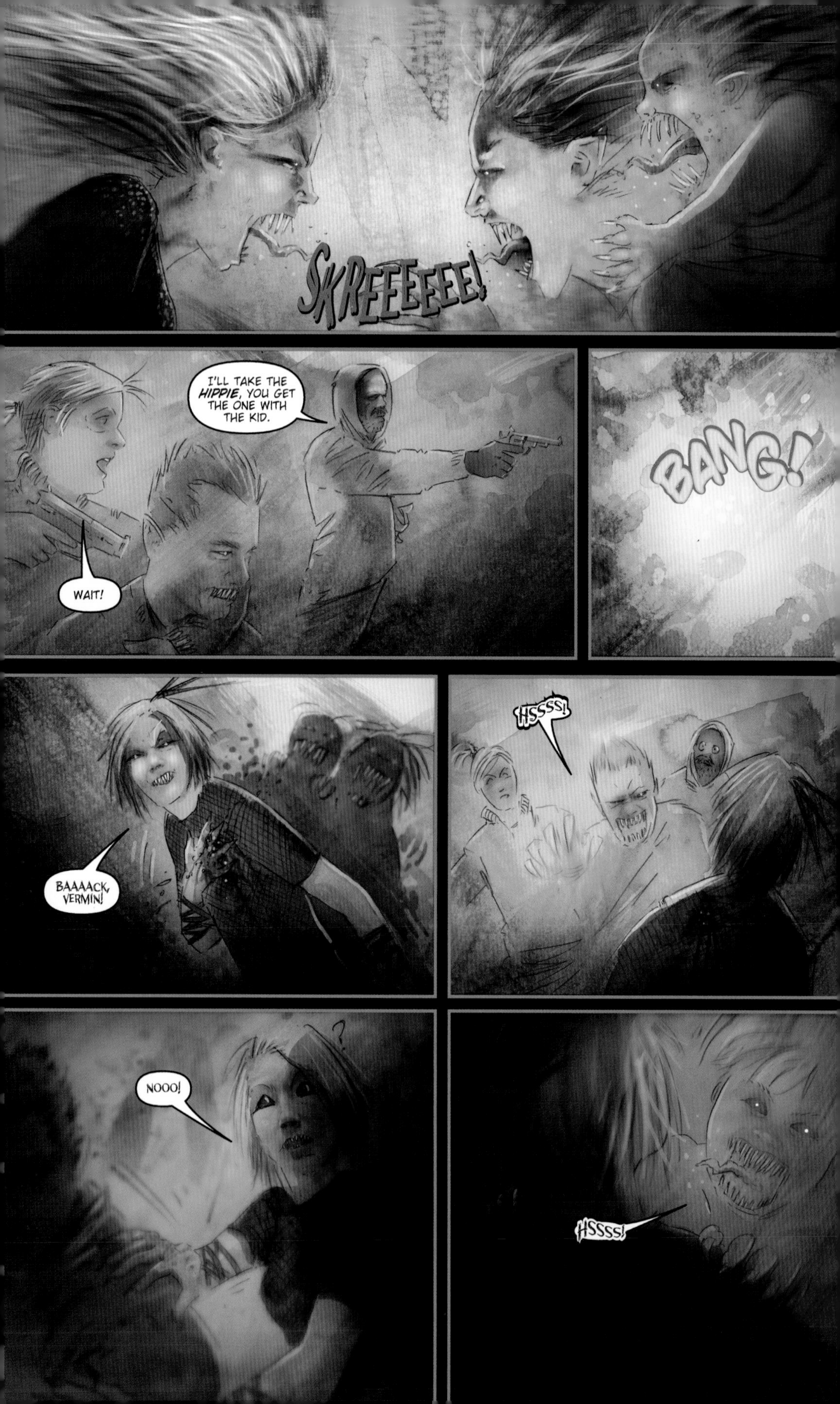
SKREEEEEEE!
I'LL TAKE THE HIPPIE, YOU GET THE ONE WITH THE KID.
WAIT!
BANG!
BAAAACK, VERMIN!
HSSSS!
NOOO!
HSSSS!

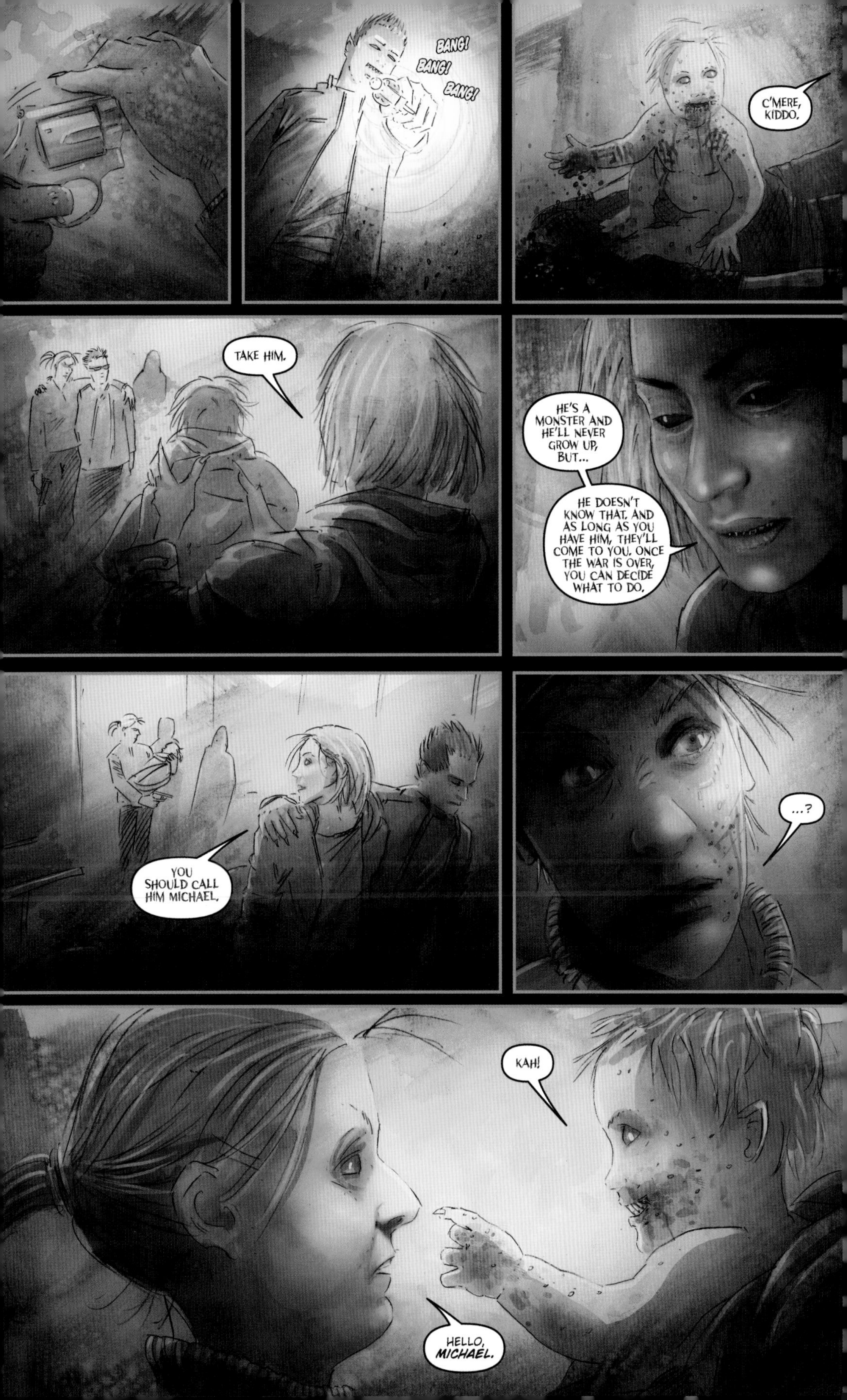
BANG!
BANG!
BANG!
C'MERE, KIDDO.
TAKE HIM.
HE'S A MONSTER AND HE'LL NEVER GROW UP, BUT...
HE DOESN'T KNOW THAT. AND AS LONG AS YOU HAVE HIM, THEY'LL COME TO YOU. ONCE THE WAR IS OVER, YOU CAN DECIDE WHAT TO DO.
YOU SHOULD CALL HIM MICHAEL.
...?
KAH!
HELLO, *MICHAEL.*

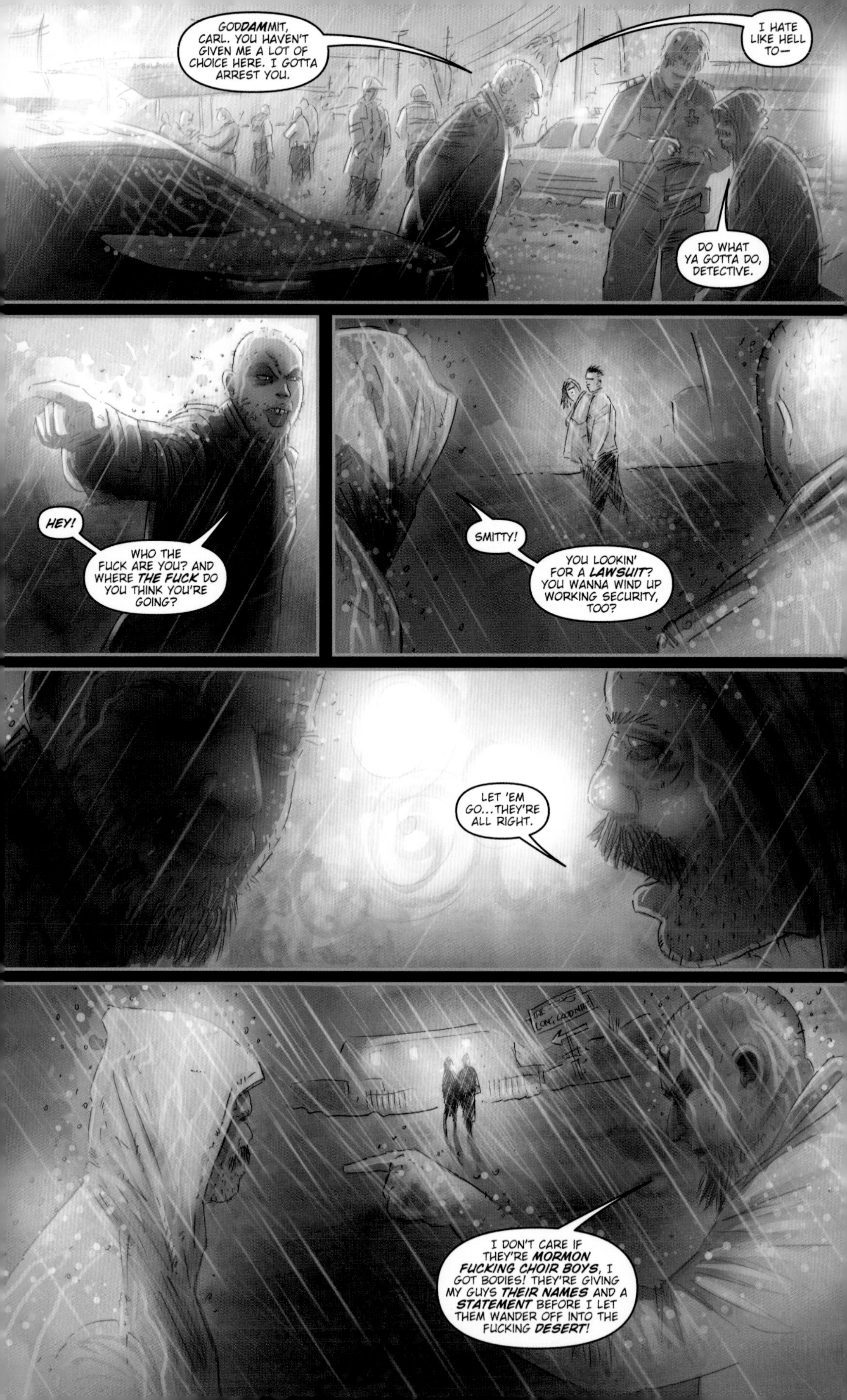
GODDAMMIT, CARL. YOU HAVEN'T GIVEN ME A LOT OF CHOICE HERE. I GOTTA ARREST YOU.
I HATE LIKE HELL TO—
DO WHAT YA GOTTA DO, DETECTIVE.
HEY!
WHO THE FUCK ARE YOU? AND WHERE THE FUCK DO YOU THINK YOU'RE GOING?
SMITTY!
YOU LOOKIN' FOR A LAWSUIT? YOU WANNA WIND UP WORKING SECURITY, TOO?
LET 'EM GO... THEY'RE ALL RIGHT.
I DON'T CARE IF THEY'RE MORMON FUCKING CHOIR BOYS, I GOT BODIES! THEY'RE GIVING MY GUYS THEIR NAMES AND A STATEMENT BEFORE I LET THEM WANDER OFF INTO THE FUCKING DESERT!

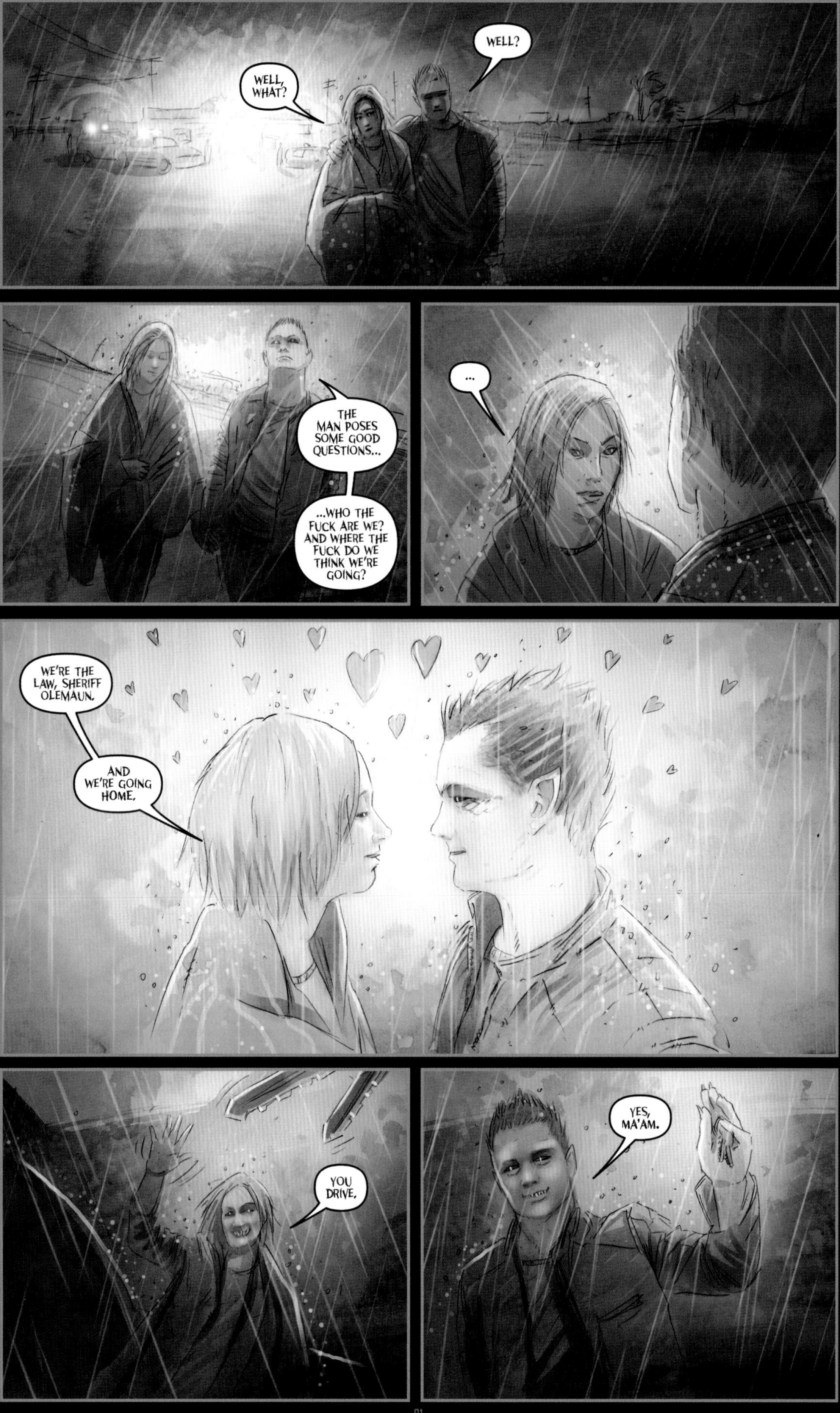
WELL?
WELL, WHAT?
THE MAN POSES SOME GOOD QUESTIONS...
...WHO THE FUCK ARE WE? AND WHERE THE FUCK DO WE THINK WE'RE GOING?
...
WE'RE THE LAW, SHERIFF OLEMAUN.
AND WE'RE GOING HOME.
YOU DRIVE.
YES, MA'AM.

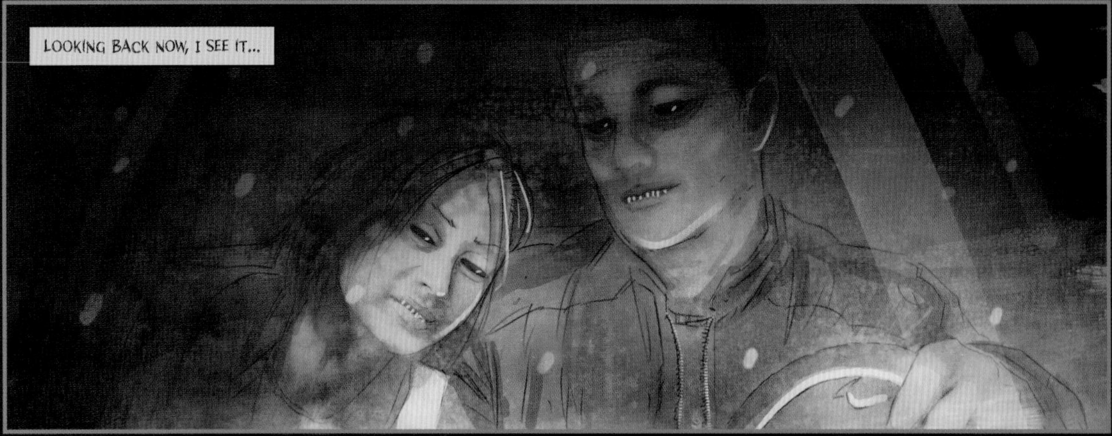
LOOKING BACK NOW, I SEE IT...

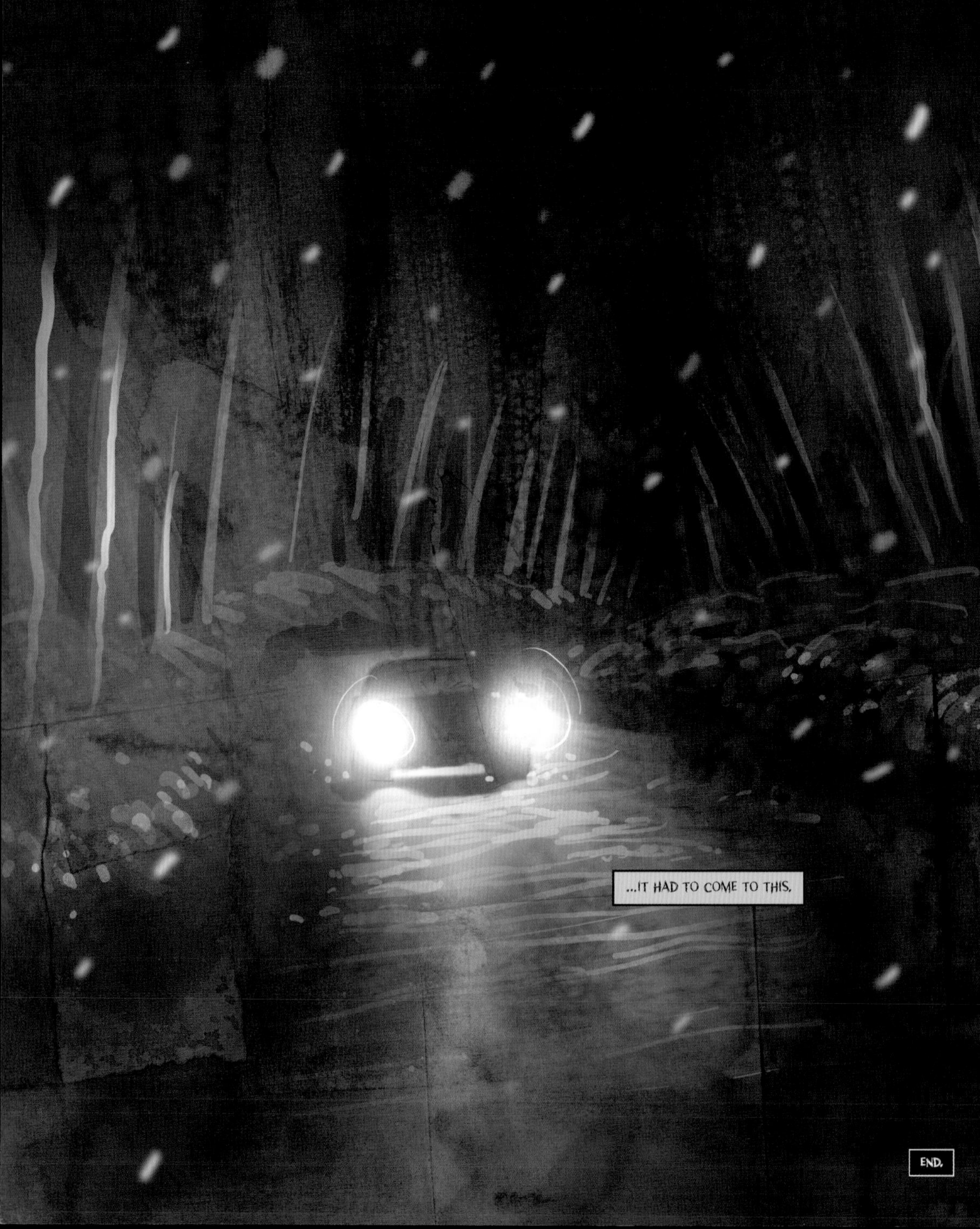
...IT HAD TO COME TO THIS.
END.

JUSTIN RANDALL
ART GALLERY

Presenting a collection of covers and artwork
for "30 Days of Night: Eben & Stella,"
from series artist, Justin Randall.

Justin Randall is a commercial illustrator, a design lecturer, and a comic book artist from Australia. He graduated from Curtin University with an Honors degree on the language of comics and has also produced feature art for magazines, posters, editorials, and book covers. His illustration techniques are a combination of traditional painting, photography and digital rendering with a Wacom drawing tablet. He has a beautiful wife called Nikki, loves horror, barely sleeps, often daydreams, and enjoys drinking booze way too much.

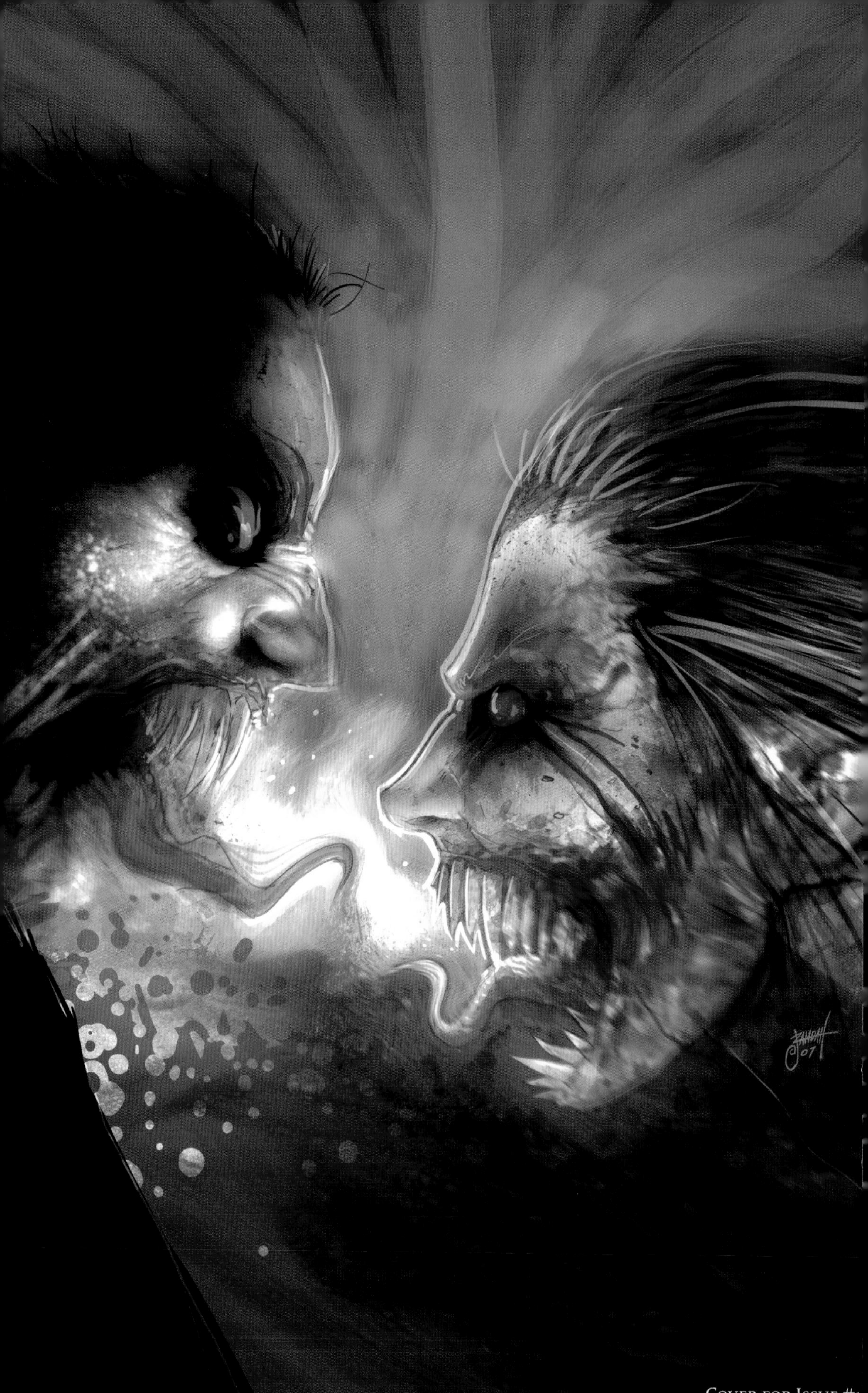

Cover for Issue #1

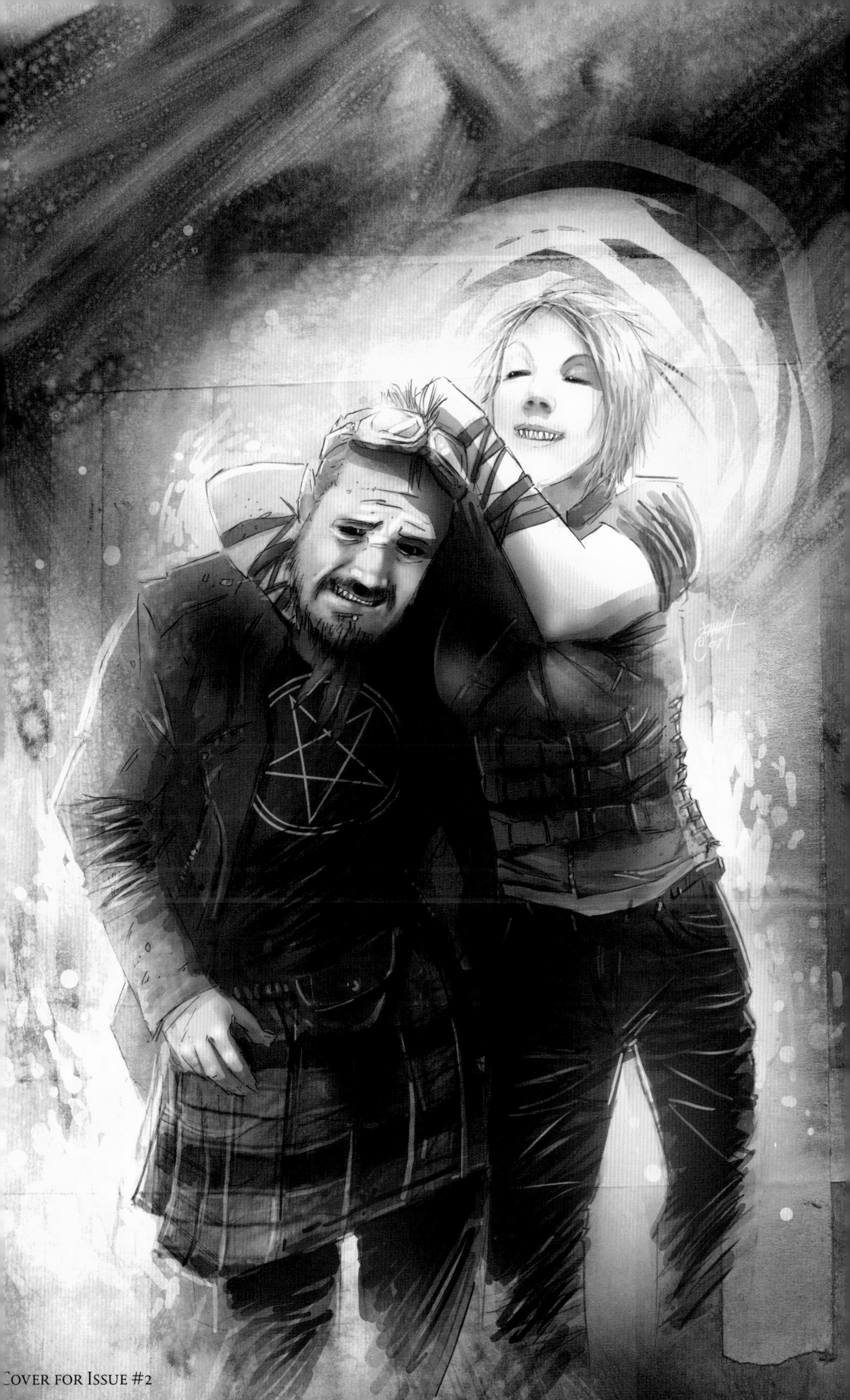

Cover for Issue #2

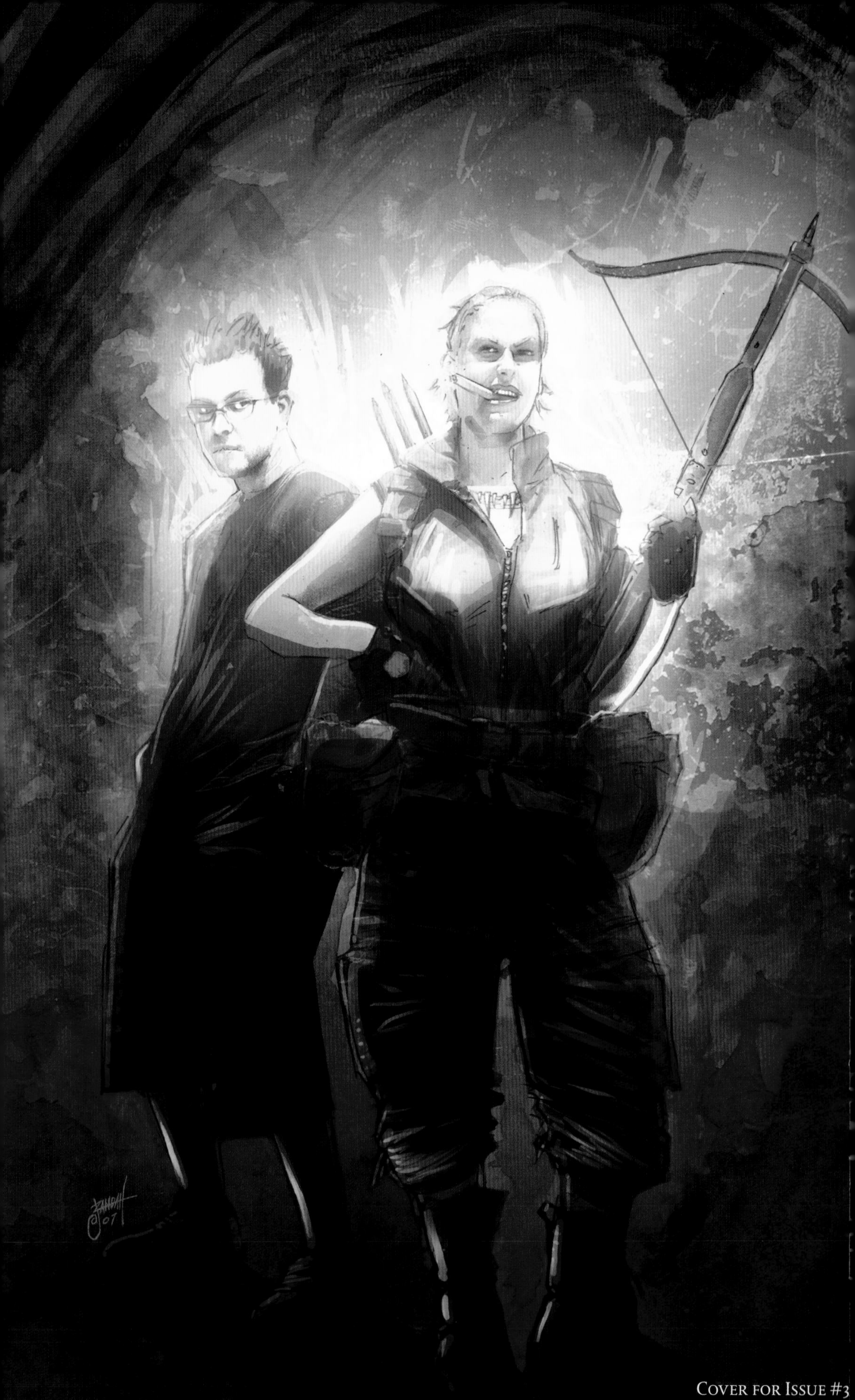

Cover for Issue #3

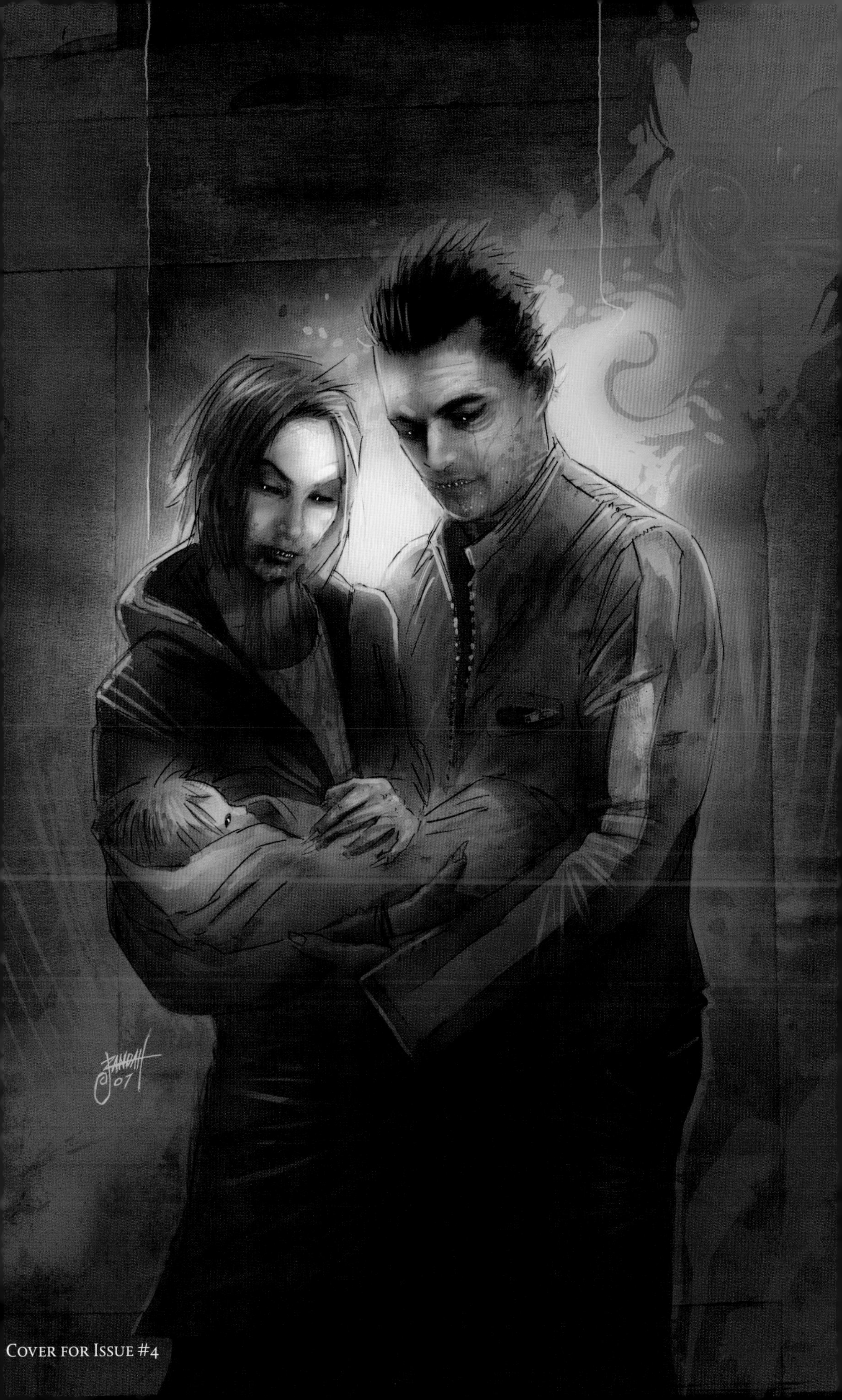

Cover for Issue #4

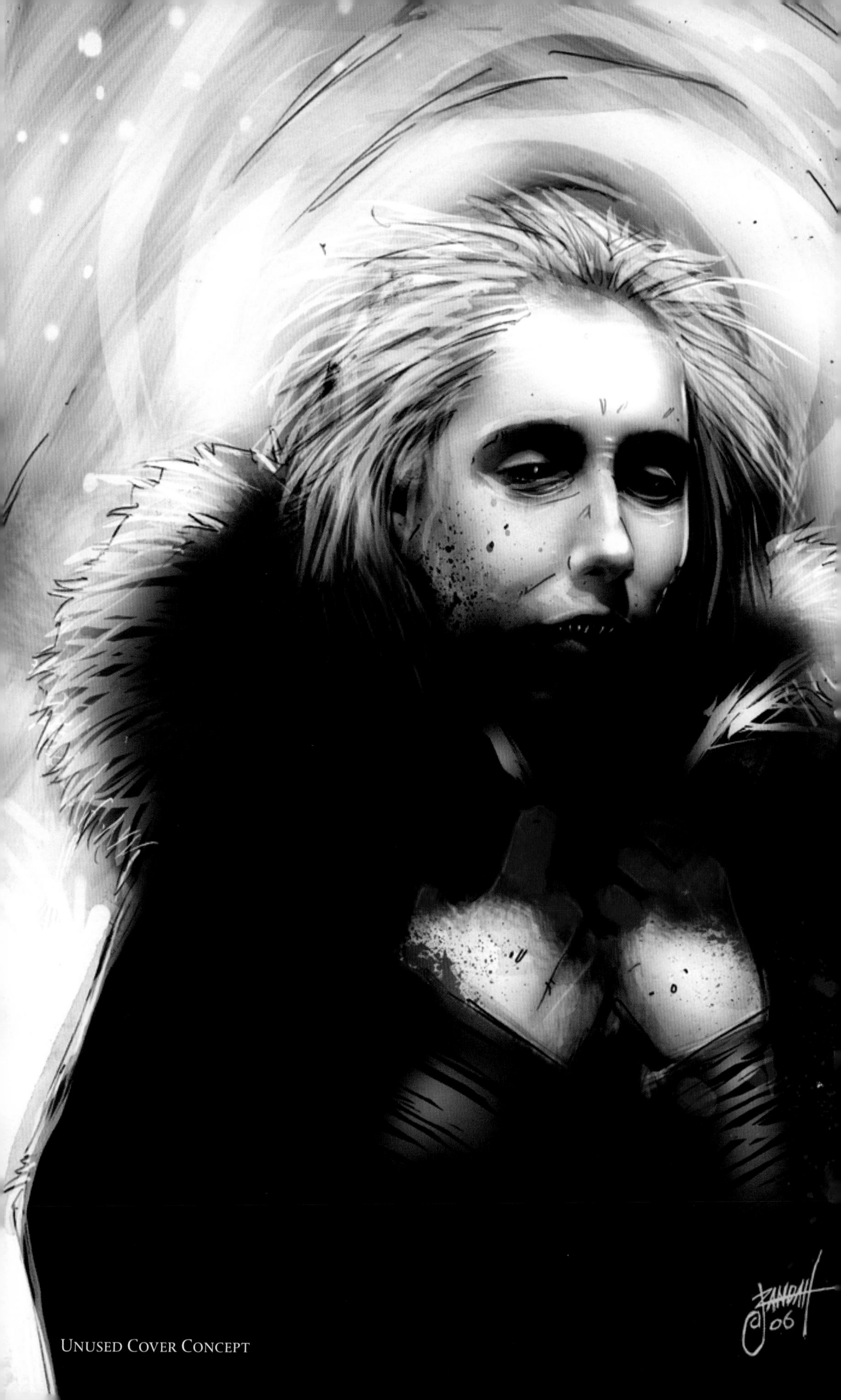

Unused Cover Concept

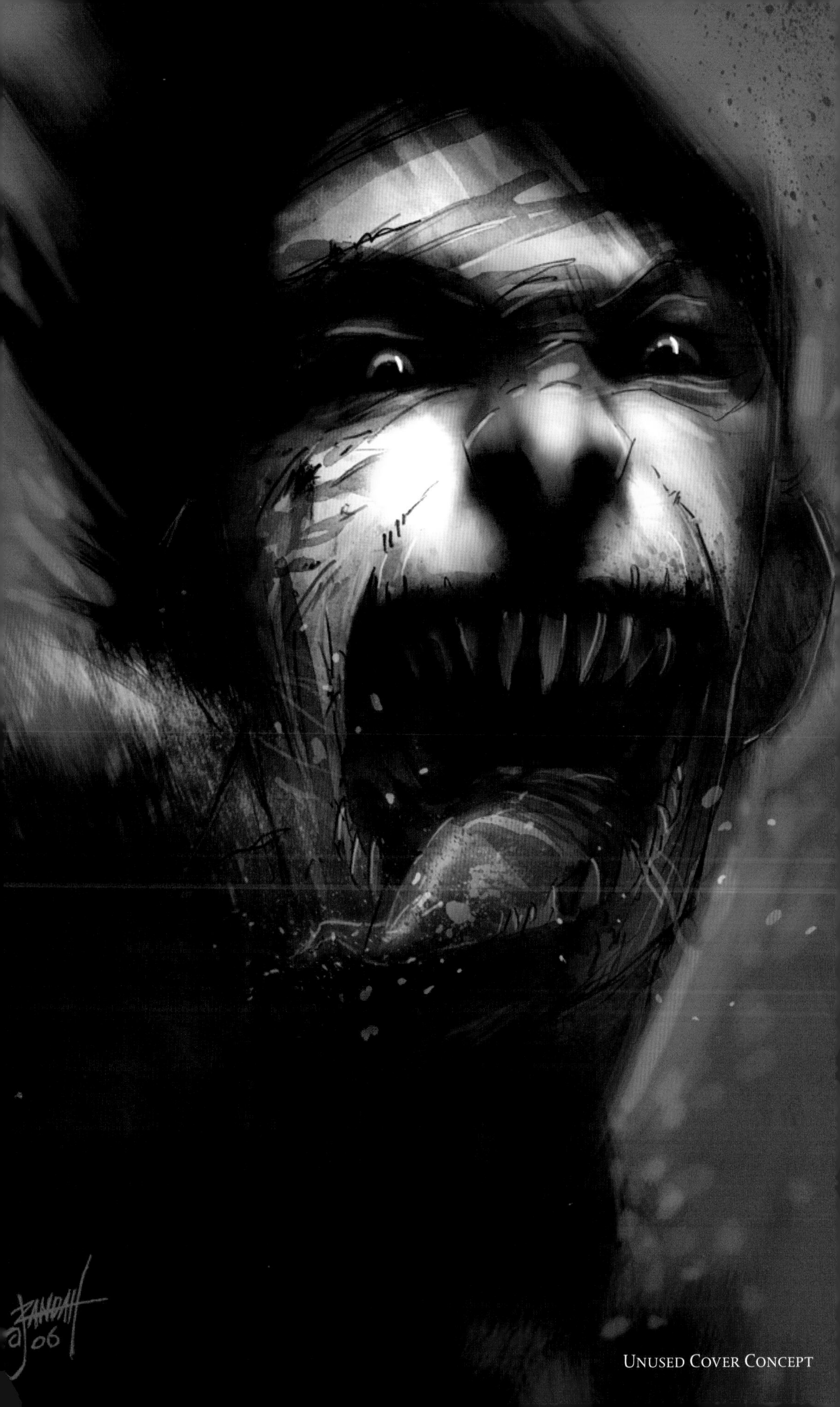

Unused Cover Concept

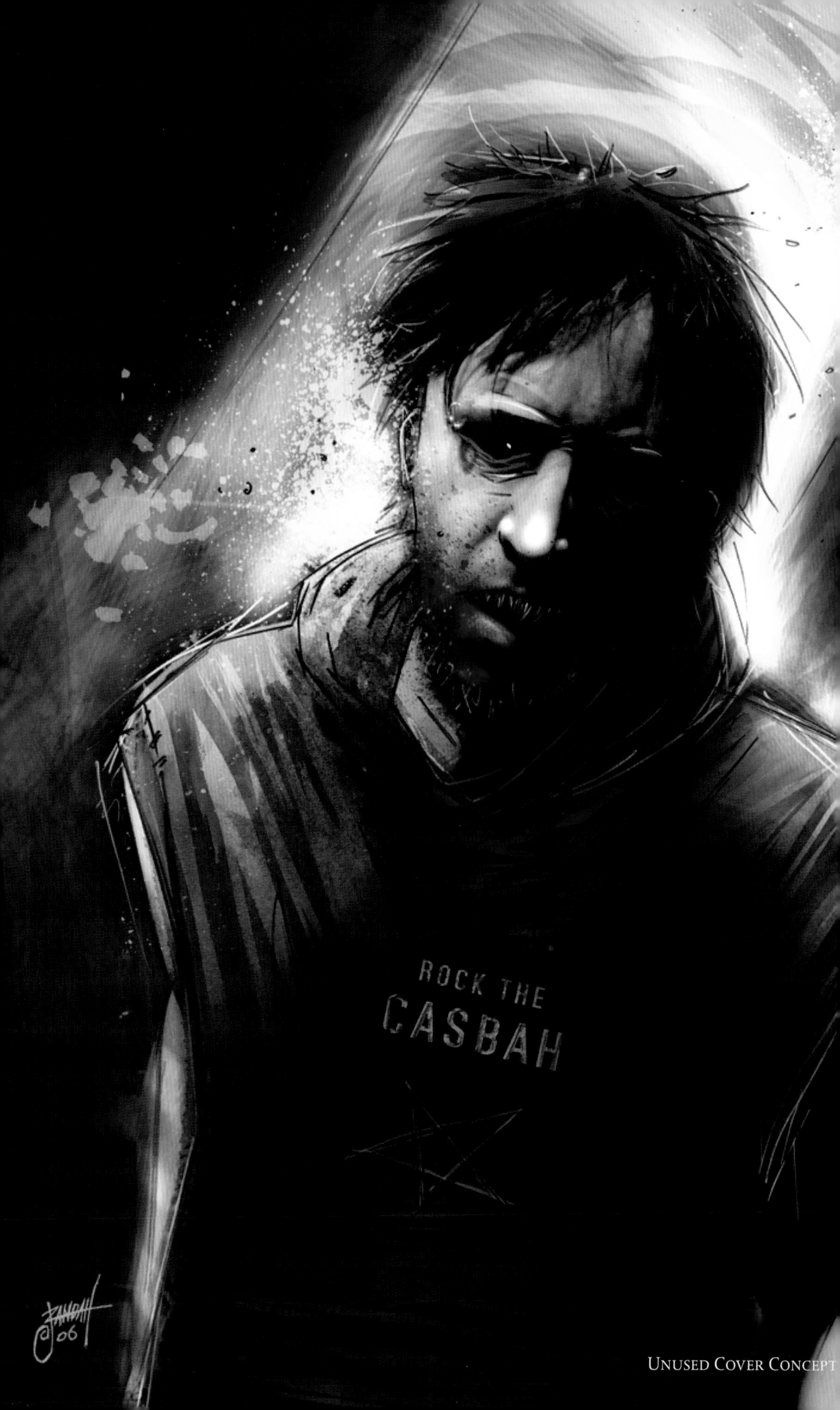
ROCK THE
CASBAH

Unused Cover Concept

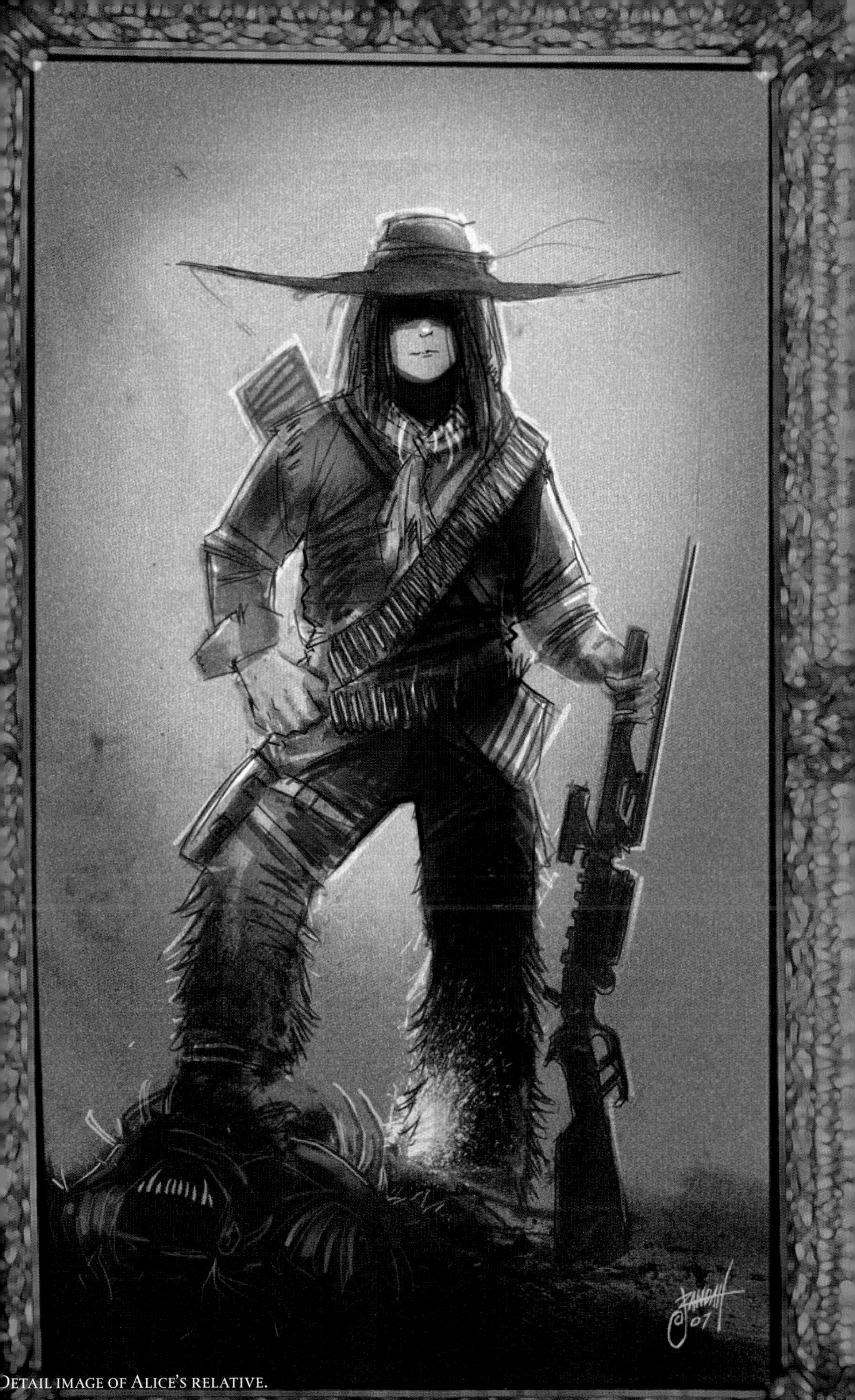

Detail image of Alice's relative.

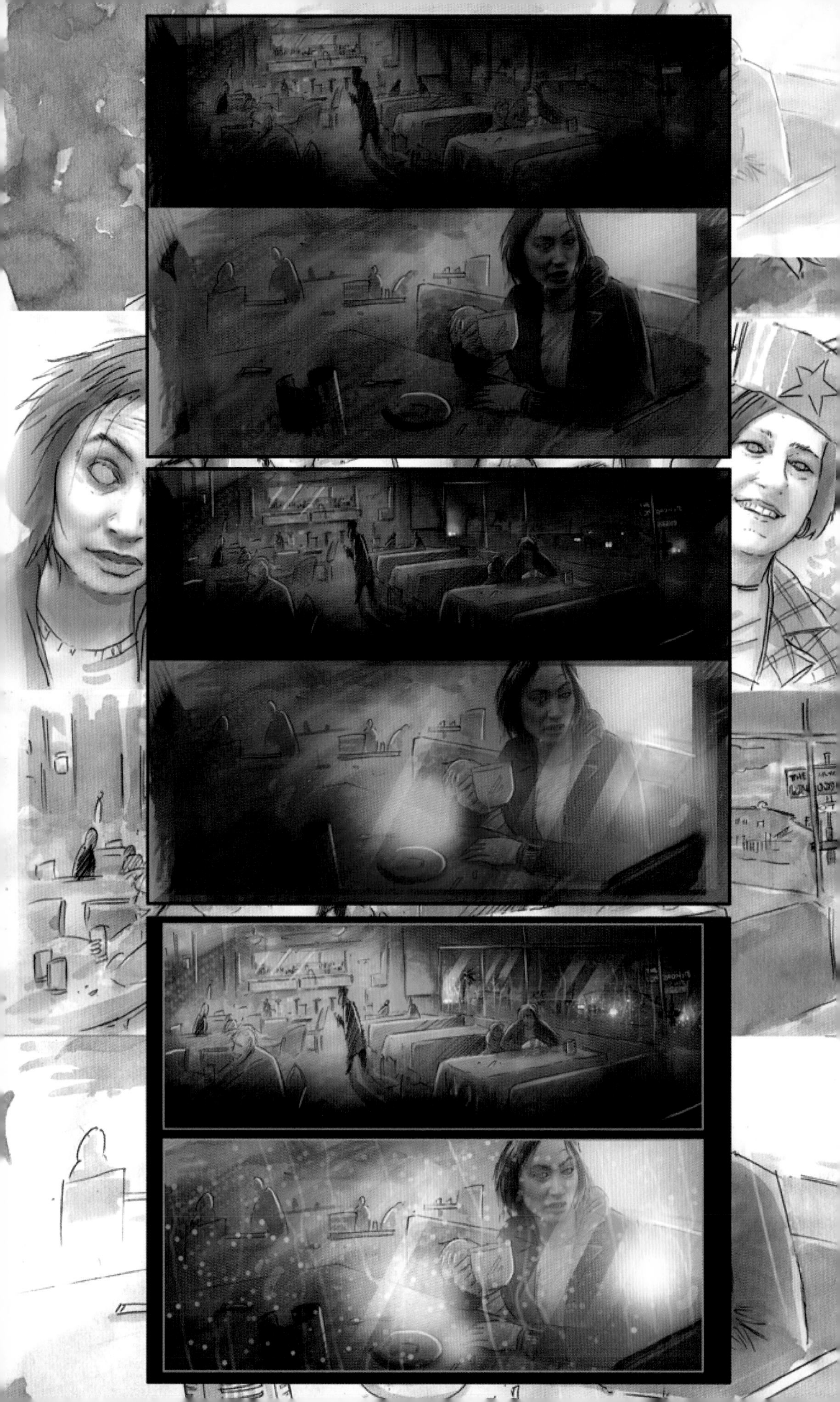

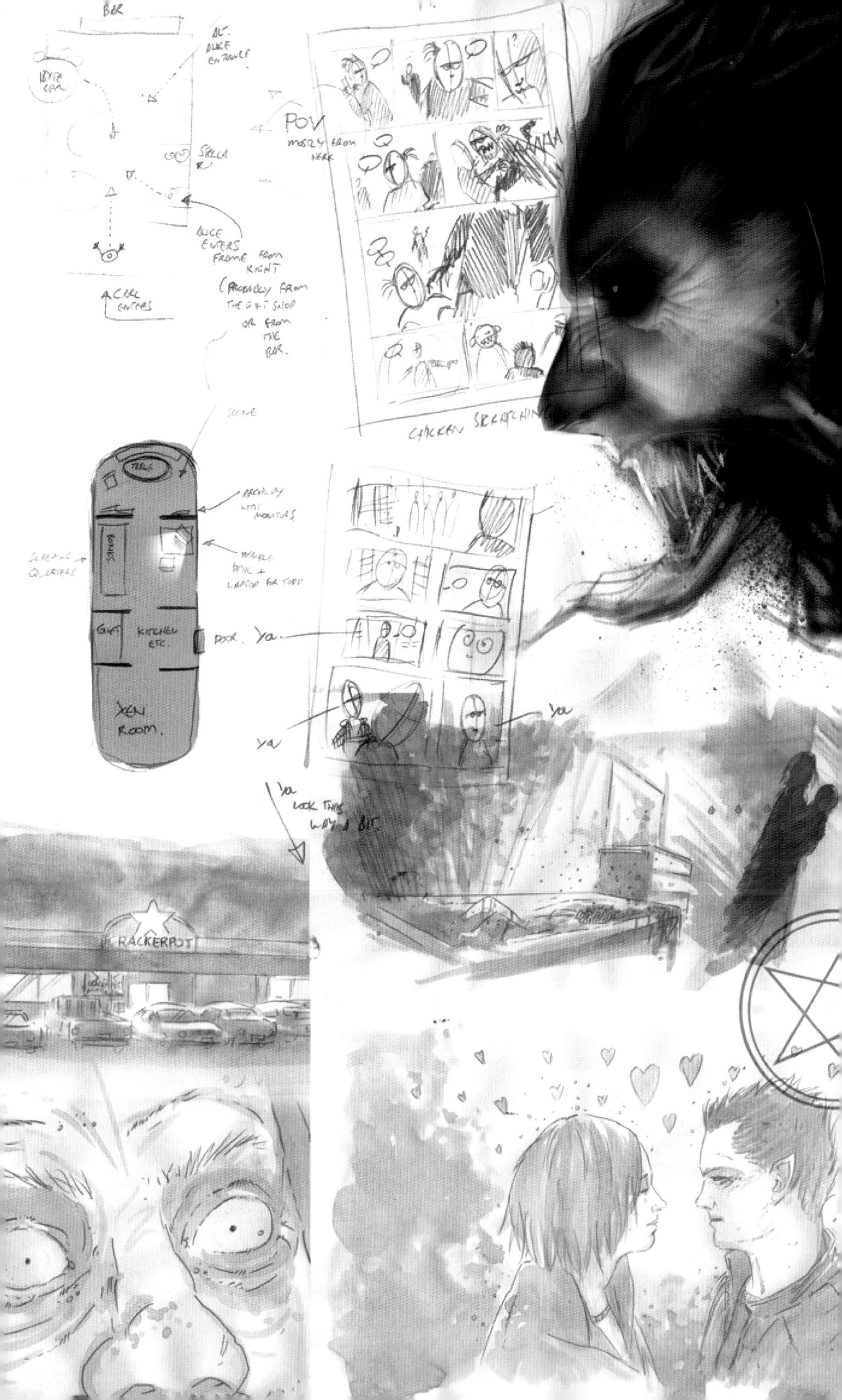
BAR
ALT. ALICE ENTRANCE
POV
STELLA
ALICE ENTERS FRAME FROM RIGHT
(PROBABLY FROM THE GIFT SHOP OR FROM THE BAR.
SCENE
TABLE
BUNKS
SLEEPING QUARTERS
GIFT
KITCHEN ETC.
DOOR. Ya
XEN ROOM.
Ya
Ya
Ya LOOK THIS WAY A BIT.

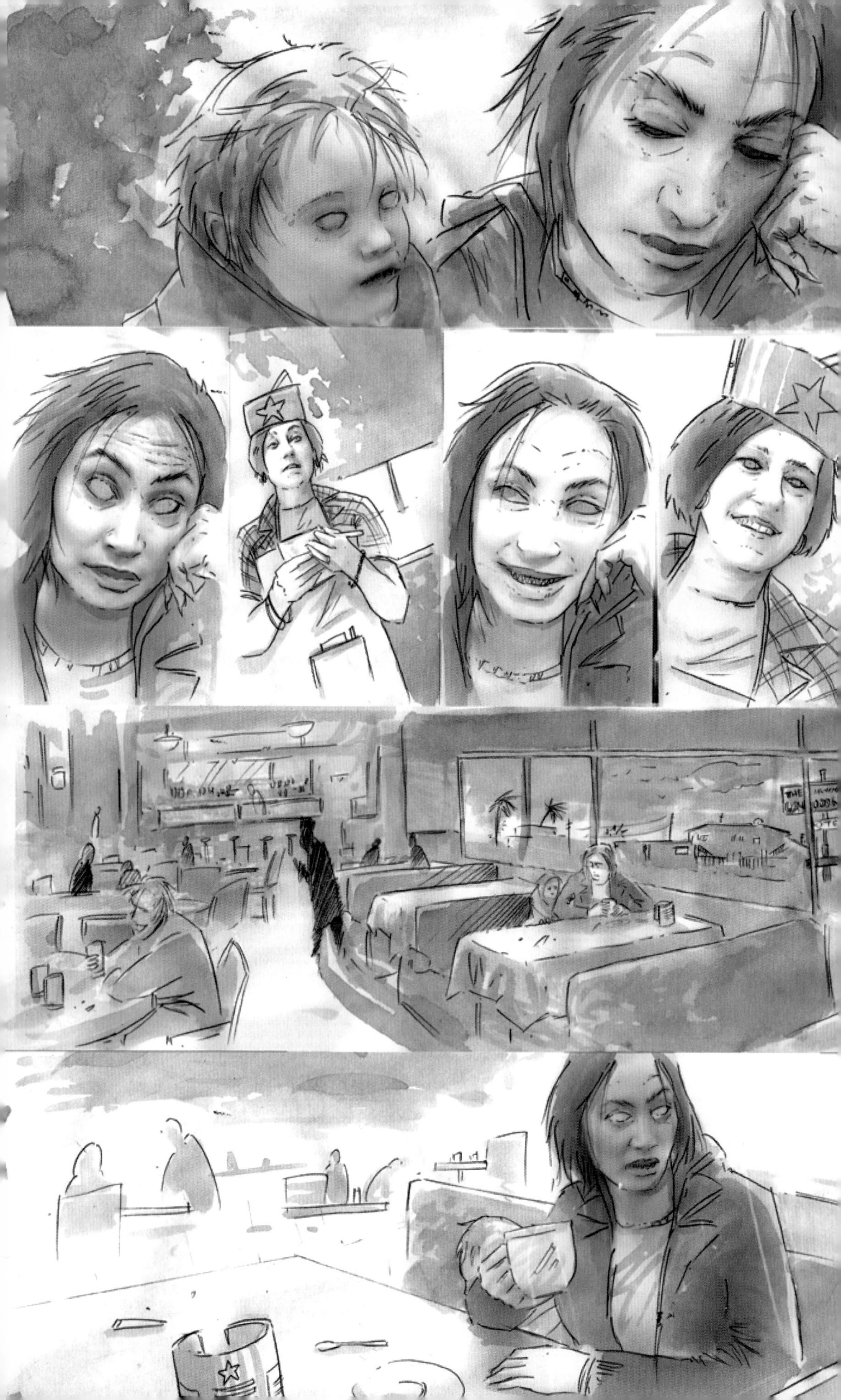